Philosophical Children
in Literary Situations

Philosophy of Childhood

Series Editors: Peter R. Costello, Providence College, and Barbara Weber, University of British Columbia

Editorial Board: David Kennedy (Montclair State University), Kirsten Jacobson (University of Maine), and Natalie Fletcher (Concordia University)

The Philosophy of Childhood series examines questions of metaphysics, epistemology, ethics, and aesthetics developed within a consideration of the meaningfulness of childhood. It formulates and develops questions such as the following: What is a child? How do children's ways of knowing emerge in their educational and family life? What ought we to do to address children? How are children's literature, athletics, and education able to articulate a sense of beauty or wonder that is particularly unique?

Recent Titles in the Series:

Philosophical Children in Literary Situations: Toward a Phenomenology of Childhood, by Peter R. Costello
Thinking, Childhood, and Time: Contemporary Perspectives on the Politics of Education, edited by Walter Kohan and Barbara Weber
Philosophy of Childhood Today: Exploring the Boundaries, edited by David Kennedy and Brock Bahler
Childlike Peace in Merleau-Ponty and Levinas: Intersubjectivity as Dialectical Spiral, by Brock Bahler

Philosophical Children in Literary Situations

Toward a Phenomenology of Childhood

Peter R. Costello

LEXINGTON BOOKS
Lanham • Boulder • New York • London

Published by Lexington Books
An imprint of The Rowman & Littlefield Publishing Group, Inc.
4501 Forbes Boulevard, Suite 200, Lanham, Maryland 20706
www.rowman.com

6 Tinworth Street, London SE11 5AL, United Kingdom

Copyright © 2020 by The Rowman & Littlefield Publishing Group, Inc.

British Library Cataloguing in Publication Information Available

Library of Congress Cataloging-in-Publication Data
Library of Congress Control Number: 2020941148

ISBN: 978-1-7936-0452-1 (cloth)
ISBN: 978-1-7936-0454-5 (pbk)
ISBN: 978-1-7936-0453-8 (electronic)

This book is dedicated to my aunt, Mary Costello, whose work with children in the city of Baltimore changed many, many lives for the better. She also has been a great support to all of us who have had the privilege to spend time with her. I love you, Mary. You always treat children as intelligent people.

Contents

Acknowledgments

This book would not have been possible without the help of many people.

First and foremost, I want to thank our two children, Anna and Laura, for discussing the children's literature with me that is featured in this book. Many of my better ideas came out of talking with them.

I also want to thank Barbara Weber and Jessica Wiskus for their feedback and encouragement on earlier versions of this book. They, and an anonymous reviewer from Lexington, were instrumental in helping guide me to a more polished version of the original draft.

In this same light, I want to thank my friends Kym Maclaren and David Ciavatta for their reading and discussion of my work. They are both excellent phenomenologists and wonderful writers.

Discussing these texts with my students at Providence College has also helped me shape my insights into these books, both phenomenological and literary. In particular I credit Stephen Mendelsohn, Chrissy Rojcewicz, Andrew Wiley, Brigid Flaherty, Julia Brown, Noah Gemma, and Linh Truong. Special thanks also go to my Providence College colleagues Tim Mahoney, Licia Carlson, Chris Arroyo, Ed Dain, and John Abbruzzese for their continued support.

For permission to republish material first appearing in their journals, I am grateful to Smiljana Narancic Kovac of *Libri et Liberi*, Walter Kohan of *Childhood and Philosophy*, and Jeffrey Hurlburt of *Phenomenological Inquiry*.

Introduction

This book seeks to combine two fields, that of literary studies and that of phenomenology. It does so by offering both a commentary on various important works of phenomenology and a phenomenological reading of six novels that are either written for children or whose main characters are children.

With its literary focus on works about children, and with its philosophical roots in the Continental philosophy tradition, this book continues the work of our earlier edited volume, *Philosophy in Children's Literature*. In that volume, however, our unified focus was primarily on literature for young children, particularly on picturebooks or early readers. By making picturebooks and early readers our focus, we made an important contribution to early childhood education. Parents or teachers could, and still can, pick up that book and enter briefly into one of a series of novel readings that could help them to set up single-class discussions—for example, of Shel Silverstein's *The Giving Tree* or Arnold Lobel's *Frog and Toad Are Friends*.

This current book, which employs readings of children's chapter books, many of which are Newbery Medal winners, and which has a single philosophical focus on phenomenology, intends a different and higher-level outcome. Instead of introducing the reader to a variety of traditions and conclusions in Continental philosophy, this book offers the reader an apprenticeship into what I believe to be the very productive and engaging phenomenological *method*. Although each chapter of this new book requires more time for thinking through some key concepts, and although each literary text under discussion is more sophisticated, I believe that the reader's dedication will be rewarded with a greater sense for what a deep reading of a longer literary text could become.

Having said that, I think it is important to note what this book is *not*. This book is not a text in the complementary, related field of Philosophy For

Children. That is, this book does not seek to chart out specific methods or exercises in the practice of doing philosophy together with children—even though it does support those practices.

This book is also not a typical book in children's literature studies. I do acknowledge a great debt to the scholars within that field, including those whose very helpful and important works I cite below. And I believe phenomenologists and children's literature scholars share common questions that orient our research—namely, the questions of what it means to be a child and of what it means to write for, with and about children within the publishing and education industries. However, my concern in this book is different from my colleagues in literary studies. While not wanting to co-opt children's literature studies for my purposes, I want to affirm that what I attempt here is a philosophical and political argument of a different kind, of which I will say more below.

What this book *is* intended to be is a narrower meditation within the philosophy of childhood, broadly construed. What it means to be a child as a *perceiving* person within the practice and institution of the family, of education, of society—this is the question central to the chapters here. As such, elementary school teachers, parents, graduate students, and scholars in the humanities, psychology, and education—anyone, really, who is interested in what it means to recognize and assist the perceptions of a child (and indeed anyone who is willing to pursue longer meditations on important works for children) will find a lasting resource in this book.

In its rather unique bringing together of phenomenology and literature, each chapter of this book can serve at least two uses. First and foremost, each chapter is part of an introduction to phenomenology as a method and as a philosophical practice. Interested readers, undergraduate and graduate students, and scholars in philosophy and the humanities will find a great deal of guided reflection on key texts and terms in the first half to two-thirds of most chapters, each of which is subtitled "Phenomenological Theory." This "introduction" to phenomenology is not intended to be cursory or superficial. Instead, it is meant to be a rich, oriented, and deep reflection.

Secondly, each chapter offers a phenomenological reading of a key children's literary text. Parents, elementary school teachers, students and scholars in literature and education will find in the second half of each chapter a number of possibilities for curricular development and research. I encourage readers who are primarily interested in the literary meditations that the book offers to turn directly to this second section of each chapter, entitled "Literary Practice." That is, it is not necessary to read the first, theoretical half of each chapter to find the second, practical half useful. And, indeed, it is my hope that these later, more practical sections in each chapter stand on their own. In any case, I offer them to assist all interested adults in developing ways of engaging children around the issues of community, gender, race, religious experience, and loss.

With respect to its attempt to introduce its readers to the theoretical insights of phenomenology, I would claim that the whole book ultimately asks what childhood means in order to answer a larger question—namely, the question of what phenomenology itself is *for*. And, by means of these chapters taken together, what phenomenology is for, I argue, is the rebuilding of our larger communities into reflections of the essential structures of our lived experience as human beings.

In other words, *phenomenology is for politics*. And it is for the creation of a specific kind of politics—one made to be in the image of the human—of the child as much as the adult. Phenomenology encourages us to make advances in our familial, educational, and civic structures such that we are increasingly able to recognize the meaningful possibilities of mutual relationships, of mutual recognition, within them. If our politics begin to reflect our perceptual and existential structures, if we make our politics more phenomenological, we might learn how not only to govern each other but also to govern ourselves with a healthy view of the collective (and not simply the family) as the home from which we emerge and to which we return.

Having situated what follows in this book with respect to related fields, and having given shape to its ultimate argument, I would like to turn now to an introduction to some of the key concepts in phenomenology that I use throughout the book. After that introduction, I will offer a summary of each chapter, including an initial discussion of each children's book treated therein.

For the purposes of this book, phenomenology is a field of Continental (read: French and German) philosophy that begins with the work of Edmund Husserl at the turn of the twentieth century. In what follows, I define some of the key Husserlian terms. I then do some of the same with those of Maurice Merleau-Ponty and Martin Heidegger. I do not intend to be exhaustive here. However, I do want to give the reader a basic framework for understanding the phenomenology employed in both the theoretical and practical sections of each chapter of the book.

In order to sketch an introduction to the thought of Husserl, I would first like to offer a brief comment on Husserl's main predecessor, Immanuel Kant. Although Immanuel Kant took up the term "phenomenon" in the eighteenth century, and though he meant by that term something similar to Husserl's term, i.e., a thing which appears or shows itself to us as perceiving subjects, still it is true that Kant used the term "phenomenon" quite differently. For Kant, the phenomenon, which appears to us as subjects, was separated from the noumenon, which names not that which appears but that which was absolutely true, the thing-in-itself, which could not ever appear.

Because of this distinction, Kant's work on phenomena was always haunted by the spectre of never really reaching the way things truly are. And his revelation of the structures of consciousness or of mind as a priori or transcendental, as producing the possibility for phenomena, never quite undid that spectre. For those a priori, transcendental structures were, like the noumena, not themselves able to be experienced.

Insofar as they were not able to be experienced, Kant's structures of consciousness, including the categories we use or the intuitions of space and time, were something like what we might now call brain events. Brain events, measured on a CT or an MRI machine, are what a doctor insists are the reasons for our thoughts or feelings. But we simply have to trust the doctor that there is a link between brain events and our thoughts and feelings. We do not experience our own brain events. The machine registers them; the doctor "reads" them. But we experience *meanings* and not our brain.

A similar criticism is possible, I believe, of Kant's epistemology. We do not experience Kantian categories or pure intuitions of space and time—not in ourselves and not in the things of our experience. Rather, the categories and pure intuitions are for Kant structures we could not do without; we *must* accept them as the conditions for what we *do* in fact experience. Just as we trust the doctor who reads the brain scans, we must trust Kant who identifies the categories.

With Husserl, the meaning of phenomenon changes. There are no noumena that we experience, so the noumenon drops out of consideration. Indeed, Husserl makes it a rule never to try to assert, to name, or to uncover anything that lies outside of experience. Instead of trying to compel us to believe in structures we cannot see, Husserl places us firmly within the *act* of seeing. Whatever Husserl presents as structures of consciousness, or essential insights into perception, we can and should find within our own experience.

For Husserl, positing or following up on the noumena, assuming that we are beings who have structures we ourselves cannot perceive and thus are not responsible for—that would be a matter for theologians or scientists. It would be for those interested in conviction or prediction. Instead, Husserl proposes a method to stay only with phenomena, only with our lived experience as we live it, and to ensure that we root any structural insights, any mention of categories or pure intuitions, within that experience.

The principle by which Husserl articulates this method is as follows:

> that every originarily giving intuition is a legitimizing source of cognition, that everything that originarily presents itself to us (so to speak in its 'bodily' actuality [*leibhaften Wirklichkeit*]) in intuition is to be accepted simply as what it gives itself to be—but also only within the limits in which it gives itself there. . . . Every statement that does no more than lend expression to such givennesses by simple explication and by means of carefully measured signifi-

cations is . . . actually an absolute beginning, called upon to serve as a foundation [*Grundlegung*] (Husserl 1983, 44).

This is the famous "principle of all principles" for Husserl. To stay within the
limits of the thing as it is given, as it "gives itself" or "presents itself" to us—
this is the goal. In recognizing givenness and the thing's agency as that which
we respond to, Husserl likewise tries to corral our linguistic usage. Words
should not create things but rather "lend expression" to givenness, to things
and perform "an absolute beginning." The goal is to found our further experiences by disclosing the meaning that the *thing leads us toward.*

For Husserl, this principle of all principles involves the discovery of our
own transcendental, essential structures of consciousness. Such structures
are, just as Kant claimed, a priori and transcendental. But the reason we are
able to discover them and to use them to "lend expression" to the given
meanings of things is that these transcendental, a priori structures of consciousness *are*, Husserl maintains, able to be experienced: "we ourselves
shall be drawn into an inner transformation, through which we will come
face to face with, to direct experience of the long-felt but constantly con-
cealed dimension of the transcendental" (Husserl 1968, 100).

Phenomenology, then, introduces us to the fact that the structures of our
consciousness are thus able to be faced directly, in "direct experience." Phenomenology is experiential; our essential structures are *not* like brain events.
We do not have to accept them without evidence.

And because they are experiential, the structures of consciousness really
allow us to see, to reach, the things themselves, and to *extend* the givenness
of things by explicating their interrelationships, their correlation, with us.
There is no hidden thing that we can assert with any experiential sense. There
are only the sides or the layers of our experience that are latent, not yet
grasped in their adequate evidence but sketched out or predelineated in ad-
vance of (and for) our future work.

Following his principle of all principles, one of the first (and one of the
main) insights Husserl discovers is something he calls *intentionality*:

> Like perception, every intentive mental process [lived experience]—just this
> makes up the fundamental part of intentionality—has its "intentional Object,"
> that is, its objective sense. Or in other words to have sense or to "intend to"
> something . . . is the fundamental characteristic of all consciousness (Husserl
> 1983, 90).

Intentionality is the name for the inherent togetherness of ourselves as
perceivers or subjects and the objects that we perceive, remember, anticipate,
imagine, etc. The "having" of sense together, the belonging together—this is
the essence of consciousness.

This inherent togetherness, this givenness of the thing and of the act of perceiving together in the unity of an overarching experience, is an insight that every other phenomenologist after Husserl retains, including Martin Heidegger and Maurice Merleau-Ponty but also including later post-phenomenological thinkers like Emmanuel Levinas and Jacques Derrida.

We experience intentionality every time we experience any concrete thing. Things are intertwined with us as consciousness because they are *given* to us as implying an already existent relationship with us. We do not create them; we respond to them. We find them within our experience as always already there, as having pre-existed our explicit awareness of them. As given, the thing tends to have a kind of agency. It irritates or excites us. And, in irritation or excitement, we experience that thing as showing itself in person or in the flesh (Husserl claims that the thing presents itself as *leibhaftig*). And so it calls to us as being of the same kind of thing as we are (our lived body for Husserl is a *Leib*).

This givenness of the thing and its togetherness with us is not an immediate or simple idea. Rather, the togetherness of consciousness and object has always already meant that any aspect of the thing we perceive is tied to a moment of who we are and what we do in order to perceive it. The givenness together is therefore also a deferred intimacy, a deferral which points to the future. In other words, the thing is, in his description, an *index* of our actions to perceive or to know it:

> The object is, so to speak, a pole of identity, always meant *expectantly* as having a sense yet to be actualized; in every moment of consciousness it is an *index* pointing to a noetic intentionality that pertains to it according to its sense (Husserl 1960, 45–46, my emphasis).

This "index" then is a yearning, a leaning, a "pointing" or referring back to the act that takes it up. It is a concretization of the future that we "expect" by means of its internal references to our own powers of perceiving and knowing.

The discovery of this correlation between noesis and noema is something that Husserl views as making possible a "radical" re-evaluation of our experience:

> the radicalness that sees in everything given beforehand as existing *an index* for a system of uncoverable constitutive *performances* is indeed the most extreme radicalness in the striving to uproot all prejudice (Husserl 1978, 276, my emphasis).

Only as recognizing the thing as projecting back onto us, as "existing" the future of our actions—only by doing that can we prevent ourselves from collapsing the thing immediately into our initial view or conception of it. By recognizing the correlation of noesis and noema as the essence of consciousness, we move, as the Husserlian dictum goes, *toward the things themselves*. We experience only a perspectival slice of any spatial thing, for example. Or we experience only one note of a song at any one moment. But we see through the perspective to the whole and we hear through the note to the song *immediately*. This is because, Husserl says, the thing gives itself to us as a whole, as corresponding or correlating itself in its total meaning to the total unity of our life. We see the whole house because we are the being that can anticipate and thus verify the other sides by walking around it. We hear the whole song because we are the being that can unify the past and the future with the present. Because of the *way* things are given with and in our consciousness, that is, we are always already aware of *more than we can account for* at any one moment.

Why are we given more than we can account for? In order to always have sufficient motivation to act, to move, to live into the unfolding of meaning in our experience. We are given more than we can account for in order to discover more, in order to have a role in the explication of the meaning of the world. We are given more in order to be part of the process of the world as it resides within our consciousness.

In order to render his description of our entanglement with things and with the world more adequately into a grammar that helps us to remember it, Husserl designates the object as it is perceived by the ancient Greek word *noema*: "perception, for example, has its noema, most basically its perceptual sense, i.e., the *perceived as perceived*" (Husserl 1983, 88). The object is not separate from my act of perceiving. Rather it is "as perceived" that the object appears at all.

And the act of perceiving is what he names, similarly, a *noesis*: "such noetic moments are, e.g., directions of regard of the pure Ego to the objects "meant" . . . furthermore, seizing upon this object, holding it fast while the regard adverts to other objects" (Husserl 1983, 88). The same experience, then, embraces a relationship, a correlation, between act and object. These do not begin as separate but as together.

When I am in a museum, looking at a painting, the actions of my eyes as they pass around the picture, the position of my body and head, the walking or sitting that I perform in the act of "taking it in," these are all noeses or noetic acts. The particular experiences of the painting from this or that position, the colors as I see them under this or that lighting, etc.—these are aspects or layers of the noema. The noesis and the noema are only separable in reflection, and only for the sake of noticing the rhythm of their togetherness, of their mutual implication.

The togetherness of subject and object, of me and the painting, is something that Husserl carries forward from his discussion of simple, static objects into his description of our dynamic experiences of our lived body and of other people. Our body is not separate from our consciousness. It *is* our consciousness. Our body is the intelligent way of having a world.

And the experience of other people makes one's own intentionality, this togetherness or non-dualism of thing and consciousness, body and mind—it makes it even richer. When I experience another person, Husserl says, I see another body there *as another consciousness*. As such, when I experience another person, I feel as if my whole consciousness, in all of its very bodily structures, in all of its perceptual positions, were doubled. But it is not exactly doubled. For if the other were really just another me, she or he would never appear as separate, as *other* to me. And I am always reminded that the other's perceptions never quite map onto my own.

The experience of the other person as this doubling, which is never quite a doubling, of the structure of my consciousness is what Husserl calls pairing: "ego and alter ego are always and necessarily given in an original pairing" (Husserl 1960, 112). It is not despite our differences but through them that we are given together. And it is by means of our imperfect pairing, our mutual implication with other people, that we always find ourselves within a relationship that situates us both.

And the essence of *any* such a pairing relationship, which Husserl calls intersubjectivity, is that by which we can come to question our paradoxical situation:

> How can a component part of the world, its human subjectivity, constitute the whole world, namely constitute it as its intentional formation . . . formed by the universal interconnection of intentionally accomplishing subjectivity, while the latter, the *subjects accomplishing in cooperation*, are themselves only a *partial* formation within the total accomplishment (Husserl 1968, 179).

By means of our ability to pair with this radically other person, each of us shares the same world. Each of us has this entire world as a meaning within our consciousness. Each of us has the world as the most significant noema of our noetic life.

And yet each of us stands on or within the world as one among many things and other people. Our consciousness, our acts of perceiving and thinking, are themselves both at least partially transparent, visible, tactile to each other *and* at least partially contested by those same other people. We see each other seeing the world. And we recognize each other as recognizing each other. And thus at one and the same time we confirm and challenge the meanings that the world comes to have.

In our acts of sharing and contesting the meanings that we experience, we begin to notice that *the world is in us* and that *we are in the world*. From this recognition comes the renewed task of having to work more systematically together. None of us will fully dominate the other or fully control the other's perception; rather, each of us experiences on behalf of the other. And so we have to refine our method of description in order to disclose the further layers of meaning that arise from the fact of our relationships.

It is because of this intertwining between a thing's noematic givenness and my noetic acts, because of the entanglement of myself and other, and because of our being both within the world while that same world is within our consciousness—it is because of all this mutual implication that the task of phenomenology for Husserl is infinite. An adequate description of any experience, of any thing in the world, of any person, of any situation—this is never fully achieved. There are always new layers to be uncovered, new implications to be realized. And each new layer of meaning offers each of us some new possible insight into the very manner and style of our experience, into the *how* of our relations to the world and to each other.

Briefly, what phenomenology discovers is this: what we can say about any lived experience with other people, any situation, is that the concepts or phrases that make its meaning explicit must come from *within* that experience, from *within* that situation if those concepts are ones that we can share effectively. Our shared categories must arise within the givens, including our givenness to each other, as something the *thing brings* to mind in our grasp of it. And instead of trying to force the experience to obey a previously assumed series of ideological positions, we should instead allow the experience itself to guide us, subordinating our speech and thinking to the way that the thing shows us we should take it up.

Martin Heidegger, a student of Husserl, takes Husserl's phenomenology more explicitly in this direction of hermeneutics. Heidegger emphasizes the fact that the structures of consciousness are ones that the human being *exists*. That is, not only are the a priori structures of consciousness able to be experienced, as Husserl asserts, but they also *disclose* the meaning of the human being to itself in the context of the human's larger (often unexpressed or unthematized) project of moving toward the meaning of Being or toward the source and end of all givenness.

Using existence and hermeneutics as his theme, then, Heidegger is able to recognize that intentionality permeates, in addition to one's perceptual and bodily life, one's emotional life as well. Our moods have a say in our perceptions. And one mood among others, anxiety, Heidegger views as actually and especially creative. Anxiety allows us to wrestle with our finitude, with the limits of our birth and death, and to create the possibility for authenticity within an explicit grasp of that finitude. By showing how consciousness is embodied in a life that has to end, we can hold in view the fact that the call of things and of the world and other people is also a call to conscience, to poetic disclosure of meaning as wrapped up with this concrete situation in which each of us has a specific role.

After Heidegger, Maurice Merleau-Ponty furthers Husserl's intentionality by bringing the structures of consciousness more clearly into the psychological and genetic realms. Merleau-Ponty clarifies Husserl's discussion of pairing when he discusses the relevance of "intercorporeality" or the way in which our conscious embodiments imply one another. A situation, for Merleau-Ponty, is not simply perceptual or existential. It is also sexual, concerned with kinetic movement, and developmental.

Studying children, people with mental illness, and people with physical disabilities, Merleau-Ponty tries to show how Husserlian insights into phenomenology have to take not just an existential path but a path that accounts for how our initial, childhood perceptions take root and support more developed, adult perceptions. For Merleau-Ponty, a child, even an infant, has relations with other persons that show a kind of premature understanding, that root the child in future dialogue. This prematuration grows out of a situation in which the experience of the child is one of shared embodiment— shared often with the mother and other parent or adult figures. In light of his own research, Merleau-Ponty tries to explain how the normal, adult individuality, which Husserl presupposes in his early analysis of consciousness, is an achievement and not an immediacy.

After Merleau-Ponty, there are a number of other significant figures who take phenomenology into specific fields—R. D. Laing takes phenomenology into psychotherapy; Edith Stein and Emmanuel Levinas, into religious studies; Jacques Derrida, into literary theory and political science. Each major figure in this larger phenomenological tradition owes a great deal to Husserl and to the establishment of the method of phenomenological description.

Of course there are many disagreements. And it may not be quite true to say that there is *one* method of phenomenology. There are a variety of approaches. However, the guiding "principle of all principles," which Husserl formulated in his first book of the *Ideas* trilogy, remains. That principle, once more, is to describe things in the manner in which they demand to be described and only within the limits in which they give themselves.

As phenomenologists, then, we are to respond to the call of things, of contexts and situations, of other people. We are to try to put aside the prejudices of our unreflective practices, national or religious or familial commitments. And we are to try to interrogate texts, things, other people in such a way as to allow that text, that thing, that other person to show itself as clearly as possible *on its own terms.*

In the following chapters, I introduce a number of the main figures I have briefly commented on here. Starting with Husserl and Merleau-Ponty, I move then to Heidegger and on to figures such as John Dewey and Paolo Freire, who have taken insights similar to Husserl's, especially with respect to intentionality, and provided us with a glimpse of a phenomenological, democratic politics, and pedagogy.

The book proceeds in stages by way of demonstrating the applicability of phenomenology to different themes. From a discussion of finitude, to community, to gender, it then works its way to religious experience and, finally, to education. In some sense, though, the book has always been implicitly about education and politics. It is just that the final chapter will thematize this as phenomenology's most authentic position and contribution.

In the first chapter, I examine the well-known, Newbery Medal–winning novel *Charlotte's Web* by E. B. White. Using Husserl's discussion of pairing and intersubjectivity, as well as his attention to the phenomenon of time-consciousness and transition, I articulate how the characters of Charlotte the spider and Wilbur the pig work together to educate each other, and the rest of the barnyard community, to the terrifying but ultimately redeeming situations of aging, of friendship, of loss, and of a life that can transcend grief. It is thus my intention here, with Husserl and with E. B. White's novel, to perform a phenomenology of time and finitude.

In the second chapter, I examine *The Mouse and His Child* by Russell Hoban. While not winning a Newbery Medal, the book has been extremely popular, spawning not only an animated movie but also, more recently, a Royal Shakespeare Company adaptation. Using Merleau-Ponty's discussion of child development and of intercorporeality, I describe how the novel sets up a phenomenology of emotion, embodiment, and community. Like *Charlotte's Web*, Hoban's novel is almost completely about animals, whether mechanized or alive. However, this focus on the animal does not prevent the reader from identifying with the characters, particularly the childlike ones. In fact, Hoban's book functions by way of differences even within the animal characters to comment upon the difficulties but also the possibilities of creating a cross-cultural community.

Following a discussion of Hoban's novel, I then move to take up a discussion of Harper Lee's Pulitzer Prize–winning novel *To Kill a Mockingbird*. Focusing on the character of Scout and her capacity to perform her own version of gender, I notice how Lee creates the possiblity for historical progress only by means of Scout's free movement. In my reading of the novel, I use Merleau-Ponty's phenomenological descriptions of sexuality and embodiment from his major work, *The Phenomenology of Perception*, and I show how Scout embodies these concepts in her life. There is of course an implicit phenomenology of education and of politics here in this chapter, and in Lee's novel, but the overall argument of this chapter is focused on how the treatment and description of sexuality requires a great deal of care in order to promote the freedom of our lived experience adequately, i.e., without causing unnecessary restriction and harm.

Having talked about a phenomenology of finitude, emotion, community, and gender, I then turn to one of religious experience. Using Madeleine L'Engle's *A Wrinkle in Time*, I discover resonances with (and concretizations of) the phenomenology of Martin Heidegger. Using Heidegger's *Being and Time* and his *Phenomenology of Religious Life*, I argue that L'Engle's main character, Meg Murry, shows quite concretely what it means for a child to explore a life of disclosure of meaning (or hermeneutics) by way of her call of conscience and of her response to a tradition of religious believers. The chapter concludes by noting how L'Engle has, like Heidegger, used the structures of religious experience as the center of her description of human experience as such.

Finally, in examining the recent Newbery Medal–winning *Merci Suárez Changes Gears* by Meg Medina, I perform a more explicit phenomenology of education and of politics. Medina's novel is about sixth-grader Merci Suárez who struggles with issues of class, gender, and race in contemporary Florida. These issues demonstrate a need for the kind of education that Husserl and Merleau-Ponty have only hinted at but which John Dewey and Paolo Freire explicitly take up. The book thus ends with a political exhortation— toward the communal re-evaluation of pedagogy as attending to the needs of finite children who desire to become free.

Chapter One

Charlotte's Web, Temporality, and the Transitions of Growth

PHENOMENOLOGICAL THEORY—
HUSSERL ON TRANSITION AND TIME-CONSCIOUSNESS

A. Introduction

In the theoretical part of this first chapter, I will introduce the reader to the thought of Edmund Husserl on time-consciousness and on transition.[1] In talking about time-consciousness, this chapter will follow up on the introduction's brief discussion of intentionality. In other words, this chapter assumes the truth of the experience of intentionality—i.e., the togetherness of consciousness and objects, of consciousness and other people, and of consciousness and world.

We experience time *because* we are already entangled beyond ourselves in the world and with the world. We experience time because our consciousness is always consciousness *of* something else. Of something that demands our moments and motion to know it more fully. But this breaking away from ourselves, this being broken open, or broken into, by the world and people and things is not without our own internal preparation.

Our hearts beat, our blood flows, our hair and bodies grow larger and stronger and, then, somewhat sadly, smaller and weaker. Our thoughts move from one to the other. Our attention passes from this note of the song to the next, from our parents and teachers to our—or another's—children.

As we move toward others and their experiences, however, we see that everything that we are makes it apparent that our entanglement with the world is, at the same time, a time that matters specifically to each of us in specific ways. Time that is "outside" or in the world, time that is shared,

13

matters to us because it maps on to the motions of time that we *already are* as these specific individuals.

We are prepared for the time of the world, for the time it takes to make friends and to lose them, to live and to become ill, because something in us *is also time*. We are time-exuders. We live as beings that hold on to the past and anticipate the future. And we are these holders and anticipators without explicit help from others. We exist time in our own lives, as those very lives.

But we also experience and exist our own time as never staying put, as always sliding away from us, as opening onto something shared. We are never, even if we are each our own time, time all on our own. Before we have noticed it, perhaps in irritation or celebration that we are sharing moments together, our internal awareness of time has already geared into the time of other people and of things and of the shared world in which we encounter everything. Our time is both our own and shared.

Time then is both a habit of motion, which we exist at every level (and in every content) of our consciousness, and also a discovery. It is a privacy and a sharing and, in the case of a death of a friend or parent or child, a grievous, forced return into solitude. Time is both our own and shared. And this is what makes it so difficult to describe.

This chapter will focus on our experience of time by focusing on our experience of transition. We move, always move, forwards and backwards toward remembered or anticipated or imagined experiences. We synthesize experiences together as we move from one to the other. We see a tree and then another one, and we pair them as a "pair of trees." We read one page and then another, and we read a story. And we have done this without recognizing it. Our time flows and so do our acts. So does the meaning of the world.

So we will attempt here to notice that flowing and that motion of making a transition. And we will see that the child, most of all the child, is immersed in transition, in becoming. And we will see White's *Charlotte's Web* as the way in which a pig, a spider, and a little girl, somewhat at the same time, begin to come to terms with their lives as transition and to become better able to perform a phenomenology. The spider, the pig, the girl—each performs an explication of meaning, specifically with regard to words in the web, as the time of their changing, of their motion, claims them here and now by means of their very *inability to rest* in that same moment that claims them.

This notion of transition has a kind of purchase even outside of phenomenology. So before I approach Husserl, I will first pursue it within a more explicitly pedagogical setting. At issue here will be the transitions that we perform in order to be a self and in order to read a word, a sentence, or a book. For in reading, we perform meaning in and through time.

In *Philosophy in the Classroom*, Lipman, Sharp, and Oscanyon argue, with a child's moral education specifically in mind, the following:

the self at any one time is always in the process of *transition*, contingent upon the means that are available to us to achieve the goals that are sought. Thus, the availability of means conditions and modifies our ideals and objectives, just as, conversely, the ends we have in view control the way we search for means to employ and the selves we are in the process of becoming (Lipman 2010, 204).

This process of transition is something that the authors note about selves in general—without a distinction between child and adult. Each human self, on this view, is more determined by its *movement* than by its points of departure and arrival. This transitional status of all selves is an important point to be unpacked, and I will spend the rest of this introduction attempting such an unpacking.

As a good deal of current research in children and education and children's literature shows, children are not little versions of adults. They are not transitional in the sense of lacking development, as being on the way to "us," as it were. To see children as undeveloped adults would be to commit oneself to the fallacy of developmentalism, more useful for categorizing and disciplining those without immediate credentials to power than to listening, understanding, and interacting.

In fact, were we to think of children as undeveloped adults, who were simply making linear moves of transition into adulthood, we would also compromise our own self-understanding. For Lipman, Sharp, and Oscanyon, the self is transitional as such. There is no static, developed "self," no endpoint, that determines adults either. On the contrary, adults cannot authentically maintain a sense of having "made it" or developed sufficiently that can allow them to stop being active, creative readers of each other or texts.

If adults are *certain* that they have fully understood a person or a text without further ado, then they are stuck—not well-developed or mature. And the self-reflection into their own "stuck" process of becoming can only come within the inevitable arrival of a painful, and ultimately unnecessarily painful, conflict of interpretations.

We can do real harm, therefore, not only to children but also to ourselves, if we attempt to construe what we experience in terms of an arbitrary, perhaps binary, system of categories. To put this point another way: we can prevent our own "process of becoming" if we do not develop the kind of supple perceptions or acts of reading that answer not to ourselves alone but to the plurality of experiences that demands to be described together with our own.

In contrast with the previous, stuck vision I have been describing, stands the possibility of seeing each self as defined by a process of transition, of evolutionary movement. To see oneself as this "process of becoming" is to liberate oneself for the kind of active, creative moments of perception or "reading" that can draw a larger community to notice its own plurality and rich possibilities for further, shared work.

How did I miss that interpretation? Who do I have to become to hear that text or that music as emotionally moving?—These are the kinds of questions we become open to when we see movement, and not development, as the definition of a self. And thus to highlight the notion of transition as the metaphysical lynchpin of humanity is productive—it allows us to see how many selves we might call on to help us flesh out our shared world.

To return to the quote from Lipman, Sharp, and Oscanyon above, we can see that a focus on transition allows us also to notice the following two things: first, we see that we are already answering to our own multi-dimensional temporal structure. We are not simply on a linear, one-directional timeline. Rather, we are, even now, dwelling within the persons we were and anticipating the persons we will be. We are constantly moving into the past and future, and we are constantly readjusting the way our past and future *selves* define and matter to us now.

We are therefore never really fully or only here and now. We are never fully *this* present self. Rather, we are moving into and out of a plurality of moments, a plurality of selves within the present moment. We are, in effect, always spreading ourselves out backwards and forwards. And this means that, far from a simple linear motion, our transitions from present to past and future have the shape of a zigzag, as we go back and forth from our present selves. Speaking phenomenologically, each self is "ecstatic" in its movement, always moving outside of itself, dancing with other versions of itself, combining with and letting go of them in various styles of living.

Second, we see that our transitional self is precisely capable of—one might almost say *designed* for—attending to our places and possible roles in a shared situation. That is, referring back again to the quote from Lipman, Sharp, and Oscanyon, we see that we are *called* to move as transitional selves between means and ends, in a zigzag fashion. We are called, therefore, to negotiate a shared world because each of us is one among many transitional selves who are all confronted together by larger situations with scarce resources. In short, we see that we share the world and each situation of our living with others, and, because of that, we are called to deploy our transitional movement between the means and ends of our own choices.

Our transitional structure thus points us to the inherent morality of shared life. We are a process of becoming. But so is the world and our situations within it. These two processes gear into one another and require our careful, attentive, moral response. Because we are capable of multi-dimensional movement, then, we are *also* capable of multi-dimensional perception and action that is called for by this world. We can and (implicitly, since we are always already *in* the world) we *must* deploy our rich selves toward the becoming of the world. We can and we must continuously reconnoiter and redefine both means and ends.

We are a process of becoming, in short, in order to answer to what this world, what this situation, is itself becoming around us. And so the notion of transition is thus triply important: 1) We move within our temporality; 2) we move within the limits of situations in which we find ourselves to be ensconced; 3) the world or the situation itself moves around us as do the others who share it with us. To remain caught in the notion of static development, to refuse to see transition as the key notion to human experience, is to become stuck or lost in oneself or in a situation, in a world, that is changing around us and calling for a changing, supple act of perception, of "reading."

Indeed, I use that word "reading" intentionally. Perhaps most noticeably we exist our transitional, moving selves in the act of reading a book—a novel like E. B. White's *Charlotte's Web*. For in the act of reading we slip from the person who we are into the characters, into the situation of the book. And when reading and responding to texts we practice self-movement and self-formation.

A book like White's *Charlotte's Web* moves us, perhaps. We feel an identification with the characters, and we develop a way of processing its key moments. Where have we gone? Who are we? These questions are difficult to answer when we are ensconced in the book. Afterwards, when we talk about our reading with others, we come to see, perhaps for the first time, who we have been, what we have noticed. And we may also see that our reading can conflict with another's.

In the case of such conflict, and finding that ours is not the only interpretative stance, we may (productively) feel compelled to return to the text again. We know we *can* do so, since the other person has already done it to a different end. And we may well *desire* to do so in order to become the person who can navigate multiple possible (and actual) responses to this same text. We learn, in the case of such conflict, that we can return to the process of self-formation in reading in order to re-engage the formation of a response.

In our re-vision, we see perhaps what we had not seen before. We see what allowed the other to see the book that way. And we see that the text has a multiplicity of openings to a variety of selves, selves who can each take up the same text differently as "means to employ" their own action in the description of a larger, shared world.

To re-view what it means to read by reading again is to find oneself in a laboratory, perhaps. A laboratory that demands, as it were, that one be more or less pleasantly engaged with a multi-layered text . . . a text that seems in the end to be as transitional as oneself is.

This novel, this story, that captured our attention gives its ending to us, perhaps, as a moment of sadness. Who am I leaving behind at the end of the story? Why cannot I continue to be who I was within the act of reading? This text, if it moves us in these ways, does not simply develop or unfold its static self. Rather, it moves (and it *moves us*) in a kind of evolution of interpretations, each of which both preserves and outstrips the others as the text lives its transitional life through us, its readers.

We are transitional selves. We take up a book as one of the means and ends that assist our "process of becoming." But the text too is transitional. It reads itself into us. It takes us up and encodes our process with its own. Who is thinking in us when we read? The text? Or our own selves? Perhaps it is too binary to try to place the power or the blame on one or the other.

B. Husserl on Transition and Temporality

On the one hand, if we go back to the quote from *Philosophy in the Classroom* above, we see that the self is transitional because the "means" to be an effective and stable self, the means to reach a set of goals, are limited. We need to wait to see what we will become, in other words, because the means we employ may not become available to us until later, if at all. We are transitional because we are moving between means and ends, like children with an allowance running back and forth through multiple stores for the most we can get for our small sum of money. Sadly, the quote implies, some of us just will not make it to a stable self, or to a satisfactory object of desire, because the means to do so were denied us.

On the other hand, the second sentence of the quoted material declares that, even absent the appropriate means, the self may still participate in its own becoming. And with hope we realize that, even a poor person, even an impoverished self without an allowance, who is bound for death as the spider Charlotte seems to be in the novel, can still legislate the tenor of its transitions. Where does this hope come from? What legitimates it?

For Lipman, Sharp, and Oscanyon, I surmise that the hope arises because the self recognizes that the availability or lack of appropriate means can "modifiy" ideals and objectives but can never fully undo them. There is something irreducible to the power of self-determined ends or goals. And, even without the means to support them, our own choices structure our becoming and our very encounter with means as such. Charlotte the spider, for example, cannot accompany her children who are to be born out of her passing. And yet that does not undo her strength in creating her *magnum opus.*

Like children, like Charlotte, we find out quickly what our allowance will "allow," and we anticipate ourselves and our desires and disappointments in our response. For example, we may change our minds in terms of what we go to buy with our allowance so that our hearts are not broken. Or we may reckon with small disappointments and refuse to buy anything at all so that we can participate in a process of hoping for later, larger acquisitions. By virtue of our power in making the move between ends and ourselves then, some of us will achieve moments of satisfaction and stability in terms of self and desired objects by means of changing the definitions of desire, self, and stability.

Of course there are no guarantees that satisfaction or stability will ensue when a child receives an allowance. But the ethical tension that the allowance affords, this being in transition with respect to self, means, and ends, is something that phenomenology recognizes as indicating an important, structural truth of the self—namely, that a motion transition occurs within and makes possible all layers or acts of selfhood. Let us now move on to consider three of those layers of selfhood in Husserl's descriptions: our involvement with things, our consciousness of internal time, and our experience of others.

Let us first consider the way the movement of transition is operative within our experience of perceived things. Husserl's description of experience in his *Ideas*, for example, notes that the perception of a table unfolds between two poles, the acts of perceiving the table (or *noeses*), and the appearances of the object, in this case the table, within those acts (or the *noema*). According to Husserl, then, the perceived table (the *noema*) only gives itself as a meaning we can recognize continuously by means of a never-ending "zigzag"[2] back and forth between noesis and noema, between the way in which the subject discovers the object and the way in which the object solicits the subject.

In this sense, the phenomenological description of experience really is the necessary motion back and forth between the poles that coalesce the self around them. Or, to put it bluntly, phenomenology describes the relationship between object and subject as the very establishment of the self in its ability to declare more or less stable positions.[3]

For example, we can experience a row of trees and then one of the trees in the row. The movement of our perception from the row to the individual is not the death of the row. Rather, the experience of the whole row, Husserl says, "is retained in grasp, in the familiar manner, as a unity which, in the *transition* [*im Übergang*] from part to part, constantly enriches itself and which coincides with itself in its different parts" (Husserl 1973, 142, my emphasis). The very unfolding of my experience, then, from wholes to parts is an experience of movement, of preserving or "retaining in grasp" the whole in order to experience and to make a judgment about its parts.

But this capacity I have in perception to move between noesis and noema, or to move between substrates and qualities or wholes and parts has deeper roots. And indeed I believe that it is in Husserl's description of time-consciousness, the second layer of subjectivity that I want to discuss, that he demonstrates how the correlation of our acts of perceiving with our perceived objects, how our coherent unfolding of one experience through changes in orientation, is guaranteed, passively, by our self-experience of our internal time.[4]

Any continuity in our acts of perception or of motion, our "going over" from one thing to another depends on an ongoing, fundamental temporal act—a synthesis, as Husserl calls it, of transition. In this synthesis of transition, we do not simply vacillate or meander from point to point in time. Rather we *maintain* the former point within the latter one. The temporal synthesis of transition that we perform is thus the process, the becoming of a *flow* of time, our time, as a unity. It is the glue, the stitching, the continuity of our selfhood.

Husserl describes this synthesis of transition explicitly in *On the Phenomenology of the Consciousness of Internal Time.* In the following discussion, Husserl is comparing the way in which the auditory experience of hearing a tone in all of its phases of increasing and decreasing intensity, pitch, volume, etc., is analogously or essentially similar to the temporal synthesis of transition from moment to moment in time-consciousness:

> Throughout this whole flow of consciousness, one and the same tone is intended as enduring, as now enduring. Beforehand . . . it is not intended. Afterwards, it is still intended for a time in retention as having been; it can be *held fast* and stand or remain fixed in our regard. The whole extent of the tone's duration . . . stands before me as something *dead*, so to speak—something no longer being vitally generated, a formation no longer animated by the generative point of the now but continuously modified and sinking back into *emptiness*. The modification of the whole extent, then, is *analogous* to or *essentially identical* with the modification that the elapsed part of the duration undergoes in the *transition* of consciousness to ever new productions during the time that the tone is actually present (Husserl 1991, 26, my emphasis).

The experience of hearing a tone, then, is fraught with the possibility of loss from the very beginning. Because it begins, the tone also ends. And because of its beginning and ending, we hold onto it and weave or stitch it together with other tones, with other experiences.

If I experience the tone directly and attentively, perhaps with some pleasure or pride if it is the tone of our child's performance of a piano piece, this does not keep the tone or the whole piece from becoming "dead" or passing out of my perception into "emptiness." Instead, part of hearing tones and melodies is hearing and *preserving* their life *in* their death *as they pass* "to ever new productions" of the world of sounds or the melody being played.

Sounds, tones, melodies, end. How do we maintain them in order to experience and remember and enjoy them? We maintain them, Husserl argues, because their passing away, their death, is "analogous or essentially identical" with the way consciousness maintains its flow of "transition" in ever new moments. We maintain them because that is what our temporal structure does. We continue, we live, we maintain. What is dead or dying to us is never simply dead. It is maintained with the horizon of memory and expectation, within the project of meaning that is essentially a flow that gathers together each moment with the others.

The synthesis of transition, then, is the "modification" of loss into narrative. It is the stitching together of the meaning of loss into the meaning of an ongoing flow. If it were not the fact that perception emulates, reproduces the very structure of temporality, we could not enjoy or be proud of the child's performance. It would simply pass away from the moment it began. Enjoyment, celebration, mourning—these are all ways of taking up the death that is at the heart of sound, of song, of life and giving it meaning because we are, to paraphrase Lewis Carroll, the timers of time.

Now this recognition of our self-stitching, of our synthesis of transition, is itself noteworthy. For, though perception essentially replicates its structure, the very skeleton of internal time does not appear to us in the same way as any other noema, as a tone or a melody. Internal time, bare transition as such, does not appear directly. It does not happen in stages. We do not get better or worse at it with practice. Rather, our basic synthesis of transition, our stitching of time is somewhat like our breathing or the pulsing of our blood. That is, our time-stitching is less reflective and more automatic than other experiences. However, it is also even less reflective and even more automatic than our breathing and blood flow.

But this does not mean that we do not experience our synthesis of transition, our stitching of time. We do. But we experience it in a different manner. More properly: the stitching of time is the experience of our lives as *flowing* in a continuity. We experience the *product* of transition as the unity of our flow.

The *fact* that we "stitch" time and the path from moment to moment, from noesis to noema, for our own self-experience is therefore clear. We witness it. We feel, even if we do not see, the *outcome*—namely, the flow and the preservation of our experience within a fairly determinate human life. But the *way* we witness the *steps* of our production of time, the way we manufacture this flow, remains almost *a secret*. We cannot catch ourselves pushing out temporality in the way we can see a spider spinning her web. We do not stitch time or perform transitions in the way that we throw a ball or walk around a table.

And yet, for all this secrecy or indirection, we can experience how this flow of time really is the grounding of the continuity of our experience and how it *must* be we that are doing it:

> This flow is something we speak of in conformity with what is constituted, but it is not something in objective time. It is *absolute subjectivity* and has the absolute properties of something to be designated metaphorically as flow. . . .

In the actuality-experience we have the primal source-point and a *continuity* of
moments of reverberation (Husserl 1991, 79).

When we speak of the experience of our internal time, we seem to be
compelled to speak of flow. The flow of our own time, of our own life
appears, we know not quite how, to our perception. The flow is almost like a
tactile impression, as if we were putting our hand in a stream and feeling the
water move around our fingers.

But something in the idea, the impression and expression of "flow,"
reaches out toward the world. It is not simply that the flow of our lives
"occurs" to us. Rather, something in the necessity of speaking about flow
reverberates outward. If we have to speak of flow, as if time were an object
like a stream we were perceiving with our hand, this is because something in
time is given as if it were an object.

It is not simply that the *word* or *metaphor* "flow" is forced upon us. It is
not simply that we must *speak* in accordance with the experience of objects.
Rather, the very experience of time is the experience of *ourselves* as *being-
or pulsing*-toward the objects themselves.

Flow is our way of being. Time is the experience in ourselves of the very
"conformity" of ourselves with objects, i.e., "with what is constituted." We
have to "speak" of our internal time, as our stitching together, *as if* it were an
object, a flow, a noema *because* time is the very movement of ourselves
toward becoming grounded within the world.

Time is the process of our becoming *like* the objects which we touch. Our
internal time is only "metaphorically" a flow. But it is so in order that we
may in fact live a life that is much more than metaphorically entwined with
objects.

Our temporality, our power of transition, is *given* to us. Our experience of
time is incontrovertible, it is lived. Time is lived, moreover, as a gift we give
to ourselves, a gift from our "absolute" to our concrete subjectivity. Time is
the permission and preparation to enter the world, as one who is akin to
objects. As giving us to ourselves as "constituted," then, time also serves as
the possibility of the preservation of that world as the things and the people
within it recede and disappear.

Time is the recognition that we are responsible for more than we can
perceive. We who perform the synthesis of transition are always already this
"absolute subjectivity" who creates tactile metaphors. And we are this tactile
metaphor of flow in order that we can run our fingers over the surfaces of
things and understand, in that kinesthetic movement, the appearance of a
thing to ourselves as these or those concrete, gendered, historical persons.

By means of our flow, things appear and are caught by us. We produce a
flow of time as a spider does of its own web. It is our doing. And yet we

cannot return to the origin of this flow, this becoming. We cannot bend ourselves to see the webbing emerging from our body.

What we can notice, however, by means of this limitation on our reflection, is that our perceptions of objects, of world, of others, depend on our temporality. The transition from object to object, from adumbration to adumbration, or from object to subject—the "allowance" of our perceptual lives—depends on a transition that underlies it that makes it possible to hold on to what is just past in the passing over to the new.

Like a child who receives an allowance from an adult, we receive our allowance as the purpose of our temporality. We move between moments in order to move between objects and ourselves.

By virtue of the transition, the flow, the continuity of time, we are transitional not as fish are. We do not make a turn and forget what we have just left behind. Rather, within our transition, the *fact* of our transition *matters* to us. We *live through* our transitions from subject to object, from other to self, because we are always already living through the moments that connect them.

We see, as we move, that what has come before is somehow, to varying degrees and in varying ways, implicit in what is now. Life is the perceptual process of fleshing out what temporality means. To read a book, for example, is to see how the unfolding of a text across the time of reading it becomes possible, desirable, etc. And like the understanding or reading of a text, or even the sides of a house as we walk around it, we too are given to ourselves as the same even as we proceed in transition from moment to moment.

With Husserl, then, what we come to see is that, if we were *not* transition with continuity *all the way down*—if our own temporality did not ground and found our perception—well, then no other relationship, and certainly no relationship of noesis and noema, could ever emerge.[5] For the very establishing of relationships is predicated on the ability we have to retain some commonality, some common thread, between the poles. And this achievement is possible only because of the very fact that the present moment in our self-experience, indeed *any and every moment* no matter what that moment is concerned with in terms of content, is biting onto the just past and the just future.[6]

Having defined the synthesis of transition of moments into the flow of internal time as "essentially similar" to the transition of tones into a melody, let us consider the motion of one further transition that brings the other two into focus. Let us now look at a motion which intersects with both absolute and concrete subjectivity, with the flow of temporality and of perception. Let us now look at how we experience other people.

C. Husserl on the Experience of Other People

Husserl's description of our experience of others, intersubjectivity, shows how we are paired with others in a relationship that, as a "passive" whole, grounds and makes sense of our differences. Within that relationship, we are each "moments" of a passing into one another, into a community or a relationship. And, as passing into one another, we enact a reciprocity of multiple acts of interconnected perception, of "awakening" and "overlaying" with others:

> essentially, already in pure *passivity*, (regardless therefore of whether they are noticed or unnoticed), as data appearing with mutual distinctness, they found phenomenologically a unity of similarity, and thus are always constituted precisely as a *pair*. . . . On more precise analysis we find essentially present here an intentional overreaching coming about genetically (and by essential necessity) as soon as the data that undergo pairing have become prominent and simultaneously intended; we find more particularly a *living mutual awakening and an overlaying* of each with the objective sense of the other. . . . As the result of this overlaying there takes place in the paired data a mutual transfer of sense, that is to say an apperception of each according to the sense of the other (Husserl 1960, 148, my emphasis).

This passivity, this pairing concretizes and directs our temporality. We do not just flow. We flow *into* and *across* one another. We do not just *have* moments. We *exist* as a moment relative to one another and relative to the newly discovered "objective sense" of each other within that relationship.

This flow, this isomorphic structure, of internal temporality that we each are is what carries us *into* our relationships with other people. Taking up the *position* of a moment in time, we each move toward one another in a kind of zigzag—not just from noesis to noema, not just from one tone to the next, but from the sense of ourselves on our own to the sense of ourselves with the others:

> Leibniz says that monads have no windows. But I mean that each monadic soul has infinitely many windows. Each understood perception of an alien lived body [*eine fremden Leibes*] is such a window. And each time, if I say, "please, beloved friend," and he answers me understandably—each time this act of speaking is a *transitioning* [*übergegangen*] out of my own I into the I of my friend and vice versa. It is a reciprocal motivation that has, that produces, between us a real unity (Husserl 1973, 473, lines 11–18, my translation and emphasis).

Husserl makes it clear, then, that the motion of transition in time-consciousness is also the motion of communication. We move back and forth toward each other. And the "real unity" between us is the reciprocity and reversibility of our movement.

Even an attempt to be alone is an attempt to reckon with (to flee) the possible glances and stares and words of others. Our very effort to leave them behind reveals them to be a part of our awareness. And so, in the face of others, we continuously move in a zigzag, from them to ourselves, from their perceptions of the world or of us to our own. And it is within this zigzag, within this series of transitional moves, that each of us within the pair can come to understand how we have a "similarity" to one another, a shared world or set of meanings, that we may well have neither seen nor anticipated.

Time, our time, then breaks us open as the continuous, living beings that we are toward the shared time of a shared world. Our own time's structure then replicates itself again as the "mutual transfer of sense" within our relationships with other people. And those same relationships are just the way that we share the opening of time together within a shared conversation or project. Like our internal time, our own meanings also slide across and onto the *shared* meanings of the world and of the relationships in which we find ourselves.

This pre-given pairing relationship, which is always already given and established as more than the sum of us as members or parts, thus guarantees, just as the absolute subjectivity of the temporal flow did, the continuity of our experience. Pairing, like temporal flow, as a manner of *living* time, just *is* the way continuity and unity function for us.[7]

It is ironic, in one way, that the relation by which we are paired with others, by which we perceive them, is, like our internal time, accomplished "passively." Sometimes it seems so necessary and desirable that it be otherwise. We are often very determined to choose reflectively those with whom we would dwell, particularly in terms of friends and loved ones. And yet, as in the act of reading, we often find ourselves committed even to arbitrary or anonymous others, even to the smallest of their gestures, like a smile we return to a smiling face in a commercial, *before* we realize what we are doing, before we realize the smile is about dish detergent.

As far as the pairing with others goes, though, even in the midst of a response that catches us unaware, there is no doubt that the response is ours. We certainly performed the return of the smile to the image of the person selling detergent. And we cannot argue the contrary of this statement very confidently: our seeing the other as meaningful is always already at least in part our activated responsibility.

If our time is that which casts us, and by means of which we cast ourselves, upon the trajectory of our own becoming, then pairing is that by which the world, our own "primordial world" engages our time and sends us forth into the shared world of common experience. Something in the totality of our experience has already broken us toward the other person. Before we were ready. Before we had a chance to figure things out. It is as if there were a primal desire that had already been awakened to the other person and had carried us toward them. The desire which remains in each case our own desire.

And that may be an important recognition here. Time and pairing, self and world, in compelling us toward shared, concrete time and experience, operate similarly as desire. We do not just suffer the structures of time and of pairing. We *want* them, we *commit* to them, we *deploy* them.

But our pairing with other people is also *not like* the synthesis of transition in internal time. In our temporality, moments are not simultaneously apprehended. The past is present within the now, but the past is present as expired, as dead. In pairing, we are present together, now, in one moment.

So time may prepare us for our transitions toward one another. But time is not the only operative synthesis here. Yes it is true that in a sense, then, the other and oneself are transitional moments of a larger time-flow—that is, the moments of our relationship. But it also remains true that we are paired *now* as *other* to one another—more like the notes in a chord than in a melody. We maintain our distance from each other in our shared chord.

Because of the sense of simultaneity in our pairing, even if we are with our beloved, she or he can often feel the time or meaning of our relationship differently than we do. We might feel it as boring, while the other might be excited. We might feel its brevity, when our friend is close to death. And we might feel quite poignantly the fact that, in her dying, she might feel only her own mortality, and the length of her suffering, and not feel or sense our shared relationship explicitly at all.

By being both an act of transition and an act of holding together with each other in the now, we thus occupy both the position of a moment (a going over or a coming back) and the position of a whole (a "window" who remains on this side of another "window"). We remain wholes, others, within our going and our coming back. And it is because of this that the thing we create together in pairing, a relationship of mutuality, is itself another unity of experience.

Our unity with another can take us for a ride or have its plans for us. Our relationship remains accountable to each of us and yet still remains apart. And thus we would have to say that neither our shared temporality nor our simultaneity—neither one—is ever simply or completely shared in its narrative. Our relationship is never just *about* time or about either of us.

Because pairing is and is not a replication of internal time, there is always room in our shared time, in a relationship, for its disruption or suspension within our experience. The other may not understand or may not return, as Husserl says, our appeal "please, beloved friend." And in that failure the motion of transition that is our *own* is thus prevented, and we can become sad or angry. For the very utterance we made was the act of intending the relationship, the being *toward* those others.

But this gap between us, this possibility of the denial of simultaneity, this tendency of the sharing or the pairing to fail or break down, attests to the very character of the members of the relationship. We are paired together *as other people.*

Husserl emphasizes this by maintaining the notion of "transcendence" as that which connects time-consciousness and pairing: "Somewhat as my memorial past . . . transcends my present, the appresented other being transcends my own being" (Husserl 1960, 115). The limited nature of the comparison—the "somewhat"—allows us to reflect on the appearance of the other person's "transcendence." Though we can move toward, or transition toward, the other person, the other I, we cannot simply achieve the kind of implication that the past or future has within a now. We are not simply two moments in a shared flow.

Nevertheless, it seems clear that the experience of our togetherness depends on our internal time-consciousness. I would not see or experience you if I did not see or experience myself in the past or the future as "somehow" moving in a transitional way, if my former self were not "paired" with myself now. And yet your transcendence to me is far beyond that of my past or future self to me. For those selves have no choice but to emerge within me. And they have very little resistance to offer. They are not simultaneous. You are. And you resist, or at least maintain your own identity, as much as you yield.

As phenomenologically initiated into the motion of transition by virtue of our temporality, then, we are given an opportunity to see how we are always in process. We are always a flow of time that is directed toward the opening of a simultaneous and shared world, whose narrative and whose passing away matters to each of us.

LITERARY PRACTICE—READING
CHARLOTTE'S WEB PHENOMENOLOGICALLY

A. Introduction—Death and Time

Gareth Matthews has written about how *Charlotte's Web* is an important story for children who are facing mortality, either in their own lives or in the lives of people they care about.[8] And one can immediately see the truth of that in the story. The whole reason for Charlotte's project of writing in her webs is to save Wilbur's life. And the threat of his death, and of time itself, looms over the book from beginning to end: "'Your father is right. The pig would probably die anyway.' Fern pushed a chair out of the way and ran outdoors. The grass was wet and the earth smelled of springtime" (White 2001, 1).

Literally beginning with the notion of mortality and time, the book declares that the earth gives off "springtime," the time of new life—and the time of reducing what is not likely to thrive in the coming months. The very first action in the book, then, the act of Mr. Arable carrying the axe toward the pig, thrusts the reader toward a certain rhythmic, automatic, and utilitarian notion of time. For Mr. Arable's farm regimen is one in which he reckons clearly and quickly, without much self-reflection, and judges what is the *appropriate* time for living things.

Wilbur as an animal is a thing that Fern's father does not identify or "pair" with, in Husserl's sense of pairing that we discussed above. Mr. Arable does not really even perceive the pig as a living thing. The pig is just a function, an object. For Mr. Arable, the animal's time is the time of the (arable) earth, of cycles, and of laws of utilitarian calculus. The time of the farmer, the time of the one who holds the axe, is *not* the time of the pig. The time of the farmer, instead, governs the time of the farm, and the farmer uses his time to cut off or end the time of the pig.

In Wilbur's vulnerability to Mr. Arable's axe, the reader can see other vulnerabilities surface. Fern claims her own pairing with the pig and demands that his vulnerability is also hers. Charlotte the spider, as we come to learn toward the end of the story, is also under the axe, so to speak. For it is her energy that is used up in caring for Wilbur and in having children of her own.

Indeed, if the book begins with Wilbur's mortality, it ends with Charlotte's. And her passing shows the reader that it is not only the demands of the farm that create vulnerability. It is also the demands of a pairing relationship, hers and Wilbur's, one worthy of people's responsibility, that wears her out. Relationships do not just take time. They exhaust it.

What is left then, in the face of these apparent vulnerabilities, is to make sense of how Charlotte and Wilbur (and to some extent Fern) relate within their own mortality to each other. And, above it all, we need to make sense of how Charlotte's voluntary sacrifice undoes a forced subservience of a lived experience of time to a rather objective, unyielding axe. Or, to say it better, we need to discover how Charlotte's act of teaching Wilbur and the other animals to *read* launches them onto the winds of an emotional, self-reinforcing pairing and its shared, discovered meanings.

B. Fern: Time, Perception, and Reading

Returning to the beginning of the book, we see how Fern grabs her father's axe and declares that she can "see no difference" (White 2001, 3) between herself and the pig. Her father's willingness to kill the one signals, at least to Fern, his willingness to kill the other.

This assertion means a great deal. At the very least it means that Fern has interrupted the normal course of events on the farm and has insisted that she too have a say in how the notion of life unfolds. Her immediate refutation of her father's claim that "A little girl is one thing, a little runty pig is another" (White 2001, 2) means that she has seen herself as paired with the pig, as living in the same time.

When her father needs to defend his subsequent decision to his son Avery, he chooses to do so by means of a familiar, farm-based time. Fern, Mr. Arable says, woke up early. As an "early riser" who "was up at daylight trying to rid the world of injustice" (White 2001, 5), Fern was thus rewarded. She in part obeyed the time of the farm and in part maintained her own time, the time of her project of justice and ethics.

It is clear, however, that Mr. Arable is uneasy. This decision will never be more than a truce with Fern and her justice-based perceptions of the world. The beginning of the novel, Fern's resistance to the axe, obviously disrupts the normal binary categories of human and animal, of family and unfamiliar.

In disrupting their categories by her reading herself into Wilbur's situation, Fern forces her family to reckon with their shared tradition. Her actions pose questions to them, implicit questions that bother them for the rest of the book: what does it mean to perceive and to raise animals? Why do we so quickly think of subordinating the animals' experience to our own? What do mortality and time mean for each one, human and animal?

In her answers to these questions, Fern also helps to form new routines and relationships with the animals. Initially, Fern seems to use the time with Wilbur to experience the time of motherhood. Even though she is a young child, Fern is "relieved . . . to know her baby would sleep covered up and would stay warm" (White 2001, 9). The pairing with Wilbur, then, has a trajectory of its own.

Perhaps out of a growing discomfort with Fern's care for Wilbur, Mr. Arable again tries to break into their relationship and tries to sell the pig at five weeks old. Again there is a conflict. The time of the farm, the time of selling the pig and ridding the farm of its care, raises itself again. And again Fern intervenes. She agrees to sell Wilbur, for six dollars, but she does not agree to abandon him.

Instead, Fern continually goes to visit Wilbur at her uncle's farm, sitting on a milk stool, "during the long afternoons, thinking and listening and watching Wilbur" (White 2001, 15). Fern thus gives her time to this pig, to her "baby." And she becomes enraptured with her new way of perceiving a barn, a set of animals, and the relationships that are formed in a barn.

This devotion of time to her perception, to Wilbur, changes everything for them both. Although Fern recedes into her silent act of witnessing, that very act of perception changes Wilbur, indeed everyone in the barnyard. What was first a universal indifference or hostility on the part of the animals toward the farm's humans becomes softened, at least for Fern: "all the animals trusted her, she was so quiet and friendly" (White 2001, 15).

I want to emphasize this fact because it is so much an imitation of the phenomenological method: Fern's careful attention to her act of perception changes how she is herself perceived. And in fact this change is helpful to the very mechanism of the book. For in Fern's act of sitting on a milk stool, she puts herself in the very position of a reader—a silent, seated witness who affirms (without taking control of) what happens.

In her quiet attentiveness, Fern becomes a way into the text for the children who read it. And she directs the reader who imitates her attention to take animals seriously, to pair with and move toward them. That is, Fern shows by example what we need to do in order to identify with Wilbur and Charlotte and to experience another perspective on what it means to be on a farm, to live, and to be toward our own deaths.

C. Webs of Madness: The Initial Experience of Disruption

Fern's attentiveness, and the challenges that come with it for her family, carries all of them into a series of disruptions that Fern could not have foreseen. As a child, Fern follows her initial emotion of righteous indignation at her father's intended murder of a runt all the way into a space outside her family—that of the barnyard.

Since Fern sees no difference between herself and Wilbur, it is perhaps unsurprising that she moves toward the animals' home. When she begins to spend more and more time at her uncle's farm, on the milk stool, however, it becomes obvious to more than just herself that Fern is leaving home.

Fern's time on the milk stool is transitional. By means of her silent witnessing in the barnyard, by means of her pairing with the animals, Fern turns toward the world at large. By the end of the book, we learn that Fern is experiencing the beginning of desire, of longing. At the fair, which serves as the climax of the novel, Fern leaves Wilbur and Charlotte behind for a boy named Henry and an exciting ride on the Ferris wheel that is the pinnacle of her young life.

Her relationship with the animals, her attentiveness to their discussions, has its own time—and its own passing. And, somewhat sadly, Wilbur and the reader both come to see that Fern uses her relationship with Wilbur and with Charlotte to care about more than them.

For those people like her mother who follow Fern, time moves too quickly and too disruptively, it seems. Relationships start forming, and then fall apart, as if on their own initiative. A pig becomes immortalized in words in a web. Her child listens to, understands, and reports the speech of animals. And, at least for Fern's mother, it is all too much to bear without help. And so Mrs. Arable goes to see a doctor, perhaps a psychiatrist, Dr. Dorian.

Everything seems to be falling apart. Everyone is vulnerable to the way that attention can affect the passage of time.

My reading, which privileges the book's act of perceiving and the disruptions that follow it—the falling apart of the tradition of the farm, Fern's leaving behind of the family, the danger of madness in Mrs. Arable and in Lurvy and the pastor, the general upholding of an animal that is meant for food as a special figure—is not an immediately obvious one. After all, the narrative progresses somewhat linearly. Wilbur is saved. And, in the end, it seems that things come back together mostly as they were before. That is, it seems there is no madness. There is, instead, a positive resolution to the initial conflict with the axe, and there is more time for love in Wilbur's new lease on life, even after Charlotte perishes.

And yet it would be a mistake, I think, to downplay the way the story, the characters, are destabilized by means of the disruptions that occur along Fern's journey of perception. Fern's time on the milk stool is as disruptive as it is gentle. And her repeated act of witnessing does not remain her private property. By way of her participation in their lives, the animals revolt and then come together in ways that far surpass what anyone had thought possible. Fern's simple act of attending to the barnyard does not stay her own story—eventually it compels everyone involved to rethink everything—including religious experience and belief.

It all starts in Wilbur's loneliness, after Fern sells Wilbur to her uncle. When Fern is not there with him Wilbur finds himself experiencing loneliness: "Wilbur didn't want food, he wanted love. He wanted a friend" (White 2001, 27). The intimacy with Fern starts Wilbur on the longer experience of desire. And that brings new relationships. One pairing affirms another, even (perhaps especially) by way of absence.

A seemingly disembodied voice promises Wilbur to be his friend. The next day, Wilbur gets up ready for a friend, very early. Unlike Fern, however, this new friend is not "an early riser" (White 2001, 35). What this new friend does do, however, which is similar to Fern's act of sitting on a milk stool, is to occupy a space that is at the borders of things. Like Fern, Charlotte is "sedentary" (White 2001, 61). She mostly sits in a doorframe, within a web. Like Fern, she is a liminal friend, who both participates with and sets herself apart from the rest of the animals.

By means of her perceptions and her choice of words, Charlotte mediates the barnyard. She congratulates the goose on the goslings. She keeps Templeton the rat in line. She teaches Wilbur new words. She promises him he will not die, after the old sheep tells Wilbur what is coming to him when the cold weather comes. Charlotte is, in a word, "versatile." And she is versatile because she never quite belongs to the farm, the barn, or the house.

But the animals' communication is something Fern reports to her family. And it is that reporting that sets off the first major disruption. Mrs. Arable worries: "I worry about Fern. Did you hear the way she rambled on about the animals, pretending that they talked?" (White 2001, 54). Even though Mr. Arable wonders whether Fern might be right, or passes it off as their child's vivid imagination, something is mounting within Mrs. Arable that will become a threat: "I think I shall ask Dr. Dorian about her the next time I see him. . . . You know perfectly well animals don't talk" (White 2001, 54). Anxiety has come to be within the home.

With the first web that has words in it, people begin to falter. Lurvy, the first one to see it, has to "set his pail down" and "felt weak" (White 2001, 77). When Lurvy brings Mr. Zuckerman to see the web, "they both began to tremble" (White 2001, 79). Mr. Zuckerman tells his wife that there is a miracle on the farm and that "the words were woven right into the web. They were actually part of the web, Edith" (White 2001, 80). There is no gainsaying the men. Edith Zuckerman protests that it is the spider who is extraordinary. But the spider disappears immediately in light of the "miracle." The word is a sign, a miracle, and it is an embodied word that announces the superiority of the animal, some pig. The word, in a sense, has been made flesh in the world on this farm.

When Mr. Zuckerman discusses the "miracle" with the pastor, the pastor insists that he be allowed to comment on it during the Sunday sermon: "I intend to speak about it in my sermon and point out the fact that this community has been visited with a wondrous animal" (White 2001, 82). The pastor feeds the fire of the "miracle" that Charlotte uses to trick the humans. But it is so disruptive, this miracle, that the Zuckermans neglect the farm: "The Zuckermans were so busy with visitors, they forgot about other things on the farm" (White 2001, 84).

With the disruption to their farm system, the Zuckermans fail to notice the animals coming together in opposition. Charlotte holds a meeting in which it is determined that the next word in the web will be "terrific." All the animals are now engaged in trying to help save Wilbur. The fact that Wilbur does not feel equal to the word is not at all relevant. The word, the disruptive word, is all that counts. It does not have to accord with reality.

When Fern reports on all the discussions the animals are having, the anxiety grows in Mrs. Arable. She wants Fern to play with other children, not to be all alone in the barn. Fern of course opposes her mother: "Alone? My best friends are in the barn cellar" (White 2001, 107). So her mother makes good on her promise of going to the doctor, to the psychiatrist.

Dr. Dorian does calm Mrs. Arable, mostly by siding with Fern. Fern's power of attention is what Dr. Dorian focuses on: "It is quite possible that an animal has spoken civilly to me and that I didn't catch the remark because I wasn't paying attention. Children pay better attention than grownups" (White 2001, 110).

Immediately after Dr. Dorian's reassurance, however, we read of the crickets singing about the impending end of summer, about the death and end of the time of thriving. There is no full release of anxiety. The very wind is full of the reminder that the present moment is already passing away. If Fern is not abnormal, she is still growing, moving out of the house to the milk stool, moving away from the milk stool toward adulthood. And if Wilbur is saved, Charlotte will be lost.

The disruption of the web is thus a pause in the system of the farm. It is a chance for reflection. The web is the site of transition and the motor of coming together as a community—both the community of the humans who, as the pastor said, are visited with an animal. And a community of animals who, with Fern, are visited with a human on a milk stool.

D. Transition to Hope: Beyond the Experience of Disruption

Charlotte's webs are not only about disruption. They are as much sites and supports for a transition to greater empowerment, to hope for a future, as the infant's use of a blanket would be for D. W. Winnicott.[9]

The webs are neither objects nor subjects, partaking as they do of both. This fact, i.e., their liminal status, allows them to have a life of their own. If they were simply disruptive, nothing would come of them. People like Fern's brother Avery would simply tear through them with a stick. But the webs also offer, in the very act of Charlotte's attempt to communicate by means of them, an opportunity for all who read them to counter the threat of loss with the experience of hope.

The webs are spun out of Charlotte's body, out of her own substance. Yet after she is finished they stand on their own. They are temporary, being designed to trap insects that will wreck at least major parts of them. Yet they are also so settled as to be permanent in their reworked continuity, unnoticed in their omnipresence in the corners of barns.

As the mechanisms that allow the words to be perceived, the webs are usually designed to be in the background. They are designed so as *not* to focus anyone's attention on them. The fly, for example, blunders into them because they *do not appear.* As such the webs retain a similarity to the infant's blanket, which, for Winnicott, is designed as a site *not* to be challenged. The blanket becomes a part of the infant's working out of her subjectivity, much as the web is Charlotte's medium of living in the world.

Then, too, like the blanket and like the web that she makes, Charlotte is a transitional friend. Her relationship with Wilbur is designed to accompany him only so far. If she is to provide him hope, she cannot be challenged or even recognized directly by humans, as Mrs. Zuckerman and Dr. Dorian do. She cannot be talked about. At most she can be perceived quietly by Fern. And, as Fern knows, Charlotte needs to be protected from Avery's stick or from people's gaze if, like the blanket, the web and Charlotte are to provide an empowering continuity for experience.

While the webs are usually designed to be in the background, the writing of a word or a phrase in the web changes the very ground of perception. It foregrounds what is not foregrounded. It stabilizes what is temporary.

While it may be true, as Mr. Zuckerman and the pastor said, that the word is woven into the web, it is also true that the web is woven into the word. The mystery of their togetherness is what produces the possibility for hope.

Reading the web changes the transitional status of the web. It allows the web to appear in a new way, to be recognized and therefore either affirmed or challenged. But in this change, the web also directs outward, toward some new form of life, toward an experience that does not remain vulnerable to the song of the crickets, to the passing of seasons.

The web as word is the very experience of hope, an experience of transcendence that does not depend on the time of the seasons or on the mortality that we each, each of us as animals, face. The web as word is an experience of simultaneity, of sharing our temporality here and now, that embraces all in the community because it is offered to all. The web as word names all as responsible for making something of this time that we are given and in that responsibility we are freed toward one another, toward a hope in what surpasses all understanding, toward *meaning* as transcending even *being*.

Such a web could not come simply from a spider's excretion or exertion, and its inspiration could certainly not come simply from arbitrary, rat-delivered garbage scraps. And this is because the web as word does not depend on its authors anymore. It is alive on the winds of the communal act of reading, of a desire to be hopeful together, to resolve upon a course of action that requires our mutual recognition.

The web as word is pointing and soliciting elsewhere. It is directing those who read it toward the question of the meaning of their conscientious, practical lives. It directs toward the future selves that they must come to be. As Charlotte tells Wilbur, her webs are her contribution to his success: "Your future is secured. You will live secure and safe, Wilbur. Nothing can harm you now" (White 2001, 163).

The web as word allows others to feel empowered by its transitional support, and it hides the mortality of those whose continuity previously depended on it. At least for a time. With a word in it, the web hides Charlotte's body, which would otherwise be laid out in the very patterns of sticky thread, like a Jackson Pollack painting expresses his arm motions in the play of the paint. With a word on it, it hides Wilbur's initial subordination to the axe. It requires belief in something surpassing the satisfaction of physical needs, in something that transcends the limit of mortality by taking it seriously, by motivating us into perceiving the miraculous within the obvious.

Fern, like Charlotte, like Charlotte's web, gains hope through her milk stool and her participation in the barn. She is launched forward through these webbed words onto the hopefulness of her own desire, of her own relationships as in the one with Henry Fussy at the top of the Ferris wheel.

E. Hope Requires Action: Mortality Is Real

For all the time I have spent in moving from disruption to hope in this reading, it seems necessary to remind myself and my reader, as E. B. White does to each reader of his book, that hope requires continued responsibility and action. Charlotte's efforts do lead to Wilbur's salvation. But they also lead to her early death. And, as White writes, "no one was with her when she died" (White 2001, 171). Wilbur must address that fact.

And so he does. The book begins and ends with mortality. It has not lost that thread. But the hope that Charlotte prepares Wilbur for, however, is something he takes up as his responsibility. The death of her friendship with him is the path to new relationships with her daughters, to a kind of continuity in his life that is "versatile" and "radiant." In Charlotte's sacrifice appears Wilbur's devotion.

The web has been left behind, as a blanket or a stuffed animal will be by an older child. There is no more need to "read" it: "Every day Wilbur would stand and look at the torn, empty web and a lump would come to his throat" (White 2001, 173). The web recedes, the word is gone, but the carrying forward of the meaning transcends. The transitional object, the transitional friend, plays the role of a growing capacity for care, for love, for meaning. Charlotte is embedded in Wilbur's life, in his habits, in his way of thinking and talking.

The time on the milk stool, like the time in the web, changes not only the perceiver but also the whole community. Charlotte's words are now Wilbur's, are now ours. And Fern, who retreats in a way so similar to that of Charlotte, allows us to see that our own position as readers is fulfilled by treasuring in our hearts what we have read as we move on to other things.

CONCLUSION

Our eight-year-old daughter, in discussing the end of the book, remarked that "I felt sad that Charlotte died but at the same time I felt happy that Wilbur saved her babies and was smart enough to do so. I learned you can change even if you don't want to change and when the future comes you will change. Kindness, tenderness, loving is the best way to make friends."

"When the future comes you will change"—the motion of transitioning for our daughter was so thoroughly learned that she saw that it was a matter of inevitability. And it was tied to her consciousness of time. To make a transition is what we are bound for. We make transitions even if we did not want to. We are the process of our time, our lives, our relationships and then have to take them up in the ways that they demand. Our transition is for the sake of taking care of ourselves and of those with whom we are placed.

With our daughter, I learned too. I learned again that it is not only that we "will change" but that we are changing all the time, by means of the others with whom we live. I learned that Wilbur learns, and changes, from Charlotte's acts. I learned to go again and read myself into the text. And there I found, clear as day, that Wilbur learns to save and to care and to change from being saved and cared for and from witnessing the change in Charlotte that is the gift of their friendship. For Charlotte tells him she wrote the words "for you because I liked you" (White 2001, 164). And because the writing helped "lift up my life a trifle" (White 2001, 164). So, in a way, Wilbur learns from Charlotte because they enforce a transitional state upon each other.

But do mothers and fathers, do teachers, do adults, feel their children "lift them up a trifle"? We ought to. For I believe that we can come to see our children as friends that we have unequal responsibilities for if we give up unstable, stuck binary categories of adult and child.

Certainly, with respect to Charlotte and Wilbur, our daughter learned from both of them, as friends who dwelled differently yet together. Reading herself into Wilbur, childlike in dependence, she learned that change is something which desire must reckon with. That tenderness, as bitter as it can be, is a way of navigating it. Reading herself into Charlotte, adult in her responsibility, she learned that care is instructive of desire, that it moves toward stability and growth.

This motion of "reading into" is a kind of passive synthesis of the order of time-consciousness or pairing for Husserl. Becoming ensconced in a novel, or a situation, or the world is not willed. But it is nevertheless something for which we are responsible. And this non-willed responsibility is instructive, and it offers us fulfillment, meaning, and danger.

It is my hope, even with the disruptions and dangers that reading texts always present, that the milk stool of our attentiveness is never left behind. Likewise, it is my hope that children, like our daughter, do not seek solely to identify with and to imitate Fern who becomes "careful to avoid childish things, like sitting on a milk stool near a pigpen" (White 2001, 183). For I think attentiveness and study is the essential, childlike character of phenomenology. When we practice careful attention to our experience, we are as much children as adults. And both of those in multiple, shifting ways.

However, if and when the stool is left behind, I hope that the "chance words" dropped by the other people in this world are ones that draw attention and care back toward some more adequate grasp of the means and ends within the situations in which we find ourselves. I hope that children enable us, in short, to see each other as both means and ends to the process of self-becoming.

NOTES

1. An earlier version of this chapter appeared as "Toward a Phenomenology of Transition: E. B. White's *Charlotte's Web* and a Child's Process of Reading Herself Into the Novel," in *Libri et Liberi* 5, no. 1 (2016): 13–36. I am grateful to the editor, Smiljana Narancic Kovac, for permission to reprint parts of the article here.

2. Though the context of this quote is Husserl's discussion of the methodology of phenomenology as a whole, I think it is apropos: "Thus we have no other choice than to proceed forward and backward in a zigzag pattern; the one must help the other in an interplay" (Husserl 1968, 58).

3. "A parallelism between noesis and noema is indeed the case, but it is such that one must describe the formations on *both* sides and in their essentially *mutual* correspondence" (Husserl 1983, 242, my emphasis). The transition imposed on the phenomenologist is thus the transition of "first one, then the other" that allows the full description to unfold, even as the noesis and noema are always already given together. This idea gets further taken up in *Analyses of Passive and Active Synthesis* where Husserl moves on from the necessary movement of explication to the transition within perception itself, the *call* of the object, through anticipation, to the responsive, noetic movement of embodied consciousness.

4. Husserl himself notes something of this kind also in the *Ideas*. There, in sections 41 and 42, he describes the way in which the adumbrations or slices of the *noema* (for example, the sides of the perceived table) belong together as a particular kind of multiplicity. But he notes that this adumbrated multiplicity of the table, while complementing and correlating with the *noetic* multiplicity of acts, is a dependent form of unity. The adumbrations in their unity *depend* on time-consciousness and its *different species* of unity in order for the perception of each adumbration to unfold as an adumbration *of* the same table. For the table to be perceived as a whole, therefore, my time-consciousness must contain my multiple acts of perceiving within me in a *different way* than each adumbration sketches out the rest of the table. Two sentences from these sections are helpful to note here. First, this: "A mental process [*Erlebnis*] is not adumbrated" (*Ideas*, 90). And then, this: "The perception itself, however, is what it is in the continuous flux of consciousness and is itself a continuous flux; continually the perceptual Now changes into the enduring consciousness of the Just-Past and simultaneously a new Now lights up, etc." (*Ideas*, 87).

5. "The now, for its part, requires its own moment of origin for its constitution. These moments are continuously united in the succession; they 'pass over into one another continuously.' The *transition* is mediated qualitatively and also temporally" (*PCIT*, 107, my emphasis). The now is thus able to originate because it is the process of transition toward itself out of the just-past now that it was emerging out of. The now is the gift of a transition that does not pause to admire its handiwork. See also Merleau-Ponty's *Phenomenology of Perception*, pp. 446ff.

6. In fact, in *Analyses Concerning Passive and Active Synthesis*, Husserl puts the relation between noesis and noema specifically in terms of transition: "let us now take a look at the formation of unity . . . by examining the *transition* of appearances, for instance, when approaching or walking around an object or in eye movement. The fundamental relationship in this *dynamic transition* is that of intention and fulfillment. The empty pointing ahead acquires its corresponding fullness. It corresponds roughly to the rich possibilities prefigured; but since its nature is determinable indeterminacy, it also brings, together with the fulfillment, a closer determination" (Husserl 2001, s.3, my emphasis). The synthesis of fulfillment is a particular concretion of the synthesis of internal time by means of absolute subjectivity.

7. "It [the Other person] brings to mind the way my body would look 'if I were there.' In this case too although the awakening does not become a memory intuition, pairing takes place. The first-awakened manner of appearance of my body is not the only thing that enters into a

pairing; my body itself does so likewise" (Husserl 1960, 118). I have argued in *Layers in Husserl's Phenomenology* that the subjunctive nature of the pairing experience makes rather explicit the function of transition within both the experience of pairing and the process of explicating it (Costello 2012). That my whole body, and not just the "take" I have on my body in this or that moment, is involved in pairing with the Other means that I must go forth and seek out the further significances of my always already established involvement with the Other, who has, as if behind my back, already gained access to my own significance.

8. *"Charlotte's Web* . . . enjoys a special place in the lives of many children battling terminal illness, as Myra Bluebond-Langner reports in her pioneering work on leukemic children" (Matthews 1994, 92).

9. Winnicott's descriptions of a transitional object could be paraphrased as follows: with her fingers rubbing the corner of her blanket, the infant started to transition toward an outside world in which there were others who always already held viewpoints on her, who shared projects with her, as in a family life. The rubbing of the blanket meant a growing capacity to access to the fact that she, the infant, did not establish those views, those projects, or that world. And her engagement with the blanket as neither object nor subject was her "allowance," her being on the way toward the means to pursue objects and relationships. It was her transitional situation—her self as a process of transition—that animated the blanket as a space of relief and growth. And the blanket seemed to allow her to settle into her patterns of fingering its corner between thumb and forefinger, etc., as if it were meant to do so. From the point of view of Winnicott, though, notably, not from that of the infant, the noematic clue of the blanket, in other words, allowed her and her parents to come to see the growing noetic patterns of her own transitional lived experience.

Chapter Two

Reading Russell Hoban's *The Mouse and His Child* as a Phenomenology of Emotion and of Community

INTRODUCTION

In the previous chapter, we attended phenomenologically to the experiences of time and of other people. Discovering the mutual implication of these experiences has allowed us to see each human relationship has multiple dimensions—that of movement (transition) and that of simultaneity (pairing).

We will now turn toward describing the experience of emotion, which enlists those previous dimensions. From there, we will make some progress toward describing a further experience of community. This community experience requires us to extend our awareness of pairing and movement, requires us to reckon well with our emotions, in order to embrace a larger, nested series of shared projects that open onto a shared world. The experience of community, in short, demands a *revolution* in the way we feel and in the way we live.[1]

In order to demonstrate a grounded, reflective, and indeed *authentic* description of emotion and community, I will turn to the phenomenology of Merleau-Ponty. His phenomenology, as I mentioned in the introduction to this book, focuses on the structure of our experience that he calls *intercorporeality*. Our bodies, in other words, interconnect, and this interconnection generates and supports our emotions as intelligent articulations of experience. Our movement toward community is therefore an emotional decision (one related to love) born of an already interconnected, shared, bodily life.

Merleau-Ponty's focus on intercorporeality and emotion appears most clearly in his essay "The Child's Relations with Others." In that essay, Merleau-Ponty continues and extends the insights of Husserl on pairing. But this extension is not mere repetition, and it is important for two reasons: first, the essay is important because it *concretizes* the notion of transition that we have talked about earlier. In living together, the motor of our togetherness is experienced as both mutual and independent, as an emotion that is ours and yet a response to another. And in being within the grip of an emotion, or an affective *situation*, we must be able to engage the transitional movement between self and others in order to *resolve* ourselves toward the development of shared, communal projects.

Secondly, Merleau-Ponty's essay is important, and unique, because it roots its phenomenological insights into intercorporeality within the *infant's* and the *child's* experiences. Enlarging upon Husserl's significant clues in this regard, Merleau-Ponty thus returns to the very genesis of our experience of emotional situations and of other persons in this essay. This move is important because it helps us to understand how the structure of pairing first gains impetus, how it develops, and even, perhaps, how it falters or gets confused *as it reaches out* toward its burgeoning expansion.

Russell Hoban's novel, *The Mouse and His Child*, seems to offer an important opportunity of pairing with Merleau-Ponty's essay. For in Hoban's novel, a child in the form of a windup mouse is joined at the hands to a father by whose motor the child moves. Only by breaking (quite literally) from the father, as Fern only threatens to do with her father and the axe at the beginning of *Charlotte's Web*, can the mouse child move from an emotional confusion toward the establishment of a more genuine community. Being broken from the father then is Hoban's way of establishing and expanding the logic of pairing more reflectively within the relationships of an intentional coming-together with others.

Reading Hoban and Merleau-Ponty together, then, I will argue that establishing a life-affirming community is the possibility that a descriptive phenomenology of emotion and of pairing extends. Such a possibility comes by means of a reflection on the genesis of phenomenological structures within concrete life and by means of a concomitant ethical reflection on what our bodies, in their being and feeling together, are trying to tell us.

PHENOMENOLOGICAL THEORY—MERLEAU-PONTY'S PHENOMENOLOGY OF CHILDHOOD RELATIONS

A. Introduction

In "The Child's Relations with Others," which is published within the collection *The Primacy of Perception,* Merleau-Ponty accomplishes two main tasks. First and foremost, he describes the genesis and development of the child's perception of other human bodies, of language, and of intercorporeality. Second, he imparts, perhaps implicitly, the value of phenomenological method insofar as it promotes the adoption of an attitude that can help adults to assist children in moving through their psychological impediments toward a loving engagement with others.[2]

B. The Child's Perception

As Merleau-Ponty describes the development of a child's perception of embodiment, he carefully anchors his discussion with the following:

> perception in the child is not a simple reflection nor the result of a process of sorting data. Rather, it is a more profound operation whereby the child organizes his experience of external events—an operation which is neither a logical nor a predicative activity (Merleau-Ponty 1964, 98).

The child's perception is "not a simple reflection." If it were *any* act of reflection, that would mean there is a divide between the child and the world and that perception could not be immediate. Because of the divide, the child would have to be aware of herself working on or "sorting" data that entered her consciousness from the outside. And if her perception operated like this, it would always lag behind the data that occurred in or from the world. With such a lag, the child could never act fluidly and immediately, could never reliably inhabit an attitude of certainty with respect to what she or he was perceiving.

The very depth or "profound" character of the act of perception indicates otherwise for Merleau-Ponty. The child, and much of the time even the adult, is not immediately aware *how* she perceives. Her focus is on the world and not on herself. As Merleau-Ponty notes in his *Phenomenology of Perception*, the infant looks at the object and not at her hand when she is learning how to grasp something (Merleau-Ponty 1962, 172). Perception, grasping, can thus (and does most often) happen all at once. There is no inherent necessity for a lag time in perception, except perhaps for situations of doubt or confusion, which are outliers. Given its fluidity, perception as it normally occurs must be *pre*-reflective, and, as such, unlike any other "process," i.e., it must be *sui generis*.

Certainly, the perceiving child does not need to speak or even to think within the "logic" or grammar of language in order to see or touch or hear the world around her. Such a requirement would be that of a "predicative activity." It would require the child to construct in thought an assertion that some thing is qualified or defined in a certain way. It would be to say, in each perception, that "S is P," i.e., to hold a subject and a predicate *separate* from each other and to accomplish the link between them through bringing perception in all its moments forward to *self-consciousness*.

Instead of a reflective, predicative act, Merleau-Ponty emphasizes, perception is an immediate gearing into the world. Perception *immediately* grasps this thing *as* something. This grasp of this-*as*-that precedes the awareness of *self*-organization required by predication. In fact, the child becomes capable of predication by means of perception, not the other way around.

As pre-predicative in the child, perception unfolds by means of passive indeterminacy. There is no clear dividing line in her own consciousness between the baby and the world in which she is thrown. Instead, the baby is perceiving on behalf of her *unity* with the world, her unity with things.

Things are already calling her to be picked up, to be put in the mouth, etc. And the baby tastes the world in the immediate way she does *because* the limits between self and world are not yet formed. If this is so, then it becomes clearer how perception requires no sentences, either in thought or in utterance. The grammar, the distinctions, of self and world has not been accomplished yet in her self-perception.

In fact, Merleau-Ponty says quite explicitly that the child's body is not yet itself organized in full:

> The consciousness of one's own body is thus fragmentary [*lacunaire*] at first and gradually becomes integrated; the corporeal schema becomes precise, re-structured, and mature little by little (Merleau-Ponty 1964, 123).

In such a fragmentary consciousness of her own body, the child's perception is given as occurring within and *as a body that is re-organizing itself.*

Her perception as fluid and immediate thus transcends her awareness of her body. Indeed, implicit in the above quote is the idea that the child's perception of things in the world organizes her self-consciousness *at the same moment* as it organizes her experience of the world.

The perception of the world transcends the body and compels the body to reorganize. The body transcends perception and refers the world back to itself. In short, the world and the child gather themselves together, within a system of mutual references, within the unity of the perceiving act.

We can see with Merleau-Ponty, then, that in the infant's process of perception the structures of temporality, what Husserl called the synthesis of transition, begin to map themselves explicitly onto the body. The experience of the object she is grasping for now roots itself forwards and backwards into the formation of her hand as a touching organ of her whole body. The just-past of the reaching moment connects itself with the holding or touching moment, the smoothness or roughness of the toy or the ball, etc. And this refers her to her body as a whole, which comes little by little into a less "fragmentary" view.

Time works on the body by way of perception instantiating the structure of time. Or, perhaps better, perception works its way into a more sophisticated experience of time, world, and self by using the time it takes to pick up and taste the world as the means to flesh out the distinctions between oneself and the world.

But perception does not simply recast the limits between self and world. The perceptual introduction of the body into a lived time and, thereby, into a grammar of reflection also simultaneously gives the child over to other people.

To achieve an "integrated" and systematic "corporeal schema" is simultaneously to be experienced as such a developing perceptual self-consciousness by others. And thus what is central for Merleau-Ponty in the infant's process of self-organizing perception is the way in which she develops her awareness of her own body within the context of *inter*-corporeality:

> the perception of one's own body creates an *imbalance* as it develops: through its *echo* in the image of the other, it awakens an appeal to the forthcoming development of the *perception of others* (Merleau-Ponty 1964, 121, my emphasis).

The body schema does not develop by way of *smooth* transitions. Rather, the sense of one's body "creates an imbalance" within the larger project of the child's perception. Her perception of the world and of her own body organize themselves only by means of leaving room for an "echo," for a reply from or a dependence on another. The baby holds its own thumb or toes in its mouth, and in the way she does that she "awakens an appeal" to the other who will take up its fingers and toes too.

The time it takes for the body to organize its world and its self-consciousness, the immediately co-given yet "fragmentary" process of uniting the body within a coherent experience of the world, is the desire for mutuality. The body is mine, predication is my possibility, only in my becoming a member of a larger process of confirmation. And thus the space, the lacuna, the gap in one's self-perception is also essentially the foundation and call for resolution within familial and social engagement.

Merleau-Ponty states this point about the child's perception developing by way of her involvement as a Husserlian phenomenon of coupling or pairing:

> the perception of others is like a "phenomenon of coupling" [*accouplement*]. . . . In perceiving the other, my body and his are coupled, resulting in a sort of action which pairs them (Merleau-Ponty 1964, 118).

Something about the embodiment of a child participates, just as it did in the character of pre-reflective self-organization, in the adult situation of being paired with others. A *perception of* another's body couples *our actual bodies* and this intertwining of perception and embodiment leads to "a sort of action."

For Merleau-Ponty this coupling in a child's perception precedes any act that takes a stand on their togetherness with others. This is to say that one's own body *is* always already moving toward an explicit rendering (pairing) of oneself with others from out of a more primordial, implicit co-givenness (coupling). And the body moves toward a more explicit rendering because the body *desires* to fill in the "lacuna" in its own self-understanding.

There are two key examples from the essay that show these points together: namely, the way in which perception drives toward self-consciousness, and the way in which perception radiates toward the others with whom she is already "coupled." The first example is that of the infant seeing the parent and yet not *immediately* himself in the mirror. The second is that of a young girl seeing her family situation reflected in the experience of a mother dog nursing her puppies.

The example of the infant in front of the mirror is an example from psychology that Merleau-Ponty takes up to reframe our understanding of the genesis of relationships. As earlier psychologists noted, he says, the infant does not see herself in the mirror until after she experiences, pre-reflectively, that she can be seen by others:

> through the acquisition of the specular image the child notices that he is *visible* for himself and others (Merleau-Ponty 1964, 136).

Before she acquires the capacity to see *her* image in the mirror, she has already been able to see her parents' image in the mirror she is looking at as they move toward the mirror. In fact, upon seeing their reflection in the mirror, she will turn around to find them because their images in the mirror match the way she sees them.

Her own image, however, even though perhaps entrancing her gaze before the appearance of the images of the parents, is not immediately available to her. She does not see herself in it. And this is because, Merleau-Ponty argues, she does not yet see the connection between the act of being seen by the parents and the instantiation or projection of this view in the mirror.

To see oneself in the mirror, then, is to take a very sophisticated step. It is a step of great organization of the bodily schema. It is the filling in of the lacuna, the appeal, to the other. For it is to perceive oneself by means of an intercorporeal relationship—to perceive oneself as how and as what others see oneself to be.

To see herself in the mirror means to see herself being seen by others. It is to see herself inserted into visibility and thus into a world in which each person's bodily life is perceptible (visibly, aurally, tactilely, etc.) to others.

The significance of this move, which happens at a very young age, cannot be underestimated. It is a move of passive synthesis, of pre-predication, which is not taught. It is the pre-reflective production of a *reflective* move by which the body's logic suddenly expands to take on an explicit "act" of pairing. If the child's body were not already "coupled" with those of the parents, she would never reach the visibility of herself. And yet there was a gap, a gap of time, that was required for her to come to herself.

And that gap of time required was the time it took for the others' views of her to "sink in," to matter, to be received in pleasure or in irritation. The gap was the space in which the others could operate by means of their repeated acts of viewing her. In this one example, then, Merleau-Ponty shows that time builds itself into the child's perceptions such that it presses forward into coherence, into taking a stand on that very time. Seeing herself as visible for others is, in a way, a giving of herself over to their time and their care.

The second example of this process in Merleau-Ponty's essay, that of the girl seeing her own situation clearly in the dog's nursing of its young, shows concretely how the child's experience of her embodiment is carried forward, extends itself, by her larger, familial involvements. Not only does she see herself as visible to others. Now she also sees herself as implicated in larger meanings that extend to the animal world, to all kinds of others, such that her future is implicated as well:

> Meeting the dog which was nursing its litter was not an indifferent experience for the child; it was a visible symbol of something analogous that was about to happen in her own world. . . . The sight of the dogs was of paramount significance by virtue of the relation to the situation in which the child was about to find herself (Merleau-Ponty 1964, 111).

The child saw the pregnancy of her own mother in the dog. And she saw herself and her future sibling(s) in the puppies. She saw the act of nursing, the caring for the young. She saw the differences in age. And she saw the bodily interdependence and similarities. Even as not a dog, she was already coupled with the dogs she saw. And she used that coupling to understand the pairing with her sibling, who was soon to be born.

In this second example, Merleau-Ponty shows that not only the child's visibility can be doubled, or filled in, as in the mirror. Her "situation" can be as well. The situation in which she finds herself is visible in the world, and it is a situation whose meaning, as visible, can be maintained in the lived connections, the matrices, of concentric relationships of meaning.

The action that her coupling had afforded her increases here. Now not only her basic visibility but her situation too leaps ahead of her into the world. Her time, as future, is rooted in the presentification of any coupling as allowing her to explicate it. Neither bodies nor situations are isolated. And the act of explication, which phenomenology takes as its reason for being, has footholds everywhere. The body is just the desire of its situation to take root by means of the pre-reflective accruing of insight.

Taking these two examples together, it is not only, then, that the child's perception has gaps that gear into and *call for* increasingly sophisticated relations with others. Rather, the child's perceptions of (and on behalf) of others *enact as if on their own* increasingly sophisticated and symbolic perceptions of (and relations with) her future and herself.

C. Pre-Maturation, Ambiguity, and Love

A child can perceive a mother dog nursing young puppies symbolically, on behalf of her own future relations with her mother and sibling(s). This is not accidental. Rather, for Merleau-Ponty, a child's perception is always characterized by a kind of "pre-maturation," which accounts for the impact of her future upon her present.

Merleau-Ponty's inclusion of this notion of pre-maturation is, again, a way of embedding genetic psychology within his phenomenology of child development. But Merleau-Ponty highlights not only the genesis of perception here. Pre-maturation also reveals an essential feature of perception— namely the way in which perception concretizes the meaning of the structures of our temporality:

> pre-maturation, the anticipation by the child of adult forms of life, is . . . almost the definition of childhood. . . . The child lives in relations that belong to his future and are not actually realizable by him (Merleau-Ponty 1964, 138).

By way of pre-maturation, childhood shows that, in its beginning stages, perception is a way of living according to the future. These future "relations" are not reflective. The child does not *know* she is living according to societal roles when she plays with Barbie dolls in a dream house. She does not explicitly understand the erotic meanings of the pop songs she memorizes at six or seven years old. Her "definition," however, is nonetheless always toward the future that impacts her without giving her the explicit tools to understand the way in which she "anticipates" and exceeds her own grasp.

But pre-maturation is more than a genetically interesting phase. Living according to relations of the future is not something a child outgrows. A fully developed, reflective adult intentionality, such as the one often described by Husserl, is such a futural process. We always perceive more than we can explicitly account for.

Seeing the whole house from here just means the ability to perceive the further sides or aspects of that same house here, *within* the ones actually, adequately in view. Indeed to see anything *as* what it appears to be is to engage the kind of futural self-structure already charted by the child. The reason to take stock of the child's pre-maturation is to notice how much further, and how much less reflectively, the child's experience exceeds what she can account for.

Unlike an adult, who can verify the intended-to sides of the thing that are implicit, a child cannot enter into such a verification, into what Husserl called a synthesis of fulfillment. The child is stuck with the future in a kind of mute enactment. As Melanie Klein notes, a child cannot explain the connection between what she does with train cars at the therapist's office and her experience of her parents' problematic erotic life. It is clear to the therapist, but not to the child. And thus the therapist forms the question, is that what mommy and daddy do, and the child nods and the anxiety diminishes.

In pre-maturation, a child lives without being able to verify the latent meanings that are shown to (and in some pre-reflective sense understood by) her. In terms of the example of the girl looking at the dog nursing its young, the child "understands" that she is going to have a new sibling in a different way after looking at the dog nursing the puppies. But she cannot phrase this understanding very well. She does not know how or why seeing the dogs' situation resolves her own.

She has no evidence she can point to that would account for her greater ease at home with her mother. However, something has definitely happened for her. She is clearly less upset, and perhaps her tendency to "steal" the things from the baby's room and hide them in her own no longer shows itself. The child is reckoning with the future within her present, and the future is experienced by her within the frames of the present.

Whatever way in which we work to describe childhood phenomenologically, then, we must allow that children perceive and act toward philosophical positions that are far richer than we might be prepared to believe. The child does not, in other words, just *happen* one day to articulate insights. She *lives* them first. And in living them first she comes to understand something of how to phrase them.[3]

But pre-maturation is not a guarantee that the child can come to greater self-awareness, can fill in the lacuna that allows her intercorporeity to assist her. There can be blocks, resistances, failures. More specifically, for Merleau-Ponty, what can prevent the child from enacting the kind of growth that allows *pre*-maturation to turn into more self-aware maturation is a kind of psychological rigidity.

This rigidity, which the child would receive from within her place within a problematic family situation, prevents the child from perceiving ambiguity as the motor of perceptual life. Instead, within a rigidity that is supported by such a situation, the child operates within a dualistic vacillation, from good to bad father or mother, from external recognition of authority to internal rebellion. The child makes little "progress" in unfolding the future and, instead, remains trapped in an increasingly depressive situation:

> Psychological rigidity can be found occasionally in all subjects, but it is only in an especially authoritarian environment that it becomes a constant conduct, of which the child cannot rid himself. In this kind of authoritarian atmosphere, the child divides the parent figure in half. On the one hand, there is the kindly image of his parents that is willingly avowed, and on the other there is the image he is struggling against (Merleau-Ponty 1964, 102).

Again, the genesis of intentionality and its opening onto the future can be blocked by an "authoritarian" family situation, which is inevitably internalized in some way by the child. The genesis of intentional structures, then, is not always fluid, univocal, and smooth. Because it is always already broken open to other people, experience itself does not protect against them. And one's own pre-mature perception can never sufficiently innoculate itself against a false "division" of what is experienced into non-communicating, dual senses. Experience must in each case be lived—and sometimes "struggled *against*"—by the child who is not yet adequate to it. Experience is finite, mortal, and limited to the bodily, intercorporeal situation in which the child finds herself.

When, however, instead of living in an authoritarian family, the child lives in a family that promotes the perception of *ambiguity*, Merleau-Ponty says, along with Melanie Klein and other psychoanalysts, the child avoids dividing the experience of the parents and instead becomes better able to allow the world to unfold as a coherent whole:

> Ambiguity is an adult phenomenon, a phenomenon of maturity, which has nothing pathological about it. It consists in admitting that the same being who is good and generous can also be annoying and imperfect (Merleau-Ponty 1964, 103).

Within a family or, say, an institution of education that allows for a tolerance of ambiguity, the child can then perceive her own life and the people and things she experiences as movements, as processes of becoming. Instead of static authorities or servants, she sees within her experience things and other people as "phenomena of transition" (Merleau-Ponty 1964, 105).

As in the previous chapter, with its emphasis on Husserl's awareness of the role of transition, we see here that for Merleau-Ponty the healthy development of intentionality is one that perceives according to our own internal, temporal structure. To see the future and its relations, to allow the future to structure the way we relate here and now, is to see the new transitional shape that emerges out of the transition of the future or the past into the present. To perceive is to allow what shows itself to continue moving toward a more sophisticated, more explicit, more "ambiguous" meaning.

Also like Husserl, Merleau-Ponty notes that a healthy embrace of ambiguity occurs within a perceiving that accords with our structure of intercorporeality. As Merleau-Ponty says explicitly, our experience of others is both a "structure" of our conscious life and a "content" of our experience. It is both: "We must consider the relation with others not only as one of the *contents* of our experience but as an actual *structure* in its own right" (Merleau-Ponty 1964, 140). Our relations with others are thus something we live as a structural openness to concrete others. We are always already ahead of ourselves *toward* them. Only this fact can explain how the child perceives the parent in the mirror without explicitly seeing or understanding her own image. Only this can explain her transition through stages into a future that has always already been in some ways, through pre-maturation, her own.

Intentionality thus engenders itself within a life that is constantly searching for "equilibrium" (Merleau-Ponty 1964, 141) and for a path forward, into more evolved and supple (read: ambiguous) values and relationships that are only sketched out or predelineated but which promise a fulfillment not only of themselves but also of us. If the child begins then with a kind of vulnerability to neurosis, to authoritarianism, it would have to be said also that she begins with a kind of power. Her perception is that power that can, if supported, move her ahead on its own motor, into ambiguity and therefore toward a more intentional, active participation in relations of mutuality.

However, Merleau-Ponty says, even if the child avoids or resolves "psychological rigidity," there may arise another possible block or resistance to a successful, ambiguous, synthetic perceptual life in the child. And that lies in jealousy.

Although jealousy is an experience that is mostly that of an older child, who has passed through infancy, nevertheless the older child who experiences jealousy retains or replicates the structure of her infantile "confusion." In its emergence, jealousy repeats and concretizes the structure of infantile indeterminacy with respect to the limits of self and other, self and world:

> For the child jealousy represents a stage wherein he participates within a total affective situation and senses the complementary life of his own *without yet knowing how to isolate or affirm his own*. He thus allows himself to be inwardly dominated by the one who plunders him. Having all told nothing of his own he defines himself *entirely in relation to others* and by the lack of what the others have (Merleau-Ponty 1964, 144, my emphasis).

Within a shared emotional situation, the child cannot determine the difference, the distinction between self and world, self and other. She "senses" her own life within that shared situation, but she cannot "isolate" or determine her own limit or the limits of the other person. The child in jealousy therefore will experience herself "entirely in relation to others." Her self-experience will not just *involve* a lacuna, a lack of another. It will be, rather, *simply* lack, i.e., "lack of what the others have."

The child has advanced beyond infant indeterminacy insofar as the child has grown capable of seeing another person *as* other and of "sensing" her own life. The very ability to enter a particular "affective situation" or emotion that is shared with (and to some extent *about*) another person, the very ability to measure the other as having something I want, is proof of that.

However, the sheer newness and magnitude of this new "stage," jealousy, uses the child's ongoing struggle with limit to resist her progress even more strongly. In psychological rigidity, the child projects a division *into the other* as the *object* (the good/bad mother or father) of her experience. But such an "authoritarian" other was always already far beyond her power. Rigidity was the way in which, in her impotence, she lashed out at the other and tried to save herself. There was no common ground, no shared object. And so self-preservation loomed large and demanded her energy.

In jealousy, by contrast, the threat to the child is both less direct and more dangerous. Jealousy is an experience not of an absolute, inconsistent authority but of a coupling and pairing in which both oneself and the other have, at least in principle, an equal claim to a mutually desired thing. Because she experiences no inherent reason for her not having it, and since the other does in fact have it, the child thus attempts to identify herself fully with the *other's relationship* with the desired thing.

Everything shows up as a response to the other's perspective, view, or project of ownership. All her efforts become ways to dislodge the thing from its relationship to the other. And thus the jealous child projects the majority of her destruction not necessarily outward onto the desired thing (which is still good and desirable—though sometimes jealousy does involve an attempt to poison the thing's desirability) but inward, preferring to conceal, damage, or spurn herself—and not the object: "When jealousy is experienced, hostile feelings are directed not so much against the primal object but rather against the rivals . . . which brings in an element of distribution" (Klein 1984, 198).

A jealous child thus makes use of her experience of the wholeness and consistency of the other person in order to continue to experience the desired object, albeit under less than ideal circumstances. As such, jealousy is the child's submersion of her self-awareness that was in the process of being worked out in relation to others and the world.

Indeed, the situation with the dominating other person, which she experiences in her emotion or mood of jealousy, does not seem to resolve itself immediately on its own. At least, it does not resolve or reveal itself to be simply a "stage" until she sees that it is *she* who "allows" the other to dominate her own self-experience. Or until something reminds her that she can define herself *with* the other in ways that reach *beyond* the focus of the particular desired (and perhaps withheld) thing. Or, finally, until she realizes that this other is only one of many who do *not* necessarily compete with her over the objects of her desire.

However difficult the child's repeated "falling" into confusion with the other may be, what Merleau-Ponty makes clear is that it is only by means of this confusion that the child can gather the strength for more explicit, more mutual relations. For love, which appears to be the focus of the whole essay on the child's relations with others, is what the child can enter into only when she understands that the relationships with others are continuous processes of negotiations. They are never fully prepared, whether by the family or by her past. And they require her to pay attention both to herself and to the other people with whom she finds herself within a loving situation:

> To consent to love or be loved is to consent also to influence someone else, to decide to a certain extent on behalf of the other. To love is inevitably to enter into an undivided situation with another (Merleau-Ponty 1964, 154).

Genetically, then, the child *can* learn from her previous situations of confusion. She can learn her limits and become empowered to decide and to be decided for. She can come to choose "an undivided situation" of self-transcendence by means of a shared relationship.

This possibility is given within the structure of each human being, but it requires concrete steps to make it explicit. Only with the right support and with the proper situations can the child move from the confusion of herself and others toward a clearer sense of how her self-awareness can be situated within creative, mutual relationships of love.[4] Within a helpful familial and educational structure that embraces ambiguity, the child can stop searching for competing "proofs" of love from a parent and start dwelling in the actions that are made possible by their relations.

Ultimately for Merleau-Ponty, a child whose perceptual, bodily, affective, and situational involvements allow for ambiguity can move toward a "non-pathological attitude" which has

> confidence above and beyond what can be proved, in resolutely skirting these doubts that can be raised about the reality of the other's sentiments, by means of the generosity of the praxis, by means of an action that proves itself in being carried out (Merleau-Ponty 1964, 155).

A child, in other words, can take on a healthy phenomenological attitude if the child's pre-mature abilities are matched with the kind of discernment that addresses her emotional needs and expressions. She can become committed to her own possibility of "praxis" or "action" as carrying the proof of her readiness for relationship. But she can do this only if the supporting home of her life is committed toward her transition into action and into self-determining interdependence with others. The role of education, then, becomes of central importance to the developing (genetic) phenomenology of one's own life.

LITERARY PRACTICE – A PHENOMENOLOGICAL READING OF *THE MOUSE AND HIS CHILD*: FROM CONFUSION TO COMMUNITY

A. Introduction

The Mouse and His Child is a story of two windup toys, a father and son, who are welded together at the hands. They arrive at a toy shop in the Christmas season and are placed in the window in order to display their motion—that of dancing in a circle with the father lifting the son higher as he turns. The mechanism for both toys is in the father's body.

The pair of windups are sold to a family whose children are expressly told not to play with them. And indeed the notion of injunctions or laws, especially as given to children, runs throughout the story. The father and son begin to have adventures, however, when the son breaks those laws by crying on the job and by asserting his own thinking against the rigid, rule-bound character of the toy world. Because of the child's crying, the cat knocks them over and smashes them, they are thrown away, and a tramp repairs them so that they no longer turn in a circle but instead move linearly, with the father pushing the son backwards.[5]

The novel ends, after many encounters with both windup toys and living animals, when the father and son have been split apart after a second fall and have been repaired and improved by their animal friends a second time so as to be self-winding. But this improvement, this achievement of being self-winding, ultimately seems less important to the two mice than the establishment of a community of beloved friends and scholars with whom they have shared their way.

B. Emotion as Intercorporeal Motor

The novel begins with an infectious dance and with a pair of philosophical questions. A tramp stands outside a toy shop window and watches the mouse and his child being wound up by a saleslady and then dancing in a circle: "As the tramp watched . . . around and around they danced gravely, and more and more slowly as the spring unwound" (Hoban 1967, 2). The tramp immediately imitates them: "with his big broken shoes printing his footsteps in the fresh snow, he solemnly danced in a circle, swinging his empty arms up and down. . . . People laughed, shook their heads, and hurried on" (Hoban 1967, 3). The dance is "grave" or "solemn" and yet also arresting. People stop.

They see the imitation. They recognize and internalize something important—hence, they laugh. An initial question arises: what does the circle of the
tramp's dance mean, since everyone else is "moving in a fixed direction"
(Hoban 1967, 3)?

The dance is infectious. It is shared. It claims the father, the son, the
tramp, and the passersby. It inaugurates an emotional or affective situation in
which bodies join. The dance is a motor for questioning and discovery.

The implicit question of the dance's meaning generates other, explicit
questions for the characters and the reader. After the mouse and his child are
first removed from their box, the child asks: "Where are we?" and then
"*What* are we, Papa?" (Hoban 1967, 4). The father mouse replies that he does
not know, but then says "We must wait and see" (Hoban 1967, 4). In his
response, the father offers no ready-made answers. He offers ambiguity and a
path toward a shared act of waiting and perceiving together.[6]

The mouse child follows at least part of the father's injunction. He "sees"
or perceives, though he does not seem to "wait." Almost immediately, the
child feels himself within the affective situations of longing, of community,
and of the threat of loss. In his education by the elephant, the child discovers
that he does not "want to go out into the world" (Hoban 1967, 6). He cries, is
upbraided by the clock, but then discovers that his fear and his lack of a
mother might be compensated by working together as a community: "'Will
you be my mama,' said the child, 'and will you sing to me all the time? And
can we all stay here together and live in the beautiful house where the party is
and not go out into the world?'" (Hoban 1967, 7).

Even though he is young, then, the mouse child senses that an experience
of genuine community can resolve a basic experience of lack. It can support
people in their flawed families, and it can celebrate togetherness. What he
does not yet see, however, and will not until much later, is that community is
not an insulation against the world but rather an impetus and manner of
"going out into" it.

In any case, the father and son are sold the next day to a family. Nothing
in the toy shop has prepared them for what is now happening. The parents
make it clear that, although they are toys, the mice "were not presents for the
children" (Hoban 1967, 8). Their very identity stripped away, "the mouse
and his child complained of the futility of dancing in an endless circle that
led nowhere" (Hoban 1967, 9).

This shared emotion between father and son, of futility, leads the child to
cry again. And the child's crying startles the cat, who breaks them. The two
are thrown away, since the motor does not run.

The same tramp who has imitated their dance finds them in the garbage,
takes them apart, and works very hard all day to get their motor working. At
last "the mouse and his child were whole again" (Hoban 1967, 11). But the
tramp has some difficulty—he cannot repair their mechanism to its original

form. Now the mouse and his child move but they move in a straight line, with the father "pushing the child backward before him" (Hoban 1967, 11). As the one who has danced their dance, the tramp now invites the mouse and his child to imitate the tramp's own movements: "Be tramps" (Hoban 1967, 12).

Of course one of the main obstacles to their moving forward as "tramps" is that only the father gets to see where they are going. The child is carried along without perceiving where they might go, where they might rest. The child, then, seems limited to emotional responses, mostly moments of sadness and fear expressed in crying.

Despite the elephant, the clock, and his father admonishing him for crying, the mouse child does not extinguish his emotions as the motor of his life. Even when they are prisoners in Manny Rat's dump, the child perceives, by means of seeing the stars for the first time, that his emotion of futility is a way of pushing them outward, beyond the reach of the dump: "But as he looked and looked upon that steady burning he was comforted a little; if he was nothing, he thought, so also was this rat and all the dump. His father's hands were firm upon his, and he resolved to see what next the great world offered" (Hoban 1967, 19). Perception in the child, then, is a way to move out of a situation of entrapment, a way to "comfort" oneself and to feel the togetherness with others as a "firmness" that allows for "resolved" progress, for resolution.

The resolution that the child seeks, within their enslavement by the rats in the dump, is for the togetherness that might be possible again in the toy shop. The child seeks, by means of his desire and his memory of feeling at home, for an enlargement of family, for a community of people who would have a different purpose than either master or slave. But the father does not yet share the resolution of the child within their affective situation. The father, instead, denies the child's emotions as opening onto reality: "the whole idea of such a quest is impossible" (Hoban 1967, 34).

For the father, this problem of the child being unable to be an equal in their shared movement is the *cause* of the impotence of the child's emotional life: "Our motor is in me. He fills the empty space inside himself with foolish dreams that cannot possibly come true" (Hoban 1967, 35). Of course, the irony here is that the father does not yet see that self-motion is not only self-loco-motion. The gaps, "the empty space," or lacunae in the child's bodily self-consciousness, and his resistance to his father, indeed the child's enforced backwards-glance, are really what gear them both into new situations.[7] Eventually, the child's efforts to hold onto the real hope of real community cause the father to retrieve, as if for the first time, an increased measure of suppleness and appreciation of ambiguity. It will be the child who guides the father into the reality of emotion as their intercorporeal motor.

By means of the child, then, who has silently held onto his dream of a re-constitution of the initial toy shop family/community, both of them grow. And the father is amazed as he too grows, for he realizes that it means that the child lives this dream of family/community, and the persistent optimism that the dream demands, as a pre-mature, yet real, shape of *both of their* past, present, and future perceptions.

The child's emotional life is rich and deep. Ironically, it is the father, who seems afraid of emotional displays, who displays a kind of pyschological rigidity. But all is not lost. As the truth of emotion as a powerful shared mechanism gradually reveals itself, the father does allow himself to see that the child's tendency to cry or to dream or to take comfort in what he sees or feels—this tendency is something the child has that is a gift, an intercorpo-real structure of motion that both of them can deploy at the same time and that has no need of re-winding. Only a certain power and pregnancy of hope in the child can bring it about: "'Maybe we shan't always be helpless, Papa,' he said. 'Maybe we'll be self-winding some day'" (Hoban 1967, 72).

C. Paired and Broken—The Move toward Ambiguity and Love

As Merleau-Ponty considers the relationship of thinking to emotion, he maintains that "the intellectual elaboration of our experience of the world is constantly supported by the affective elaboration of our inter-human rela-tions" (Merleau-Ponty 1964, 112–113). The two are in constant communica-tion. Thinking elaborates because it is supported by emotion. Both elaborate. Thinking is about the world. Emotion is about relations with others. Togeth-er, they build up the narrative of our lives that is the way we share the same world together, the way that ideas, for example, are only worked out together in emotions of friendship, opposition, and resolution.

What I will do here is to show in the mouse child's development a radical shift in his perceptions and speech after he is broken apart from the father. In so doing, I will determine that the image of the father and son joined at the hands is one of a very intense and specific kind of coupling or pairing—but it is only an initial one that their emotional life together elaborates.

While they are joined at the hands, the gaps within the child, and the difference in position that they occupy while moving, whether in a line or a circle, promote a kind of growth. When the father and son are stuck on the bottom of the pond, the father despairs. The world just is the pond. There is no way out. However, the child refuses this rigidity.

And the child uses his emotion to elaborate his relation with the father, with the muskrat, with the frog, with the turtle, and with the apparently infinitely repeating images of dogs on the can of dog food. His emotions assist his thinking, his relationships build toward a new idea, and a new set of commitments, of affective vectors and of actions, emerges that then takes hold of both father and son.

At first it seems that the new idea of freedom is only the child's. And, contrary to Merleau-Ponty, the new idea seems *not* to be born of emotional elaboration. After all, Serpentina, the turtle, admonishes the father and child: "Each of us, sunk in the mud however deep, must rise on the propulsion of his own thought. Each of us must journey through the dogs, beyond the dots, and to the truth alone" (Hoban 1967, 104). But this wisdom is clearly false. The turtle sleeps in the mud immediately after uttering it.

What does happen is that the son can see the can while the father cannot. The son sees on behalf of them both, just as the father pushed the son backwards from having their joint mechanism in himself. The child's emotion and thinking then are borne out of his responsibility, his desire to lift them both up. The father has emotion but it is "painful to him, as if a spring within his mind were wound up achingly tight. Powerless to act, he could not convert that coiled energy to motion" (Hoban 1967, 108). The elaboration must be done by the child, but not on his own.

Within a profound appreciation of the ambiguity of his experience, the child does come to a self-realization. And this seems to be something he does completely on his own and completely about himself: "If I'm big enough to stand in the mud all this time and contemplate infinity . . . I'm big enough to look at the other side of nothing" (Hoban 1967, 110).

And with that, when the label is removed from the can of dog food with its infinitely repeating dog images, the child finds not a truth of himself alone but a truth of his relationship with his father.

The child sees himself for the first time by means of seeing himself together with his father in their simultaneous reflection in the now bare and shiny tin can: "he had never seen himself before, but he recognized his father, and therefore knew himself. 'Ah,' he said, 'there's nothing on the other side of nothing but us'" (Hoban 1967, 111). It is this seeing of his whole affective situation in the label's removal, of the whole of himself in relation to his father's reflection in the bare can, that allows the child to form the idea of freedom and of community more explicitly. Feeling his relation with his father as charting a new path enables the child to see how to get out of the pond.

There is "us" on the other side of nothing. We *are*. And he carefully executes their escape by means of a coin, some fishing line, and Miss Mudd's assistance. In using his relationship with his father as an affective truth, the child becomes capable of thinking, of showing his own motor, and of moving toward more mutual relationships.

But the way out of the pond involves tragedy and dislocation. It involves the end of a certain perception of family. Having emerged far enough out of the pond by means of dim-witted fish, the father and child are taken as food by a hawk. As they are flying, the child then orchestrates their fall from the hawk's talons. And in so doing the child wills their demise as a couple.

Even in launching them to the ground, however, the child mouse retains the meaningfulness of their prior attachment, as just before they fall, he says to his father, with all the profound care and impotence of a parent: "I've got you! You won't fall" (Hoban 1967, 118). The child has seen their "undivided situation," to echo the description of love in Merleau-Ponty's essay, and has moved, by enacting his love, to take a stand and to decide for the father. The father and the son have thus changed roles, and the child has found that their future together is worth the loss of the present.

When a moment later the coupling is broken, the segregation that they experience is profound: "the dump leaped and shuddered in their vision as the impact broke their grip on each other's hands, split their bodies open, and flung them violently apart. The scattered pieces of the mouse and his child lay on the path . . . and they saw and heard no more" (Hoban 1967, 119). The vulnerability, the reconfiguration of their experience is total. The schema that develops among the ruins of their connection will forever replace the one that joined their hands.

However, this segregation is not absolute; rather, it is repaired and made sense of. It inaugurates a community in which neither segregation nor union is ever complete.[8] In fact, after the fall, what now finds its way into their lives is their greater and more intimate community and co-perceptions by means of the mediation of their shared friendships.

Unlike the communities, then, of the toy shop or the mob-like dump, the community that the mouse and his child work together to form after freeing themselves from the pond is no longer simply about either protection or profit. This community is richer and *sui generis*: "something new and different emerged from the concerted efforts of the little family" (Hoban 1967, 157). What was to be a home turns to a hotel; what was to be a refuge from war turns into education. And they are reminded that what joins the community together is not an easily manipulated notion of familial roles (uncle, sister, mother, father, son, daughter) but "good *friends* to wind you" (Hoban 1967, 161).

Within the newness of their community, the mouse and his child now declare that they "aren't toys anymore . . . toys are to be played with, and we aren't. . . . Now we have come to that place where the scattering is regathered" (Hoban 1967, 131). There is a "we," a love that proves itself in its history and its praxis, by means of their relations with other characters. And it is these larger sets of relations that allow them to go beyond the relation of original and copy, of originator and issue in their relation with each other. Theirs is now a "we" that implies shared perception of suffering, of endurance and that gives them the possibility of loving—loving others outside the family and loving the fact that they are a new, singular kind of thing.

And of course it is all because of intercorporeality that community emerges. It is not "reasoning" that bands people together alone. As Manny Rat attests in his new, humbled role, "You have to have a feel for fings" (Hoban 1967, 163).

NOTES

1. An earlier version of this chapter appeared as "Russell Hoban's *The Mouse and His Child* as Phenomenological Novel," in *Childhood and Philosophy* 11, no. 21 (2015): 93–103. I am grateful to editor Walter Kohan for permission to use parts of that original version here.

2. Matthew Lipman's exhortation in *Philosophy in the Classroom* to teachers is something I think Merleau-Ponty would find appropriate, given his phenomenological description of a child's affective life. Lipman says the following: When a child asks what is death, we should appreciate that "the fact that children can raise such questions indicates that they begin with a thirst for holistic explanations, and it is patronizing, to say the least, not to try to help them develop concepts equal in generality to the questions they ask" (Lipman 1994, 29). Pair this statement of Lipman's with the opening of *The Mouse and His Child*, where the mouse child searches for such holistic explanations, and one can see the relevance of the novel to teaching philosophy to children almost immediately.

3. Peter R. Costello discusses this operative motif within Arnold Lobel's Frog and Toad stories in "Gift-Giving, Waiting, and Walking," in *Philosophy in Children's Literature*.

4. See Winnicott's essay "Transitional Objects and Transitional Phenomena" in *Playing and Reality*. See also Kirsten Jacobson on the relationship between toys, transition, and reality in her article on *The Velveteen Rabbit* in Costello, ed.

5. Maria Nikolajeva, in "Toward Linearity," notes that it is precisely the opposition of circular and linear motion in the novel that drives the novel's complexity: "Going out is linear, dancing in circles by definition circular; this contradiction sets up the whole movement of the book" (Allison 2000, 65). I might note that Nikolajeva seems to downplay the long moments of being still—in the box before the toys are unpacked; in the pond before the insight into what is behind infinity, etc.

6. John Stephens, in "Questions of 'What' and 'Where,' and Contexts of 'Meaning' for the *Mouse and His Child* in the Late Twentieth Century," acknowledges the philosophical importance of these questions early on in the novel. Stephens classifies this as a "modernist" novel with a "modernist conception of subjectivity, but now with a strong emphasis placed on the dependence of selfhood on intersubjective relationships" (Allison 2000, 47).

7. The child sees the past, the father the future. Together, they form a shared present.

8. As Merleau-Ponty notes, "there is a first phase, which we call pre-communication, in which there is not one individual over against another but rather an anonymous collectivity, an undifferentiated group life. Next, on the basis of this initial community, both by the objectification of one's own body and the constitution of the other in his difference, there occurs a segregation, a distinction of individuals—a process which, moreover, as we shall see, is never completely finished" (Merleau-Ponty 1964, 119).

Chapter Three

A Phenomenology of Sexuality and Movement in *To Kill a Mockingbird*

INTRODUCTION

In the previous chapters, I have shown how the thought of Edmund Husserl and Maurice Merleau-Ponty can be useful to developing a phenomenological reading of some important pieces of children's literature. In this chapter, I want to continue that demonstration. But I want to continue in a different manner.

Here, instead of waiting to perform a literary analysis until *after* an explication of a phenomenological text or series of themes, I want to weave the phenomenological and literary analysis together from the start. In this way, I believe the reader will begin to see more concretely how phenomenology is much more than a series of arguments or beliefs. At least for me, phenomenology, rather, is a way of perceiving or, more precisely, a way of *expanding* one's perception.

Building upon the previous discussions of intercorporeality and temporality in texts by Merleau-Ponty and Husserl, I now approach Harper Lee's *To Kill a Mockingbird* from a phenomenological standpoint. First, I note the main character's (Scout Finch's) transitional, process-oriented subjectivity in general. In doing so, I claim that it is Scout's transitional character, her active transferences, her intentionality as embodied and mobile—all of these—that enable her to think in ways that surprise and enlighten the adults in her life.

Second, I will look more specifically at Scout's fluidity with respect to her own understanding and deployment of gender. As transitional, Scout can move not just between people or between areas of the community but also between roles and categories. And she can establish her home, freedom, and self-understanding most clearly when she is not forced to maintain allegiance to just one or the other.

In looking at Scout as a transitional subject, then, I align my reading of Harper Lee's novel with work in philosophy for children. As David Kennedy, a prominent figure in this field, asserts about a child in general, I believe Scout is an example of "an experimental being, in rapid and continual reorganization—a being in which the elements of self are in dialogue—both internally and with the external world" (Kennedy 2002).

Reading *To Kill a Mockingbird*, then, with a foot in both the thought of phenomenology and the thought of philosophy for children, I articulate a meditation on how this one child, Scout, thinks in a non-static mode as a developing person. As such I encourage the reader to take a further step along the journey charted in the second chapter of this book—the journey toward perceiving the intentionality of human consciousness as embodied in a genetic, developmental life within a family and within a community.

As I engage with the character of Scout, I use almost exclusively material from Merleau-Ponty's seminal work, *The Phenomenology of Perception*. What I make most use of from that book are these two insights: first, Merleau-Ponty's extension of Husserlian intentionality to movement (or motor intentionality); and, second, his analysis of sexuality and gender. Both are original insights of Merleau-Ponty that remain important for a burgeoning phenomenology of childhood and of education, which this book is developing across each chapter. I conclude this chapter by claiming that a successful educational system or program must take people seriously as dynamic beings and must gear into or engage their motions, desire, and gendered self-understanding.

SCOUT AS SCOUTING THE TERRAIN

Throughout the novel by Harper Lee, Scout moves into and out of most of the places in the town of Maycomb. And, as she moves, Scout weaves together the experiences of many of the town's citizens. Indeed, I would argue, it is because we identify with Scout as readers that we become able, simply by witnessing her creative *style* of moving, to see the novel as a complex, layered whole that resists a single interpretation and that demands that we reflect on it.

Unfortunately for Scout, however, and unfortunately for us who identify with and feel for her, this movement of hers, and her creative response to situations and her engagement with us as readers, often occurs by means of—or in response to—her whole body being monitored, shamed, punished, hurt, or threatened. Very often in the novel, Scout's movements, like her thoughts, are judged as being those of a "girl," or of one who ought to become more girl-like. And all too often we who learn with her are relegated to participating in her punishment by means of our silent gaze and silent co-feeling.

Nevertheless, as I have intimated earlier, the novel, Scout herself, also makes liberation possible. The novel only makes progress by means of Scout's movements and her ability to retain the significance of each movement within the passage to the next. If our silent act of reading makes us a party to her punishment, our silent witness also can become (once we are finished reading and get a chance to reflect on what we have experienced) an embrace of Scout's bodily resistance. And that resistance comes in the way Scout epitomizes the concept that Merleau-Ponty develops called "motor intentionality." As I will go on to show, Scout narrates her deployment of "motor intentionality" as an intelligent scouting of the terrain of the town of Maycomb.

In his *Phenomenology of Perception*, Merleau-Ponty describes motor intentionality as a compulsory conceptual admission. This compulsion is one phenomenologists experience because we desire to do justice to the lived experiences of all humans—of children, of those with disabilities, and of those who have "normal" perceptual experience—all of these—together. If we are to do this work, if we are to do justice to perceptual experience as it is lived in these very different situations, then we must admit that there is the following:

> between movement as a third person process and thought as a representation of
> movement, an anticipation or a grasp of the result assured by the body itself as
> a motor power [. . .] or a "motor intentionality" (Merleau-Ponty 2012, 113).

At the most fundamental, lived level, thinking and moving are not separated for Merleau-Ponty. Their occurrence within the same person, within a single gesture of waving to a friend or within a project of typing a paper, for example—this entails the admission that thought and movement are always already present within actions as meaningful, within meaning as enacted.

For Merleau-Ponty, Husserl's emphasis on intentionality must be extended beyond perception and thought to movement. Indeed human movement and thought are *given* together. We live their togetherness before we separate them. Perhaps it is only the artist, like Auguste Rodin, who can thematize the posture of thinking. But it has a posture. And after we see Rodin's sculpture, we are left with the insight that thinking has always already been a certain set of bodily motions.

Before any reflection on the distinguishability of movement and thought, then, we can experience that we are intelligently moving beings. And what the study of Scout in this novel shows is that Scout's movement too is itself always already a kind of thinking which, as a *living* kind of thinking, "does not consist in the act of subsuming under a category" (Merleau-Ponty 2012, 130).

We take it as a given then that the union of thought and movement precedes their distinction for Merleau-Ponty. Using this insight of his enables us to see that Scout's movements are both pre-reflective, i.e., that they are not predicative in their essence, and yet *still intelligent*. Then, from this insight, we can see that Scout's pre-reflective, intelligent movements do in fact, like the organist whom Merleau-Ponty uses as an example, "consecrate" or unify the town of Maycomb, herself, and the people she interacts with: "[hers] are gestures of consecration: they put forth affective vectors, they discover emotional sources, and they create an expressive space" (Merleau-Ponty 2012, 147).

Like the organist Merleau-Ponty describes, Scout makes philosophical and affective gestures in her movements. Her emotions are intelligent responses to her situation. And thus Scout's body, her (e)motions, and her ability to inhabit the spaces between the categories of people in Maycomb—all these allow her to show, above all, the truth of our embodiment: "our body . . . is the very movement of expression, it projects significations on the outside by giving them a place and sees to it that they begin to exist as things" (Merleau-Ponty 2012, 147).

There is some truth to saying that Scout is not a simple unity; for there really are at least three Scouts in the novel. The very first chapter introduces us to the coming instability in the process of the narration. For the one who speaks there purports to be an adult woman who claims to tell this whole tale again after some period of reflection and after talking to Jem.

What the narrator relates by way of a first person account then is a reflective, rehearsed, family-based narrative that focuses itself on Scout's experiences. It weaves in and out of a girl's, a woman's, and a family's account of bodily movement (focused at the beginning and end on Jem's broken arm). The story, then, is overdetermined; it demands we return to and reflect on its overdetermination after we have, after at least one Scout has, moved through it.[1]

The novel's overdetermination, however, does not prevent its continuation. We simply forget about this in order to move through. And so the narrator recedes in favor of the six-year-old Scout who goes to school for the first time.

And the first main figure that the six-year-old Scout introduces us to within the context of going to school is Miss Caroline, the first grade teacher. At only six years old, Scout reads to Miss Caroline fluidly, out of the newspaper. And the teacher disapproves. Because of her disapproval, Miss Caroline not only disciplines Scout's body—singling her out for the gazes of others—but she also inserts herself into Scout's relation to her father. That is,

Miss Caroline tries to tear Scout from her father for the sake of Miss Caroline's own benefit.

This inhibition of Scout's movement by which she joins home and school in one whole, shakes the six-year-old to her core. Out of her experience of discipline and punishment, however, Scout reacts as one who refuses to be compartmentalized. Instead of becoming obedient and taking on the division required, she rejects the very institution of Miss Caroline's education.

The reason she rejects Miss Caroline is that Scout experiences herself just as naturally a part of learning as she was naturally a part of Sunday services or her father's love. In Miss Caroline's intervention, what education becomes for Scout is compulsion—and Scout deploys her whole being against that compulsion in order to gather again her wholeness: "Now that I was compelled to think about it, reading was something that just came to me, as learning to fasten the seat of my union suit without looking around, or achieving two bows from a snarl of shoelaces" (Lee 1999, 19). Miss Caroline's compulsion returns Scout to the wholeness of her body, to the way her hands and fingers learn to accommodate her body with clothing.

The irony of course is Miss Caroline has everything wrong; it is Miss Caroline who cannot teach effectively, not Atticus. The "Dewey Decimal System" (Lee 1999, 20) that Jem tells Scout of is really the educational reforms initiated by John Dewey that precisely took children's experience into account in order to promote a learning that drew the concepts out of lived experience rather than the other way around.[2] This humor, however, betrays a tragedy—it is not Scout who cannot read properly. Rather, it is Miss Caroline who is unable to read Dewey clearly since she is so worried about her own body, her own presence being respected and honored. She, Caroline, sacrifices the bodies of herself and of Scout for recognition within a patriarchal situation.

Already we see that education begins, for Scout, in movement and relationship. It begins in unreflective, bodily habit. Education does not begin with interdiction, programme, and obedience. And it does not begin with a kind of shame-based reflection that seeks to tear the child away from her other, important spaces in order to maintain the educative space as the primary one.

The older Scout then reminds herself and us of another fact about her premature abilities—this time concerning her ability to write: "Calpurnia was to blame for this" (Lee 1999, 20). Scout writes because Calpurnia gave Scout the opportunity to copy the Bible for the promise of some desired food. Education then was inseparable from desire—for closeness, for tasty food.

But Scout begins to have her own views on Calpurnia now in light of Miss Caroline. For the growing Scout, Calpurnia's efforts at educating her were also about punishment. Scout's body, then, learned to learn on its own as a whole, as a body from which desire and indignation issued, but as a body that went far beyond those—a body which was not to be bargained for with short-term rewards or punishments.

Miss Caroline's punishment, too, was something Scout learned from. But she learned about it on her own, by moving from Caroline back to Calpurnia. Scout learned because she was a child, able to put her whole body and being into a task that would open her onto the world. Scout learned because she took multiple teachers into her heart and then left them behind just as easily. Scout learned because she *taught herself* by means of her ability to unite the situations in which she found herself.

Scout moves between methods of "teaching" that require her to recognize her body in its standing out or in its desires and needs. But in the move she offers herself some capacity to hold onto multiple situations and to hone close to their essence. Because of all this learning, much of it happening right there on the spot in the first grade classroom, she speaks on behalf of Walter Cunningham, whom Miss Caroline also misunderstands.

Scout speaks because of her home life. She speaks because of having been a witness to a serious conversation between Atticus and Mr. Cunningham about "entailments." Eventually, her holding on to this word is precisely what saves her father, Tom Robinson, and her brother and Dill on the steps of the courthouse in front of the mob. And it saves Walter here.

Indeed, Scout keeps words like "entailments" in her heart because in them she enlightens or encodes an entire situation or range of situations, an entire family or two families, and a way of relating the world to them. "Entailments" is what happens when Scout moves into and out of the family into the world—entailments gathers up the situation of the Depression, the honesty and integrity of the Cunninghams, and the patience and wisdom of Atticus. It "entails" the unity of the whole town and the economic pressures that everyone is set up to experience.

And this is what this philosophical child does (as have Fern, Wilbur, and the mouse child before them). She gives attention. And not just to the teacher. Her whole body, her whole being is geared toward the world. She gives that world attention and she receives back from it the mystery of its meaning. And thus Scout has a gift that she gives the town—her attention. And she gifts and re-gifts that attention over and over, from the age of six, to the age of the current adult narrator.

Scout attends because she cannot help but to do so. She attends and holds on to "entailments" because that is the way, following Merleau-Ponty, that her body operates: "it is a knot of living significations and not the law of a certain number of covariant terms" (Merleau-Ponty 2012, 153). And giving attention is not only in the moment but occurs by means of bringing the past and the future to bear on the present.

To stand up for Walter is a philosophical, ethical move that a six-year-old does without reflection (much as Fern did for Wilbur). It is a complex thought that the adult Scout can only relate in awe even to herself, for it displays a powerful phenomenological truth, namely that the "category" of right action for Scout "must be rooted in the givens" (Merleau-Ponty 2012, 154).

A little later in the novel, the weaving together of her defense of Walter, her fighting with Walter, and her stinging rebuke by Calpurnia in defense of Walter's pouring syrup on his meal—the weaving together of all this shows that Scout learns only by moving and by her body. It is in being called to the kitchen, talking with Calpurnia, and then being spanked on her way back that Scout attends to Walter as a person who is blessed with certain intelligence about farming and hampered from his own intelligence in other contexts by means of bodily necessity.

Scout learns that they needed him in the fields. They needed him at home. And so he could not learn, and so he eats a different manner and has no understanding of what "company" is. Scout learns both on and with her body what that category "company" means by means of Walter. And so by means of the experience of company, and of rebuke, Scout deploys what Merleau-Ponty describes as "the acquisition of a certain style of vision, a new use of one's own body . . . [which signifies that] our body is not an object for an 'I think': it is a totality of lived significations that moves toward its equilibrium" (Merleau-Ponty 2012, 155). As her body "moves toward equilibrium" in learning what company means, six-year-old Scout "hates" Calpurnia for her stinging smack, for her defense of Walter, and for her defense of the need to be empathetic and civil. That is, Scout hates Calpurnia until she sees Little Chuck Little mediate the classroom for Miss Caroline.

Like Walter, Chuck is poor but straightforward and intelligent. It is in Little's assistance to the pupil who had lice and to Miss Caroline, attending to the teacher's bodily life by getting her some water and walking her back to her desk, that Scout recovers herself and moves toward and beyond her resentment of Calpurnia. Scout connects Calpurnia to Little Chuck Little and figures a way to move with and through them into another pattern, one in which she has Chuck and Calpurnia for "company."

Atticus tries to formalize Scout's pattern of transcending her situation into other, more sophisticated situations by means of explaining the notion of empathy to Scout: "You never really understand a person until you consider things from his point of view [. . .] until you climb into his skin and walk around in it" (Lee 1999, 33). This is of course what the six-year-old has been doing all along, on and off, but Atticus's formalization of her already engaged practice into words allows Scout to reflect on it and to make it into a more consistent and a more effective habit.

In the whole course of the novel, Scout will always move ahead and transcend. And in doing so she will sometimes be triumphant and sometimes be vulnerable. She will be attacked for her union with Atticus and, perhaps because of his formalization of her movement by way of the concept "empathy," ultimately, by Bob Ewell—a person for whom empathy is a movement he can neither perform nor allow.[3] But Scout is precisely capable of transcendence by means of her vulnerability and by means of the limit of Atticus's formalization. Scout is not forced to relate to others but instead offered tools to help her explore her own experience. She is appealed to as a necessary part of the family's whole motion, and the limitations of that family are what she also reflects upon along the way.

Atticus tells her that she is not to leave school after the first day. Learning comes through the desire to move into "a new environment" and the stamina to take one's empathy and create that new environment by means of one's attention to all those involved. Scout has that desire, and thus Atticus forces her only through a kind of appeal and of persuasion, which requests that his daughter take up something between force and freedom in order to move beyond even himself as her father.

For of course the revelation that her father "never went to school" (Lee 1999, 5) also has to be very interesting to Scout. The lawyer who is self-taught advises her to go to school. This is a contradiction that she must herself resolve by participating in both environments. And thus Scout moves and learns to think in more fluid ways, by means of gaps in her father's life, gaps in the family, gaps in her understanding, gaps in the community.

Her mother's death, for example, is the gap that allows Calpurnia to teach and to be hated and to be taken back; her mother's death and Atticus's own reluctance to deploy the forces of commonly understood practices and concepts like gender—these are also the gap that allows for androgyny to become a deployable tactic for Scout. And it is her androgyny that allows Scout to scout out further terrain and more complex negotiations.

With all of this in the background, then, Scout moves between people and what they say and do, and thus she assembles tools to help her explore her own experience. She is even able to discover the limitations of her own family and to reflect on how her own motions propel her beyond them.

SCOUT IS A GIRL—SCOUT IS NOT A GIRL: ANDROGYNY AS A SYNTHESIS, GENDER AS A TRAP

Throughout the novel, Scout is tied, it would seem, to the practices of gender. Multiple people are trying to get her to wear dresses, to participate in Missionary Society meetings, to stop playing roughly, to become more feminine. Her original way of thinking, I would say, lies in the way she simply refuses to play those games with the girls and women of the community and, instead, decides to interpret her own body in her own way. In doing this, Scout instantiates what Merleau-Ponty argues is the basic power of bodily life, namely that the body's own power of self-interpretation undergirds any concepts we could form about how it operates: "If one can still speak of an interpretation in the perception of one's own body, then it would be necessary to say that it *interprets itself*" (Merleau-Ponty 2012, 151, my emphasis).

As we will see in the remaining chapters of this book, Merleau-Ponty makes an important move forward here. The body is a hermeneutic power. It is a self-interpreting existence that is made up of (and exudes) meaning. The body is the law of its own logic, of its own development. And we are forever catching up to its implicit motor within its movements.

But motor intentionality is not the only intentionality of the body. Movement and perception are joined by a third flow, a third corridor of intentionality—that of sexuality. Sexuality, too, is a way of rooting oneself in the world and a way of the world rooting itself in us.

If we follow Merleau-Ponty in his discussion of the body as a sexed being, we see that the adult human who engages in meaningful understanding of sexual or erotic situations displays "erotic 'comprehension' that is not of the order of the understanding" (Merleau-Ponty 2012, 159). Instead, the adult who navigates sexuality expresses an intentionality "that follows the general movement of existence and that weakens along with it" (Merleau-Ponty 2012, 159). Erotic intentionality, then, is a kind of "original" intelligence that the body deploys as a whole, and sexual or gendered life is for Merleau-Ponty "the vital roots of perception, motricity, and representation" (Merleau-Ponty 2012, 160).

Continuing along with his genetic phenomenology that he begins with his description of childhood, then, Merleau-Ponty shows the way sexuality forms "the vital roots" of all other intentional pathways. Desire, which we should understand as always already implied in the heart of any discussion of sexuality, underlies all intentionality. It is the structure of yearning, leaning, being-toward the things that we experience from within our own resources—it is this structure of desire that forms the foundation for intentionality.

Within the novel, Scout is a child, but she is nonetheless always already participating in gender and in erotic perceptions by means of other women, by means of Dill who asked to marry her, kisses her, and talks about having a baby with her at nine years old. And certainly in the way she resists a gendered definition of herself, Scout shows, as a child, that "her manner of being toward the world . . . is projected in her sexuality" (Merleau-Ponty 2012, 161).

If Scout is able to scout the terrain of the town, to offer philosophical insights, to think critically, then, this is because, I argue, she deploys an original intentionality with respect not only to her motions but also to her gender. For in her resistance and in her creativity as to gender lie the very foundations of her "perception, motricity, and representation." She moves fluidly with respect to gender, and thus she moves as a primary and creative perceiver into places others cannot go. She thinks thoughts others cannot have.

Such a fluid movement, however, requires that she also navigate others' reactions to her and the limitations that sexuality and gender as such set upon her. She cannot simply "get out" of being a girl. She cannot simply transcend gender. What she can do, though, is transcend the way others live "being a girl" in order to make space for thinking through—all at once we might say—the critical intersection of sexuality, race, class, and community. For Scout, as for Merleau-Ponty, the issue of her gender is never closed: "Sexuality cannot be transcended, and yet there is no self-enclosed sexuality" (Merleau-Ponty 2012, 174).

While the attack on her at the end of the novel by Ewell signifies the vulnerability of the girl and the woman to the murderous categories instituted by white, male patriarchy, Scout can and does continue to embody the "revisiting" of gender that Merleau-Ponty might point us to:

> human existence will lead us to revisit our usual notion of necessity and of contingency. . . . All that we are, we are on the basis of a factual situation that we make our own and that we ceaselessly transform through a sort of escape that is never an unconditioned freedom (Merleau-Ponty 2012, 174).

Scout transforms herself and those around her, and perhaps us as readers, by means of her changing of "necessity" *back into* "contingency." She escapes the clutches of her aunt, the Missionary Society, and the Ewells by means of donning, for a moment and on her own terms, the powerful and occasionally protective costumes of gender only to *discard* them and move beyond them.

Close to the beginning of the novel, in one of the first attempts to "enclose" Scout in a subordinate position as a girl, Jem tries to pay Scout back for contradicting him by pushing her far too strongly down the road when Scout is inside a tire. While in the tire, Scout's body is contorted, bent over on itself, wrapped inside a thing. While inside, she is at the mercy of Jem's push.

Because Jem pushes in anger and from a desire to subjugate her, the tire goes too fast and too far, and Scout is hurt enough not to bring the tire with her when she extricates herself. She forces Jem to retrieve it from the Radley yard, which then creates a crisis in Jem's own sense of masculinity.

Responding to the necessity of retrieving the tire, Jem is of course frightened. But to hide it he tries to humiliate Scout in front of Dill: "'I swear, Scout, sometimes you act so much like a girl it's mortifying'" (Lee 1999, 42). Scout hears this and is silent about the fact that "there was more to it than he knew" (Lee 1999, 42).

The summer of the tire incident, the children play the Radley drama. Scout is relegated initially to minor female parts. But gradually she begins to play the male parts, including that of a judge, a role close to that of her father. When the children are caught by Atticus, the ensuing argument Jem has with Scout involves him again telling her her gender: "Jem told me I was being a girl, that girls always imagined things, that's why other people hated them so, and if I started behaving like one I could just go off and find some to play with" (Lee 1999, 44).

Dill also takes on Jem's attitude toward Scout. Scout then begins to know gender by what it prevents her from doing—from playing with the boys, from being free to disregard gender as a reason to think about her body—and moves toward Miss Maudie Atkinson. This movement toward an adult woman is the first of four such "movements" in the novel.[4] I will call them "experiments" here, because in moving toward and dwelling with each of these four women, Scout begins to think more creatively and with more sophistication about what it means to be a girl and a boy, a woman and a man, and to transcend herself and others by means of the results of these experiments.[5]

Miss Maudie is the first "experiment" with gender that Scout takes on after the tire incident and her interaction with the teacher Miss Caroline. Miss Maudie lives her gender with relative freedom—she routinely rejects Uncle Jack's offers of marriage, and she loudly rejects the foot-washing Baptists and their condemnation that "women are a sin by definition" (Lee 1999, 50).

Scout learns from Miss Maudie about nut-grass and about aging (the gold teeth and the bridgework that she is shown). She also learns about dressing—men's overalls in the garden, lady's beauty in the evening. Finally, she learns generosity (Miss Maudie bakes and makes little cakes for the three children) and to watch the stars in the evening. Maudie teaches her the way that a woman can enjoy pleasures such as gardening and still be a faithful Christian.

But Scout is not Miss Maudie. And so Scout does not rest on her porch and watch. It is not only Miss Maudie who must reckon with gender. And, besides, Jem does not let Scout rest with her new friendship with Miss Maudie. Nothing seems to overcome the accusation of being a girl. Gender is not defined simply by older, single ladies and their garden clippers. No, after becoming closer to Miss Maudie, she is on a different path—toward a synthesis that is far more androgynous.

The novel highlights this with a sense of humor. As Scout deals with gender, Miss Maudie reckons with the snow sculpture the children have made. Alternately made to look like Mr. Avery and Miss Maudie, the snow person is something Miss Maudie terms a "morphodite," which recalls the word's original—"hermaphrodite." Like "entailments," this word is something Scout carries with her, as being the name for what she is creating together with her family. The road to transition, it seems, is littered with (good) syntaxes.

Scout's second experiment with gender comes when she and Jem spend time with Mrs. Rachel Dubose. When the children go over to Miss Rachel's to read to her and to atone for Jem's chopping off the tops of her camelias, Scout is able to take her father's admonition to "try fighting with your head for a change" (Lee 1999, 86). She fights by applying his admonition and attending to what it has to be like for a woman to fight a morphine addiction and to be caught within the vicious habits of speech that such an addiction wreaks upon and from its victim.

Mrs. Dubose begins her new relationship with the children by yelling at Scout that "you should be in a dress and camisole" (Lee 1999, 116). But what Scout learns ultimately, with the help of Jem and Atticus, is to disregard what Miss Rachel says, to not be frozen in place by the terms she uses, but to deploy reflection upon how her own experiences can overcome adult aggression.

In her reflection on Miss Rachel's willing giving-over of herself, Scout finds that what it means to be a woman can be to concentrate her whole body and mind on something and move out of it; she can be the one to regain her confidence and self-assurance. And she can do so, Miss Rachel, by means of reading with children, by means of the assistance of children.

Because Atticus further developed her experiment with Miss Rachel, Scout learned that a woman, particularly a dying woman trying to beat her morphine addiction, can show courage: "I wanted you to see what real courage is, instead of getting the idea that courage is a man with a gun in his hand. [. . .] She was the bravest person I ever knew" (Lee 1999, 128). And thus Atticus and Mrs. Dubose help Scout meditate what it means to be a female—a camelia that will return to its glory by means of the inordinate power of her life to push beyond the bounds of its own frailty.

In the third experiment, Scout attends Sunday service with Calpurnia and Jem at First Purchase African M. E. Church in the Quarters. Just before going, Scout marvels at Calpurnia as a woman and thinks that "by watching her I began to think there was some skill involved in being a girl" (Lee 1999, 131–132). Once inside the church, however, Scout is worried by the fact that she "again was confronted with the Impurity of Women doctrine" (Lee 1999, 138). It will be Calpurnia, though, that restores Scout's notion of "skill" and helps Scout reject the patriarchal garbage.

For certainly Scout's resistance to this theme, that women are impure, comes in the person of Calpurnia, who lives a "double life" and "speaks two languages" according to Scout (Lee 1999, 143). Calpurnia resists the preacher's forced reflection by being learned, by speaking appropriately to whomever she encounters in the language of that setting, and by refusing to reduce different situations to each other. The impurity of women doctrine is false and harmful. Worse—it means to be a serious truth but does not see how ridiculous it is. In the face of real, strong women, as in the face of Calpurnia, misogynistic clergy are no different than (sad) clowns.

To continue her rejection of the impurity doctrine, and thus her assistance to Scout, Calpurnia also knows the virtue of silence: "It's not necessary to tell all you know. It's not ladylike" (Lee 1999, 143). Calpurnia is the move beyond Miss Maudie and Miss Rachel. Both of those women are restricted to their own homes, but Calpurnia mediates two worlds. If Scout is to become more than a single or an unhappy woman, she must do likewise. She must mediate, speak multiple languages or layers, learn when to be silent, and be reconciled to the necessity of doing so.

In her fourth and final experiment, Scout lives with Aunt Alexandra and learns to take on both Alexandra's world and her strength as a buffer to the family. Alexandra comes to help the children when Atticus is taking Tom Robinson's case. But Alexandra cannot (and does not want to) perform the mediation that Calpurnia can do. Her sense of gender, of race, and of class restricts her.

Not having her (new) friend Maudie's strength, Alexandra also cannot see as clearly as Maudie; nor can she demonstrate courage like Rachel. Alexandra's strength lies in her "fit" with the majority of the white citizens of Maycomb: "Aunt Alexandra fitted into the world of Maycomb like a hand into a glove, but never into the world of Jem and me" (Lee 1999, 150). Alexandra's strength and ability to buffer the children and Atticus from the white citizens of Maycomb, however, forces Atticus into a mother's role that he cannot perform easily. When he goes to Scout to soften Alexandra's harsh dictates, Scout replies thusly: "Atticus was only a man. It takes a woman to do that kind of work" (Lee 1999, 153).

There is no mediation possible, then, between Alexandra and Scout. Scout's mother is dead. All hope of a shared sense of gender with her mother, a family definition as it were, is lost. So, even as Aunt Alexandra buffers the children from the rest of society, Scout must either take up Alexandra's dictates in some way or simply suffer.

Scout does learn something from Aunt Alexandra, though. Perhaps a good many things. First and foremost, Scout learns from Alexandra the general way in which she ought to relate to the white women of Maycomb within the Missionary Society, one that forms the double of the sewing circle by the same name at First Purchase. And that way comes by way of dresses, serving tea, and syrupy invective: "I felt the starched walls of a pink cotton penitentiary closing in on me" (Lee 1999, 156). By the process of elimination, perhaps, Scout learns from Alexandra and from these other tea-drinkers in more detail what it means to "think like a girl."

But quite apart from learning the specifics of gender as imprisonment, what Alexandra also shows her is something similar to what Dill shows by way of hiding in her room: "They needed me" (Lee 1999, 163). This child's certainty in being needed roots itself in Scout's ability to move between all these situations, all these people. To be a girl for Scout is not just to be hampered by needless rules determined by patriarchy. To be a girl is also to care, to set oneself up as a strong buffer, to support, and to protect—in short, to be indispensable.

Given who Scout is moving to become, it is no surprise to the reader of the novel that Alexandra's attempt to force Scout to be a girl and to serve the ladies and dress up in dresses mostly fails. But something about the way in which Alexandra listens to Maudie when Atticus and Calpurnia leave to tell Helen that Tom is dead changes something in Scout. That is, something in Alexandra's listening and in her support of her brother helps Scout apply the lessons from Calpurnia about how to remain silent, how not to say all she knows, how to mediate, how to agree, for the moment, to be a girl.

Combining all the powers of the four experiments, Scout becomes capable, when the situation demands it, when her father needs her to be one, when it serves the unity of the Quarters and the town together—Scout becomes capable of applying herself to the synthesis of herself as girl and not-girl. In the face of necessity, Scout is resolute, and she is the mistress of her domain: "After all, if Aunty could be a lady at a time like this, so could I" (Lee 1999, 272).

Scout's understanding of gender then involves something of a continuum and a choice. To be a girl or a lady is part of her life and it is a set of skills she can deploy. But it is not something that she wants to be caught in—like a tire or a ham costume. Indeed, Scout sees gender as a danger if it remains an enforced series of roles.

As a final movement of Scout's gender play, if we look carefully at the comic and tragic role of the ham that Scout plays in Mrs. Grace Merriweather's Halloween pageant, and if we were to see the figure of the ham as a metaphor for the figure of a life as a girl, we see the real danger of gender that Scout must escape. Perhaps it requires some footwork, as it were, to see meat as the image of an enforced feminine gender. But the choice might serve us well.

To be dressed as a ham demands Scout give over all choice: "it was a close fit; if my nose itched I couldn't scratch, and once inside I could not get out of it alone" (Lee 1999, 291). To be a ham is precisely for Scout to be seen as "meat," as a body that is fully objectified, to be disposed of and consumed by its owner. To be a ham is to be, in some senses, a body that is only meant to be looked at. And thus to be a ham is to be utterly vulnerable to the desires of others and to their practices of consumption.

Like the ham, gender is "a close fit," and it takes over bodily desires (e.g., to scratch certain itches) and disciplines them. To be a lady is not to scratch when one itches. It is to give over one's self-definition to others and to be unable to work out of or remove it by oneself. Basically, and perhaps this is no real footwork, gender is the encasement of the body in some costume that is, in the case of girls, designed for objectification and for the satisfaction of the male gaze and male desire. It is the caesura of real communication: "'You all right in there, Scout?' asked Cecil. 'You sound so far off'" (Lee 1999, 296).

Scout is not meant to be a ham. To cut off her bodily and thoughtful self-determination is to put her (and her ability to think) to sleep. And so, of course, she falls asleep, comically, and then falls to the ground under the attack of Ewell. The costume in a sense protects her from Ewell's switch-blade but it ensnares not only her but also Jem: "I was so entangled we didn't get very far" (Lee 1999, 301).

But Scout, at least the nine-year-old Scout, is not yet caught in gender as she was caught in the ham. And she does receive a good deal of help—from Arthur Radley, from Aunt Alexandra, from Jem. With their help, she gets out of the costume: "It was a relief to be out" (Lee 1999, 303). Once "out" Scout almost immediately sees the costume had its advantages, as it is only with it that Heck Tate can unhesitatingly identify Ewell as the perpetrator without Arthur being called to testify: "I wondered why he had those marks on him. His sleeves were perforated with little holes" (Lee 1999, 309). It is the costume, Heck Tate says, that saved Scout's life: "a shiny clean line stood out on the dull wire" (Lee 1999, 309).

So gender can assist and entrap. It can be assumed or put on. But when it is assumed gender requires assistance to let go of. For Scout, as she grows, gender will always be a problem, a vulnerability, a tactic, and a power. Gender will always be multiple and never simply be derived from her own experience and her own desires. Because of these facts, how she relates to gender will be unforeseen and creative.

But all her experiments, all her thinking about gender, will bring her to bear on herself and on her world as an androgynous person. From her experi-mentations and her own thinking, Scout holds that no role should simply entrap, no role should simply be assumed as someone else's choice. But by means of those same experiments and thoughts, Scout also shows that no role can simply be rejected either—for the simple reason that we live with other people in a democratic society of laws that require us to look on each other as equals. And thus does Scout embody Merleau-Ponty's final comment about sexuality which I am applying to gender: "No one is fully saved, and no one is fully lost" (Merleau-Ponty 2012, 174).

A PHILOSOPHICAL CHILD:
HOW CHILDREN LEAD BY THINKING

Scout leads the adults in the novel to see how they need to pay attention to the motions, the perceptions, and the thinking of children. Beating up Francis for his name-calling of Atticus, for example, combined Uncle Jack's discussion of "provocation" being a necessary cause for swearing with Scout's inherent sense of honor for Atticus. Scout was behaving ethically according to her own attending to what adults said and to what the experience demanded, and she threw her whole body into the process.

Jack's attempt to shame her, to beat her behind, was a mis-estimation of children's thought. Where he saw simple, uncontrolled fury, Scout was deploying careful consideration. And, although we as readers see Jack's mistake after Scout's thoughtful explanation, I think that we most clearly see her thinking and her mediation not within the family but outside of it, particularly when she joins Atticus outside the jail in front of the mob. There she defends Jem from being beaten by a member of the mob (presumably by kicking that person in the testicles) and then disperses the mob by speaking directly and eloquently to Mr. Cunningham.

By Scout's selecting one person, Cunningham, and reciting to him the way they are connected (by his son Walter's being in her class at school and by his whole family's previous dependence on Atticus) she allows mutual recognition to replace hatred. She does the work that Merleau-Ponty mentions here: "Hegel says each one seeks the death of the other. For this battle to even begin [. . .] they must have a common ground, and they must remember their peaceful coexistence in the world of childhood" (Merleau-Ponty 2012, 372).

Merleau-Ponty's mention of Hegel here should remind us of another root of phenomenology that we have not yet talked about. If Husserl's own lineage should be drawn by way of opposing or supplementing the transcendental ego and categories of Kant's epistemology, certainly Merleau-Ponty's lineage draws a good deal of its power from Hegel's focus on the shapes of Spirit.

I want to talk briefly about this Hegelian lineage here because it informs the way the rest of the book will take shape. In his *Phenomenology of Spirit*, Hegel shows how our description, our understanding of our experience is compelled to move in a certain logical and historical progression through what he calls "shapes" of consciousness and self-consciousness. We cannot, for example, say that something "is" or "is not" without employing the notion of Being and Nothingness. But this means that we must already be caught up not merely in the conflict between what is and what is not but also certain ways in which we can transcend their opposition by means of a more sophisticated view that we are already employing.

The process of consciousness, of our phenomenological attempt to describe the meaning of experience, through these shapes is something that Merleau-Ponty is performing in his own way in his writing on phenomenology. Though not arranged systematically as Hegel did, Merleau-Ponty time and time again is focused on giving Husserlian phenomenology a grounding in the development of human beings and in the experience of their bodily life. What ends up shining through Merleau-Ponty for me is the way our bodies educate us as to the possible ways in which we can become ourselves. In so doing, Merleau-Ponty launches us on a trajectory toward real "mutual recognition" as we can encounter it here and now in particular institutions.

This motor of mutual recognition was Hegel's basic theme throughout his work, and it is certainly the center of the discussion of the master and slave that Merleau-Ponty mentions above. It is mutual recognition that Scout thus demands in her position as a child and it is what the entire town of Maycomb is having to come to terms with. Sexuality then is a motor of perception, and it is a motor that can carry us toward one another as toward a community of equals.

To pick up the thread of the narrative, in light of Hegel's and Merleau-Ponty's discussion of mutual recognition, let us note the following: Scout's speech to these men in front of the courthouse is a speech about mutual recognition. Scout is able to return these fighting men to their own children and perhaps their own childhood, and she is able to do so by way of her own memory and thinking. She has remembered the word "entailments" from her father's conversation with Cunningham. And she has remembered her own previous movements in the tire and in her four experiments with the older women in the town. This in turn supports and motivates her to enter the situation with the expectation of being listened to. It motivates her to put forth her body and mind as a whole. For she is not bound as in the tire. Rather, she is free to leap "triumphantly into a ring of people I had never seen before" (Lee 1999, 173) such that "I slowly awoke to the fact that I was addressing the entire aggregation" (Lee 1999, 175).

Scout risks and speaks because she has a fundamental belief, rooted in the world of childhood, that each needs the other. This allows her to bring Atticus and Cunningham together because she remembers that Atticus said to Cunningham "that you all'd ride it out together" (Lee 1999, 176). To bring the living room conversation into the public square, to bring previous relationships into present ones, to be brave and to do something with your whole body—this was to Scout as natural as reading or breathing.

What she rushed to do initially, though, becomes harder to do as she continues. Her body changes—she realizes that they are all looking at her. But Cunningham is moved to remember, and he "takes her by the shoulders" (Lee 1999, 176) with a consciousness, at least in himself, that the mob is not who they are, or whom they are meant to be, most fundamentally. Rather, with Cunningham, the men in the mob are returned to themselves by way of Scout finding herself and her voice in speaking to them. Dignity retakes violence because a child was capable of saying more than she knew while saying precisely what she knew.

When Scout returns home she is returned to the episodes of that evening by way of reflection: "The full meaning of the night's events hit me and I began crying. Jem was awfully nice about it: for once he didn't remind me that people nearly nine years old didn't do things like that" (Lee 1999, 178). Reflection teaches her that she, that children as such, speak out of their situation and out of their knowing without first being fully united with themselves. Their self-consciousness, their need and capacity for reflection, develops by way of their already enacted actions and speech.

And this means precisely that children are in a position to be most philosophical. What they say and think is *intended not just for their current selves but also for their future selves*. And thus they speak ambiguously, with more than one direction meant at a time, and generatively, with more than one meaning speaking through their interaction with the world.

Scout returned Mr. Cunningham to his past (his relation with Atticus) and to the institutions of the town (the school where Walter and Scout attend class). But this return was more for Scout about pushing what she thought forward, into another kind of community that did not lend itself to the formation of mobs. What she thought and said was for the sake of the community her adult self could find with her present one, for the sake of her future town's preservation of the unity of the different situations and people.

Scout's appeal to the past so that they could live a future together is what dissipates the mob. And it allows the adults to reflect on how no adult, not even Atticus or the shotgun-wielding Mr. Underwood, could do what Scout as a child did: "a gang of wild animals *can* be stopped, simply because they're still human. Hmp, maybe we need a police force of children [. . .] you children last night made Walter Cunningham stand in my shoes for a minute. That was enough" (Lee 1999, 180).

Atticus is right in part. Scout was applying Atticus's earlier admonition about empathy. But he is wrong too. The children are not trying to be the police. The children are able to return the men to their senses because they are moving beyond the urgency of that moment toward a future in which entailments end, toward a shared vision of prosperity that will have had a past of riding it out together. Scout is thoughtful not just because she gets Cunningham to be empathetic but also (and more importantly) because she imagines the synthesis of Atticus and Cunningham, an imagination that is rational, a concept that is democratic.

Later, when Scout and Dill leave the trial because Dill feels sick and Scout proclaims that she understands the sexual nature of the charges against

Tom Robinson, Scout shows again what it means to be thoughtful in her own way. This comes in her conversation with Mr. Dolphus.

Dolphus is just pretending to be a drunk, having only Coca-Cola in the paper sack. But he tells the children honestly why he does it: "I live like I do because that's the way I want to live" (Lee 1999, 229). This admission allows Scout and Dill to see why the breaking of racial norms and codes could happen. It could happen because it fulfills people's desires to be free, to love whom they choose.

Scout asks Dolphus why he told them his secret. It is because Dill cried "about the simple hell people give other people" (Lee 1999, 229). Children then have a power to think that is unmotivated by coercion and punishment. It is more universal because its categories arise from within their experience instead of from without. It is less interested in power over other people and is satisfied with combining the power of people toward some more sophisticated situation of living.

This power has already been on display in the courtroom when Scout relates Mayella to a person who is of mixed race and even to herself. In fact, throughout the novel, as in this description, Harper Lee says how thoughts "came to" or "occurred" to Scout. That is, Lee seems to entail, children's thinking is more fluid and immediate. Their thoughts are not controlled, occasional, and properly reflective. Rather, at least in Lee's novel, *thoughts think themselves* into children, and children extend themselves into thoughts as a response to the call of the situation, of the world.

Within the context of the trial, Atticus's thinking as a lawyer is prepared, rehearsed, formalized, and careful. His thinking is in service to the truth. But his thinking is insufficient. Atticus's thoughts are insufficient because they must subordinate themselves to a judge and jury. They occur within the framework of the judicial system. Atticus begs them, pleads with them. He acknowledges that what he thinks, what he says, does not fully operate yet in the realm of the universal by the very *attempt* he is making to allow the thought to take hold in all the adults and in the community *as* universal.

Scout's thinking, a child's, is not the thinking of law. It does not aim to persuade or to punish or to be universal in the way Atticus's thoughts do. A child's situation is one in which there is no hope to persuade the godlike adults who take things as settled, who only live in the moment. So the only way Scout's thoughts grab her as universal is by not playing the game of argumentation. Scout's thoughts are universal because they immediately appear as if they were *already* everyone's: "the perception of others and the intersubjective world are only problematic for adults. The child lives in a world that she believes is immediately accessible to everyone around her. She is unaware of herself and, for that matter, of others as private subjectivities" (Merleau-Ponty 2012, 311).

A child thinks universally about the meaning of what occurs. A child thinks universally because that is what they swim in—a truth that enfolds them as the universe's truth, as coming from the world to them. And they see these truths because they are accorded a strange kind of freedom by the very fact of the situation of childhood. The child plays. And in playing, whether at melancholy or at comedy, the child reaches toward something essential because the essential has *always already reached out to her.*

All we would need to do to understand the originality of Scout's thinking, to understand the androgyny or gender-bending of Scout, would be to see Scout's thought as pointing to her growing grasp of the commonality and the difference between herself and Mayella. For certainly Harper Lee and Atticus have set us up to see Mayella and Scout as potential foils.

First, the commonality: Scout and Mayella shared something important. They shared the *need* to transcend codes that were not themselves self-conscious, codes that produced the opposite of self-consciousness and freedom, toward a community that came home to itself and evolved its codes in response to a developing self-consciousness, a developing freedom, of all the individuals that comprised it.

And now the difference: unlike Scout, Mayella could not move her whole body and mind toward anything but more violence. Mayella could not move beyond the walls of the home and the context of the dump. She was so used to being used, trapped, abused, and dominated (particularly by her father) that she could only think mean, reduced, narrow thoughts. Mayella was no longer a child and no longer thought like one, even if the structures of her situation bore every similarity to childhood. She was no child because she thought like a mean parent who wanted what he ought never to have allowed himself to have had.

Mayella had no Atticus as a father. And that was why she could not move beyond herself and why she resented him. Scout had an Atticus, and that is why she could move beyond, transcend, both herself and him.

But children like Scout, despite their philosophical acuity, despite their creative thoughts, are not simply saviors. They will not lead us into heaven. And this is because children have very real limits. They go to bed at 8 PM. They get tired. And they do not yet understand on their own the import of the things that they think or that get thought through them.

Yes, they think on behalf of more than themselves. But they also get caught by the limitations of their own bodies and cannot finish what they start: "I toyed with the idea of asking everyone below to concentrate on setting Tom Robinson free, but thought if they were as tired as I, it wouldn't work" (Lee 1999, 240).

Scout applies what Atticus and Jem and any interlocutor says within her own thinking. She intends to focus her desire on the community thinking together. And she believes in that possibility. But she also knows thinking is bodily. And it cannot happen at night, when she is sleepy. As Merleau-Ponty describes it, motor intentionality and living thought always has its limits: "My body is this meaningful core that behaves as a general function and that nevertheless exists and that is susceptible to illness. In the body we have to learn to recognize this knotting together of essence and existence" (Merleau-Ponty 2012, 148).

One child cannot do all this thinking or this moving—one child cannot do this—alone. And all children—all people—get tired. Calpurnia is tired. Atticus is tired. The people of color in the balcony are tired. Tom Robinson is tired. The judge himself always looks tired. There are roadblocks everywhere. How can thinking become communal? How can it become intersubjective and dialogical? How can it transcend the body? It seems in the novel that everything mitigates against thought becoming communal.

But Scout, like all philosophical children, does not accept defeat. Her thinking is future-oriented and remains consistently engaged. After the trial, Scout sees the inherent contradictions in a teacher who is for the Jews but against people of color; she sees the contradiction of the missionary circle members who are for the people of Mrunas but against those of the Quarters. And she stakes out her claim to thinking as inherently requiring consistency and self-transformation. For Scout, thought is a response to a tension or contradiction in a situation, a response that works to resolve contradiction into a more sophisticated shape.

WHEN SCOUT RETURNS:
CHOOSING THE WAY FORWARD

This chapter has been the attempt to blend together two strands of analysis: literary and phenomenological. Using Maurice Merleau-Ponty, I have tried to suggest that the character of Scout in *To Kill a Mockingbird* is in fact a successful example of a child who "thinks like a girl" where neither "thinking" nor "girl" are watered down, pejorative, or failed echoes of more patriarchal, traditional definitions of thinking or experience. Scout thinks on her feet, in front of the mob, in front of the class, and in the moments during and following Ewell's attack on her and Jem. She thinks in ways the adults do not, presumably because the adults do not feel able to move with as much freedom as she does.

Using literary criticism, I have tried to show how the character of Scout "thinks" by way of her fluid transitions between genders, between social contexts, and between selves (the narrator being both child and adult). Scout both is and is not a girl, and she embodies a kind of thinking in her resistance to set binary categories. Perhaps, as some critics have argued, Scout is a "tomboy" or "queer." But I have a hunch that Scout herself, at least a certain

Scout, might take umbrage at that, insofar as queering Scout might also be an entrapment.[6] In any case, Scout's movement within her own redefinition of gender is, I believe, where the power of her character and of her thinking lies and not in our formalization of her categorical structure.

Now I will try to suggest some further thoughts about pedagogy. Following Merleau-Ponty, I would define authentic reflection as "radical." And radical reflection, which "is conscious of its dependence on an unreflected life" (Merleau-Ponty 2012, lxxviii), simply tries to organize a thinking that is always prior, bodily, immediate, and foundational to the very attempt at systematicity. As the proponent of radical reflection, phenomenology is a philosophy "for which the world is always 'already there' prior to reflection—like an inalienable presence—and whose entire effort is to rediscover this naïve contact with the world in order to finally raise it to philosophical status" (Merleau-Ponty 2012, lxx).

Scout acts intelligently and thus can be led—and can lead herself—into radical reflection. Assisting Scout in this way would allow Scout to become like her name—i.e., like a scout to a group of cartographers. The mapping that adults would do would therefore always be secondary, since there is a very real dependence of mathematics or of "geography with regard to the landscape where we first learned what a forest, a meadow or a river is" (Merleau-Ponty 2012, lxxii).

Now I am certainly not the only phenomenologist to pursue this line of thought with respect to Merleau-Ponty's notion of radical reflection or thinking in general. In *The Roots of Thinking*, phenomenologist Maxine Sheets-Johnstone describes thought as inherently bodily: "Analysis of the hominid evolutionary record will show that basic human concepts, including those of word and number, ultimately revert to the body as semantic template. What was—and is—originally thought was—and is—founded on a bodily logos" (Sheets-Johnstone 2010, 7–8).

This "reversion" or "foundation" is what Scout lives out. Her body and her movement carry her to places of thinking that will sustain her for a long time to come. And whatever her final definitions of things like "democracy" or "Maycomb" will be, it is certain that her definitions will carry the echo of her embodiment (and all her experiences of powers and punishments) within them.

As a motion-oriented thinker, who proceeds without a rigorous or well-defined method of reflection (as evidenced by the way the narrator slips in and out of the story), Scout seems to demonstrate, further, what Sheets-Johnstone calls "analogical thinking": "In analogical thinking, there is a transfer of meaning from one framework to another, or at the simplest level, from one thing to another. [. . .] To perceive is not only to *extract* meaning but may involve a *transfer* of meaning. The transference is of critical significance. Just such transference is at the root of concepts" (Sheets-Johnstone

2010, 61). Scout transfers as she moves. She is herself the transfer of con-texts and significances. And thus she weaves meaning around her and trails it after her.

In weaving the meaning of the contexts and categories that structure the town and the situation of Tom Robinson's condemnation, Scout thereby creates a kind of dance. She pirouettes onto the stage of Mrs. Merriweather's pageant as the ham and shakes the Judge at least from his sleep—i.e., he has a fit of laughing. Scout's dance, a dance in general, is necessarily nonreflec-tive (lest we stumble) but is nonetheless the product of practice, deftness, and intentionality. And it is thus that Scout shows not only that movement is thinking but that thinking is also movement: "thinking in movement is foun-dational to being a body" (Sheets-Johnstone 2011, 494).

So how might we use all this to create educational environments for children? Well, if Scout is androgynous, if she moves fluidly and creatively between gender roles and resists being categorized simplistically, we might well think about how this kind of resistance and motion is a natural and valuable part of many (perhaps all) children's own situation and thinking. We should, therefore, see gender fluidity as offering creative enterprises for children, and not attempt to discipline them into binaries. But this is obvious and simplistic.

Whatever they are, children not only move between genders. They also move back and forth between family and school, between family and friends, between themselves as called upon to be one thing (daughter or son, student or playmate, good or bad, etc.) and themselves as multiple. Encouraging the child to remain in motion, to tie together multiple contexts by means of their experience—supporting the child in her or his multiplicity—might well be to enable the child to learn in a way that is helpful and that motivates untapped creativity.

Forcing children to reflect too early, or too often, might hinder them. Insisting on critical reflection as a practice in a way that reduces their tenden-cy to "dance" could hamper their creativity. Changing the notion of philoso-phy and of thought, however, to a praxis of embodied synthesis and a series of experiments that the children themselves have a say in how to synthe-size—this might well enable children to hold more. To hold on to more. To hold themselves up.

If Scout learns by moving, as well as by holding together "entailments" or "provocation" from Atticus or Jack while speaking with Cunningham in the mob or fighting Francis at Aunt Alexandra and Uncle Jimmy's house, then we adults who would assist them could attempt a curriculum that fosters both such movement (change) and such synthesis (holding together). In so doing, we might well come to see that we could never establish a canon of texts or a program that would have to be read and discussed by children without their input.

The successful classroom text will, perhaps like the novel *To Kill a Mockingbird*, so irritate or promote identification that those children who read and discuss it will discover something new. They will discover themselves always already in process with it, always already taking up the text as partner, moving toward its quarters, dancing with it, singing with it, and bringing it home to some new place. These texts in their success with children will support our own growing certainty that children are their own modes of being and that, in their own register and in their own temporality, children are original and creative thinkers.

NOTES

1. Neil Heims puts this point about the narrator and reflection in the following way: "There is a flow of experience and there needs to follow upon experience the disposition to examine it and to reflect upon it. . . . The conjunction of connection and detachment required for the exercise of perspective is fittingly represented . . . by the duality of the narrative voice" (Heims 2010, 51–52).

2. See David Kennedy's "John Dewey on Children, Childhood, and Education" in which he argues that Dewey strove toward "that encounter between adults and children called education in which both are transformed and through which a "future new society of changed purposes and desires may be created by a deliberate, humane treatment of the impulses of youth" (Kennedy 2006, 215).

3. Katie Rose Guest Pryal in "Walking in Another's Skin: Failure of Empathy in *To Kill a Mockingbird*" notes that Atticus fails both to define and to embody empathy sufficiently. The only character, Pryal says, who almost succeeds in bringing empathy almost to view for the reader is Lula, who challenges the Finch children when Calpurnia brings them to First Purchase (Pryal 2010, 186 ff.).

4. See the brief article "Just a Lady" by Michele Ware that makes the same basic point: "various female characters influence Scout's social development and exemplify the range of gender roles available to her" (Ware 2003, 287).

5. Laura Hakala more systematically characterizes each of these four women as types of gender roles for Scout in her MA thesis entitled *Scouting for a Tomboy: Gender-Bending Behaviors in Harper Lee's* To Kill a Mockingbird.

6. However, I do read Imani Perry's take on the novel and the film as a rich and helpful resource: "in this cast of queerly beautiful subjects with complex humanities we find the basis for arguing against the stratification of American life" (Perry 2013, 102).

Chapter Four

A Phenomenology of Religious Experience in *A Wrinkle in Time*

INTRODUCTION

In this chapter, I turn to a consideration of the phenomenology of Martin Heidegger. Because I am treating a new set of texts, and because Heidegger's terminology and style do not form an immediate kinship with those of Husserl or Merleau-Ponty, I return here in this chapter to the structure of the first two chapters. First, I will articulate what is at stake in Heidegger's texts, and then I will move on to a literary analysis of a related children's novel—in this case Madeleine L'Engle's famous *A Wrinkle in Time*.

If phenomenology is a method that is effective at describing all experience, at making explicit the meanings that lay implicit in our first perceptions of things, of ourselves, and of other persons, then phenomenology ought to be able to offer us something valuable in its descriptions of our religious experience. This chapter is an attempt to show that it does.

In fact, one way of tracing phenomenology's origin is through its kinship with hermeneutics. Hermeneutics began centuries ago as a way of relating to texts, particularly religious ones; however, in the nineteenth century hermeneutics significantly developed its methodology. No longer was hermeneutics only about certain religious texts. Rather, hermeneutics also became interested in the situation of the reader, and the nineteenth-century hermeneutic reflections involved a revamping both of epistemology as concerning the author-reader relationship as well as of a historical-critical approach through the writings of thinkers such as Dilthey and Schleiermacher.

When these philosophers reflected both on the stance of the reader and on the text simultaneously, they came to propose a rigorous, methodical deployment of the famous hermeneutic circle—i.e., the back-and-forth method of reading the whole by means of the parts and the parts by means of the whole. In fact, what I see in the field of hermeneutics is a deployment of the hermeneutic circle not just within the text but also within the reader's relationship with the text—the circle of the reader within the text and the text within the reader.

In any case, the way I see the relationship between phenomenology and hermeneutics in the nineteenth century is this: hermeneutics gave birth to phenomenology because hermeneutics attempted decades before to see the reader as within the circle of literary experience and thereby to bracket the dogmatic assumptions that tend to accrue across a tradition's (particularly a religious tradition's) development of interpretation. In bracketing those assumptions, hermeneutics then worked phenomenologically to allow the (sacred) text to speak on its own terms, to offer new aspects or moments of itself that allowed contemporary readers to take up that text again, to notice what continues to live in, and to reshape and re-organize the tradition of interpretation in connection with contemporary lived experience.

The way that hermeneutics allowed the text to speak for itself, the way hermeneutics deployed the hermeneutic circle, presaged the (now familiar) phenomenological zigzag motion between the perceiver and the perceived. This zigzag was deployed by hermeneutics in two ways: historically and essentially. First, hermeneutics moved between the present time in which the reader found herself and the historical context in which the text was written, between the expectations that the community of current readers or believers had for this text and the acknowledgment that those readers or believers were themselves further and further removed from the original audience or communities in which the texts emerged for the first time. Second, and reciprocally, hermeneutics moved between the essence, the perpetually intuited (and presumed) heart of the text, and those historically selected, salient moments that insisted on re-negotiating that essence with respect to their own prominence in a contemporary lived experience or a religious situation.

This reciprocal motion back and forth, from reader to text, and from essence to historical situation, is a movement that phenomenology continued to develop in the twentieth century, beginning with Edmund Husserl. Edmund Husserl himself mentions the zigzag method of phenomenology quite often—though for Husserl the movement is more general, and occurs as the movement from the noesis (or act of perceiving) to the noema (or perceived object)—instead of simply from the reader to the text or to the tradition.

All that is to say, however, that there is a hermeneutic method built in to phenomenology. So much so that we as phenomenologists now tend to take hermeneutics for granted as a kind of focus or direction that phenomenology might take as it tries to comment on literary or religious texts. An example of how this is so—that is, an example of how hermeneutics is embedded in a contemporary phenomenological reading of sacred texts—might be the way we understand our reading of the Christian Gospels to change when we focus on some of the characters or the lived experiences in the stories of Jesus' life. In focusing our attention as readers of the Gospels on one part or moment—perhaps on the women with whom Jesus comes into contact—we begin to see, perhaps for the first time, something new. We see that Jesus had a great deal to say to and about women. He appeared to empathize with them, to move toward their situation, to inquire about that situation, and even to share it. He defended them from stoning or from manipulation. He spoke and shared water and food with them. He healed and walked with them. Noticing these accounts, one might read Jesus' own attempts to relate himself to the lived experience of women as making apparent a shift in the essence of the Gospels as such. That is, if one were to read the Gospels in this way, then one might come to the conclusion as a contemporary reader that Jesus valued many of the things that contemporary feminists do.

As surprising as that conclusion might be, one could also repeat the same exercise in the hermeneutics of the Gospels with respect to other, related intuitions. We might learn a lot by focusing on the way Jesus mentions or interacts with children or with people with diseases or disabilities in the Gospels—and especially on Jesus' inclusion of them.

That being said, however, there is still a question at hand. Although phenomenology may identify itself with a certain method of textual hermeneutics when phenomenology confronts texts, what does the hermeneutics of texts have to do with the phenomenological description of religious experience itself? Surely, not all religious experience is mediated through the sacred text(s) of a religion. In fact, much of what sacred texts are written about are themselves religious experiences. The genesis of the sacred text, in other words, seems to lie in a number of crucial experiences. Not only that, but to many people (people who might consider themselves religious) sacred texts open onto the possibility of *more* religious experiences, on new or renewed experiences of the divine or of God.

However, perhaps asserting that last point is to try to make too fine a distinction between texts and experiences. Experiences are themselves a text for phenomenology, as the previous chapters in this book have shown. They are even, one might say, the only text worth reading to phenomenology. And indeed it is this identification—the experience as text—that provides the viewpoint of the surpassing of hermeneutics offered by phenomenology. Or, one might say the following: it is because our lived experiences are themselves texts to be described, to be understood as a whole-part relation, that we could ever come to have texts. It is because of our experiential structure that texts come to be cited in relation to them, much as Jesus himself quotes Isaiah or the Torah in order to determine the meaning of what is occurring as the enactment of his life.

Within the larger project of exploring lived experience as text, what I hope to do in this chapter is to consider a very famous American novel for children by Madeleine L'Engle, *A Wrinkle in Time*, and to explicate the religious experiences in it, especially those of Meg Murry, its protagonist and a young girl. I will do so by assuming the kinship of Madeleine L'Engle with phenomenology. In making this assumption, I hope to show something essential about the way phenomenology can open us up as readers to experiences of time, of the divine and of each other in a way that encourages us to see these three things as moments of a whole.

The lens through which I will attempt to make allies of L'Engle's novel and phenomenology is constructed out of a reading of two texts by Martin Heidegger. As I mentioned above, because these texts are extremely difficult to read for the first time, and because of their importance, I will go back to the method I engaged in the first two chapters of this book—namely, I will first explicate the Heideggeran texts and then analyze *A Wrinkle in Time* by means of their insights.

The first text, entitled simply *Being and Time*, is one that I use to discuss the link between what it means to be a human being and what it means to experience or to live time. This connection, between humans and time, is obviously something L'Engle's book contemplates (even in its title). And using Heidegger's book allows me to delimit some general structures the novel evinces that should promote L'Engle's novel as more philosophical than much mainstream science fiction. In short, I will show, thanks to Heidegger, that it is because we *are* time, and because we are, in Heidegger's language, *care*, that our lived experience already has the character of a kind of time travel. Tessering or wrinkling ourselves, we begin to contemplate the time of God and of the good.

There are obvious developments in this chapter of the Husserlian notion of transition and of absolute consciousness temporalizing itself, which we discussed in the first chapter of this book. However, Heidegger's discussion does not simply echo or presuppose Husserl's understanding. In fact, for Heidegger it is not really the consciousness of time that is central. Rather, it is the way we *are* time. As such, Heidegger's discussion of time has a lot to do with Merleau-Ponty's discussion of motion or sexuality.

The second text I go on to discuss here in this chapter, Heidegger's *The Phenomenology of Religious Life*, contains Heidegger's commentary on two Christian texts, St. Paul's letters to the Galatians and to the Thessalonians. These readings by Heidegger help us to concretize and deploy his structural discussion in *Being and Time* toward our own understanding of religious experience, especially but not only Christian ones. In using this second book, I direct the reader's focus to how the religious experience is a situation that takes up temporal structures and both produces and reshapes our relation to the divine and to each other. More specifically, using this second text, I will show how Meg Murry's growth in *A Wrinkle in Time*, her growth toward the divine and the good, is made possible by a coming to terms with religious experience as a commitment to a shared stance—one of Heideggerian anticipatory resolution.

This chapter therefore has four parts: in the first two, I explicate Heidegger's two works. In the third, I present a reading of L'Engle's novel. And in the last section, I offer a brief way forward, using phenomenology, to continue to open up religious experiences to what I hope is a process of sympathetic description.

PHENOMENOLOGICAL THEORY:
HEIDEGGER ON TIME AND RELIGIOUS EXPERIENCE

A. *Being and Time*: Time, Care, and Stretching Out (Together Toward God)

To be human for Heidegger is to have one's own existence or one's own being be an issue that is always before oneself: "*Dasein* is a being which is concerned in its being about that being" (Heidegger 1996, 185). What we are, and how we are what we are, is always our concern. We are never datable, definable, exhaustible. We are, our experience is, for us an ongoing text that we must continue to explore and to describe.

For Heidegger, however, I am concerned about my being, I am constantly paying attention to the how or the there (*Da-*) of my being (*Sein*), because I find myself always already "thrown" outside of myself: "thrownness is meant to suggest the facticity of its being *delivered over*" (Heidegger 1996, 131, my emphasis). I find myself already under way, already in the midst of a world, of a total of actual and possible situations. I find myself "delivered over" as this particular "factical" person, with these or those parents and prospects. I did not choose to be delivered to the world now or here, in this family or addressing this problem. And yet here I am.

This thrownness, this being delivered over to the world, being in the middle and in the midst of the world—this is something Heidegger stresses as a way I live my being. I am already, from the inside as it were, opened out toward the totality of my contexts, my contacts, my situations. I am "delivered over" to the world and to all that occurs within it, and I cannot choose to deny the world.

Part of being "delivered over" to the world means that I cannot determine which is more important, me or the world. Rather, the distinction is to some extent meaningless as we are mutually implied within one another. At best, I can say that I am "being-in-the-world," with all the ways that those hyphens in that phrase point out my internal unity with the world. At best, I can say that I am embedded within what Heidegger calls worldhood: "'World' is . . .

a characteristic of *Dasein* itself" (Heidegger 1996, 64). Very often (and fundamentally) I do not know how I got here, in the world. But here I am.

Being, as Heidegger says, "thrown" into the world, I am oriented not just toward this or that memory or expectation, toward this or that project, but toward time as such. "Veiled" from myself as I am, I am thrown not just toward one memory or expectation, but toward the entire way in which my origin or birth and my end or my death are both implied in my life, how they are both "disclosed" and "veiled" from me *at the same time*: "this character of being of Da-sein which is *veiled* in its whence and whither but in itself all the more openly *disclosed*, this 'that it is,' [is] the thrownness of this being *into* its there" (Heidegger 1996, 131, my emphasis).

My way of being, my way of being implicated in a world, is not to be a thing locked in itself. My way of being is to be thrown "into" my world. It is to be intentionally directed from my hair to my toes. My way of being is to form an arc. An arc of worldly directedness. And it is to have to take up the meaning of my existence. It is to have to try to turn "veiled" time into the time of "disclosure" or hermeneutics. My life is a project of establishing the meaning of my facticity, of my time here and now, as well as there and then.

My existence as *Dasein*, in other words, is a way of working out my being-veiled. I project myself in the world toward possibilities or projects that cannot ever get me away from my own lack of definition, from the nothingness that is at the heart of my self-awareness. But these same projects are not futile. Each of them is an attempt to use that concealment, the nothingness that I am in order to generate meanings that can narrate me into a meaningful story that reckons with my lack of definition.

Another way of saying this: Because I am concerned about my birth and my death, I am, as *Dasein*, *toward* not only the world and things in it as if separable but also *toward* myself as embracing that world as a *whole*. I try to narrate myself because I *want* to be whole. And I want to be whole because I can witness the entirety of the world as within my own structure. I am meant for the world, and thus I am meant to be and to be whole.

However, because I am both being-in-the-world and yet fundamentally indeterminate in my meaning, I am *toward* my wholeness without being able to become that whole. As a finite human being, I will never be a whole person or a whole story until I die. And when I die and my life forms a whole narrative, for example in an obituary, I will not be witness to it: "when *Dasein* reaches its wholeness in death, it simultaneously *loses* the being of the there" (Heidegger 1996, 226, my emphasis).

"Loss" structures my existence. After my death, I will only be a whole for the others who write it or speak it. I will never be that story myself. And yet being certain of that does not prevent my narrative attempts. I am, e.g., a husband, a father, a professor, a friend. As such, finding myself already both veiled and disclosive, lacking and creative, I am motivated to gather myself to myself, to take a stand and give meaning to those "roles," and thus to become a whole that I have already "seen" myself to be, at least peripherally.

My being is existence—and an ecstatic, striving existence at that. No "role" is predetermined, even as billions of people might be said to be living similar roles. And thus in whatever projects I find myself in, I am always in process.

At the moment I understand something about being a professor, say, I slip away from myself, I read a review of my work, I feel deflated or empowered, and I find myself reinterpreting that role. At the moment I am engaged in something here and now, I feel the pressure of the future reaching into what I am doing, situating it or spoiling it with the understanding that it cannot last, that nothing gold can stay. And so I feel myself slipping into a consideration of the to-come. My being-*toward* is an essential part of my whole being. And I am constantly deploying a hermeneutics toward myself. Just existing *is* a hermeneutics. It is a reaching toward a *whole* that is only ever *partially* revealed.

Because I am ecstatically and hermeneutically structured, though, because I am both separated and united with myself, because I am whole and part and hermeneutic circle all at the same time—because of this, because I live in that separated unity with myself, I also realize that I am separated and united not only with myself but also with things and with the world. My wholeness is a possibility of interrelations.

A thing, for example a hammer, is never simply my appendage or tool. A thing, a hammer, is also its own manner of being that requires that I take it up, that I respond to it. This required response is a kind of engagement or involvement. But this engagement is only ever partial and always subject to conditions not in my control. When the hammer breaks—and it will break— then I see that my relationship with it is only ever partial, only ever for a time. My use of things, and even of other people, is only ever temporary, partial, and subordinated to projects that themselves wear out, become finished or boring.

Still, however, this insight is powerful. Even if one project wears me out, or if I retire from it in boredom or fatigue, still there is no sense in which I am ever bereft of projects or ever fully removed from the world or from things. The very success of using the hammer to build, say, a bookcase is a way I show that I am not just a being but a being-in-the-world, who is forever immersed in the world, *striving* toward things, toward projects, toward the redefinition of that same, whole world that I find myself in.

It is because I can recognize my being-toward or my striving that I understand myself not as fusing with things, with what does not have the same kind of being that I, *Dasein*, do. Rather, I find myself as interpreting those beings and, by extension, myself. I am not just hermeneutics of self. I am the hermeneutics of the world. I am the world coming back to itself by virtue of me being thrown into it.

As a hermeneutics of the world, though, I am also thrown beyond the world toward other people. In fact, it is because my internal relationship with the world throws me toward things and other people that I find myself thrown not just into self-discovery but into hermeneutics as a kind of dialogue with myself and others: "the world of *Dasein* is a with-world. Being-in is being-with others" (Heidegger 1996, 116).

This breaking-open to others from within my own being as *Dasein* has already been accomplished in my being-in-the-world. As having projects within a world that is essentially a "with-world," I always already speak, describe, and understand. My hammer, even though it is not a pencil or pen or keyboard, traces an arc of meaning as I build the bookcase, which is of course intended as a housing for the project of reading and discussing what others see and know. But what is not yet accomplished in the structure of my being-in-the-world—what is not yet revealed in building the bookcase—is the *way* in which I could, by taking myself to be a whole who has a part to play in each situation, read, discuss, and thereby *release* the meaning of our shared world to myself and others.

When I do that, when I move beyond building furniture and take up discourse as my more important way of being thrown into a shared world—that is, when I take hold of and deploy my stance or my perspective on the world I am intertwined with—I not only reveal myself as having a world. I also reveal the world itself to be discoverable by my action.

In the face of the world, I enact a response that means to narrate a whole not just of or for myself but for others. Something about my wholeness resides in my striving to provide dialogue, to affirm or challenge other persons in their consciousness of themselves as also being-in-the-world, as also having a stance toward wholeness that could define our togetherness. To take on my world-character by entering into meaningful dialogue is thereby to enact a kind of leap: "there is the possibility of a concern which does not so much leap in for the other as leap ahead of him . . . not in order to take 'care' away from him but rather to authentically give it back as such" (Heidegger 1996, 119). Such a possibility is poetic and creative, and it frees each *Dasein* who is already thrown together in the world. It frees each of us to engage in a hermeneutics of self and of community, a freedom of each to become a whole within a larger whole of inter-relations.

All of this is a very brief, basic summary of much of the earlier sections of *Being and Time*. It is my attempt to say that the human's ability to take up things and take on a place in the world is to take on a project, a hermeneutic project of striving for the whole even when it seems the whole exceeds our grasp. It is my attempt to say, with Heidegger, that the life of *Dasein* is for the possibility of *caring* about and for things and other people such that each of us, and multiple people together, can reach out for tools, a foothold, friends, a God, etc. Indeed, this engagement in my own project, in my projection, of becoming a whole in the world is what Heidegger later in *Being and Time* develops as "care." And I return to cite the text here because for Heidegger it is a huge move forward in understanding what we are as *Dasein*:

> becoming what one can be in being free for one's ownmost possibilities—is an "accomplishment" of "care." But equiprimordially care determines the fundamental mode of this being according to which it is *delivered over* to the world taken care of. The "ambiguity" of "care" refers to a single basic constitution in its essentially twofold structure of *thrown project* (Heidegger 1996, 192, my emphasis).

I am care insofar as I accomplish my "ownmost possibility" or my project of doing something as the meaning of my existence. But I am not simply united with or in control of myself as care. In caring about a project, I am "delivered over" by my own caring. I am "delivered over" to the world and to the others who might just as well support as persecute me. This world, these others—these are just as much an agent in my engagement, in my narrating my story, as I am. And although I have something to say about the meaning, the hermeneutics of my being, and that of the world and of the others within it, so too does the world.

So far we have followed Heidegger in defining *Dasein* as striving and thrown, as relational and as a whole, i.e., as care. By reading ourselves in these terms we see our agency and self-determination as located and made possible by our situatedness. Now we will see how, as such a being that is being-in-the-world, in a world with others who also have their plans for us, we can be lost and unable to comprehend these phenomenological insights.

Because I am a whole only peripherally, only by not being simply at one with myself; because I am projected into a world in which I care for things, and in which I busy myself by engaging with and responding to others, I can also lose, conceal, fragment myself. Running away from the lack of self-definition that is constitutively part of my ecstatic being, running away from the fact that I can never simply be my past or my future, I can find that I lose myself in my character as "thrown project" in the world.

I can lose myself in my own emotions, such as fear or indifference, when projects seem to lose their grip. I can lose myself in a non-reflective relationship to others in general, to an idle way of talking and bypass specific others who could also, along with me, become free to shift the terms of our situatedness. In all of these possibilities, I lose myself—and it seems that I do so in order that I do not have to think about my radical incompleteness as the heart, the character of my being.

When I am so lost, I become unable even to remember the desire to narrate the whole that I am. I can remain unwilling and largely unable to view my self-imposed task as the hermeneutics of self, world, and others. I can deny myself the experience of my finitude that, by some miracle, always already knows itself as finitude. In denying myself that experience of myself, I would therefore remain closed off from the way in which my self-knowing can and does (even in indifference or in flight) strive beyond finitude toward Being as such, toward the divine.

But what also can happen, in my lostness or in my attempt to immerse myself in things and in the world, since I am not at one with myself, is that I can recognize that it is impossible for me to be fully lost. At any moment, when the hammer breaks, or when someone else walks in who demands my attention be turned away from my woodworking or my reading, I can call myself back to myself and back to my having to take account of my being. I can be called back to the transcendence of my *Dasein*, by means of what Heidegger calls "conscience": "the call of conscience has the character of *summoning Dasein* to its ownmost potentiality-of-being-a-self, by summoning it to its ownmost quality of being a lack" (Heidegger 1996, 268).

In such a call of conscience, I experience some internal tension. I am "summoned" as if by another person, another force. Conscience calls often in the face of another person being present to me. But each time I hear the voice of conscience as my own. What is this transcendent and yet immanent voice?

Conscience appears to "summon" me to the fact that I lack the principle or the rigor to be a self yet. Conscience calls because I am not yet equal to myself. And often I resist that call.

Perhaps I did not *want* to attend to the other person when I was hammering. Or perhaps I *flee from* the opportunity to reckon with the way in which my being is never going to be subsumed under my project. Yet even despite my active desires here and now there is something in me that is restless, that does not simply unite with my work.

Again, I experience this restlessness as the certainty that the call of conscience originates *from* me myself. It is not only the other walking into the room who calls me to her. But also it is me who calls myself toward her on behalf of the whole of me that surpasses any particular desire not to be involved.

For Heidegger, then, in conscience, the whole of what I am now (and yet) to be calls toward that part of me that has been engaging in this or that project. Conscience is the hermeneutic circle of self-understanding enacting itself.

As that whole that I both am and am not-yet, I had to call myself as if I were not the call itself—in order to get myself to listen. And yet the call of conscience is definitively me calling myself back toward the whole that I am in the background. It is never *not* me that calls me toward self-recognition, to a sense of self that is to be more perfectible, more complicated than I am taking myself to be: "the call without doubt does not come from someone else who is with me in the world. The call comes from me and *yet over me*" (Heidegger 1996, 265, my emphasis).

Perhaps this sense of the call as originating both "from me" and also "over me" allows for *Dasein* to show itself the way in which its lostness, or as Heidegger says, fallenness, makes possible the call to self as echoing the call of a transcendent, of the divine. In any case, the call of conscience, by which I enact my care toward my own wholeness, my own being, marks out for me the fact that I am already living a distinction between authenticity and inauthenticity.

Most of the time, with an irrevocable naturalness and necessity in order to project my being toward its function as "thrown project," I find myself lost in what I am doing, lost in the world, in an emotion, in my particular projects. In such a moment or an attitude I am inauthentic.

However, in the moments when I feel called by conscience, when I move within my being toward myself as whole, then I try not to lose myself. Rather, I try to attend to the entire structure of my existence, of *Dasein*, as a global project of disclosing meaning within the situation in which I find myself. This global project, this striving to wholeness, is a moment or an attitude of authenticity.

If the call of conscience calls me back to my authentic possibility of being a whole, then the call awakens me to the meaning of myself. It awakens me to the fact that I am not standing on solid ground, formed by another. It awakens in me, even if I have never thought about this before, the awareness that the foundation of my own experience is always an issue for me and that, at the heart of me, there is a "lack," a definitive nothingness that makes possible my ability to perceive any real being or thing.

Conscience shows me that my wholeness is not a substance but a verb, an act of existence. I exist as a whole that is never at one with itself, as a unity only to be promised because I am never yet that which I take myself to be. This structure of a non-substantive existence makes possible being routinely lost, inauthentic because this getting lost is how existence returns to itself and learns about itself. It is, structurally, a story very similar to the parable of the prodigal son. The young man needed to lose himself in order to find his way back.

This presence of conscience and its return (or my conversion back to it) is ongoing. It is a structure of my being for Heidegger. As such, conscience points out my lack and, for Heidegger, my guilt. More precisely, the guilt that I am in my being means that any project I undertake is, in a way, not a sin but an understandable attempt to avoid looking directly at the sun of my existence, a turning away from myself, even if it does not feel that way. And so, in a return to authenticity as a call of conscience, in a return to the hermeneutics of the whole that is a life and not a thing, I find that my essential structure as a whole is one of guilt: "only because *Dasein* is guilty in the ground of its being, and closes itself off from itself as thrown and fallen prey, is conscience possible, if indeed the call basically gives us to understand this being guilty" (Heidegger 1996, 275). It is because I "close myself off" that I can call myself back. It is because I am limited, finite, that I must continuously remind myself that I fail to be self-sufficient, either perceptually or ethically.

The call of conscience thus summons me back from lostness in the world, back from "falling prey" to the way things are usually talked about or performed by everyone. It summons me back to my own global situation as something I need to wrestle with and disclose to myself and to others. If I am a Catholic, I am not in this religion in exactly the same way as anyone else is. Rather, this religion is another thing I take a stand on and can project myself into with respect to my own wholeness, my style, my preferred charism, etc.: "Understanding the call, *Dasein* listens to its ownmost possibility of existence. It has chosen itself" (Heidegger 1996, 276).

Because of the structure of my being, then, I am committed by means of "listening" to my existential structure, to what Heidegger calls "care." Care is the grasp of my structure, my being, as a *whole*: "being-in-the-world is *essentially* care" (Heidegger 1996, 192, my emphasis). Care is the "essence" of my existence. It is the witnessing of everything that I always already am as deployed here and now in any one project. Care is the way in which I am simultaneously both *toward* things, other people, and world and *toward* myself at the same time. Care is the way that my self is always in process, always desiring further narration, always to-come *as* this being thrown outside of itself in the world.

Care is the method of breathing out and in. Care is the unity of thrownness *and* conscience, that being thrown outward and being called back. Care is the systole and diastole of the zigzag that I am. As care, I am "anxious" about myself. I feel anxiety about the unfinished nature of my wholeness that I am required to stand on and set forth. Care is the anxiety that I can never care enough. I can always and again reckon with my finitude, my limitations.

As care, given my attention to my own potentiality for being a whole self, I can, within any given situation, either live "authentically" or "inauthentically." If I am inauthentic, I leave off a consideration of my process-oriented self. If I am authentic, I can by means of care become, to use Heidegger's language, "resolute."

This resoluteness is a calm, measured responsiveness to the anxiety-producing demands of the situation in which I find myself. And this responsiveness is also a commitment to disclosing what it is that I must do, here and now, in order to continue to explore what I am in relation to what or who is there with me: "Resolution is precisely the *disclosive* projection and determination of the actual factical possibility" (Heidegger 1996, 285, my emphasis).

In other words, in being called to myself, I am being ordered and empowered, by the self that I am and have been and will be, to "disclose" the meaning of the situation such that what I ought to do in response can be disclosed as if for the first time. To be resolute is to gather oneself as a whole and respond, as that whole, to the potential meanings that the situation reveals, withholds, and calls for by means of my own call to myself.

Resolution is an attitude of my authentic wholeness, a possibility of gathering myself together and reflectively acknowledging my finite capacity not as crippling me but as offering me a foothold, a relevance to the situation that I find as already existing. Resolution is a hermeneutics of self in situation. In such a hermeneutics, a hermeneutics within the limits of my finite being, within a "disclosing" of the situation by means of a disclosure of my authentic self, I begin to create a kind of poetry.

Resolutely, calmly, clearly, I create a way of perceiving or of describing that does not simply take up how most people view things. And the reason for that is that the general or everyday way in which people approach situations is inauthentic.

To be a human is thus to have to reckon with my being as something that is at the same time self-understanding. I do not *fully* understand myself and so am capable of projecting myself into a project of understanding myself, my being, my meaning: "The meaning of being of *Dasein* is not something different from it, unattached and 'outside' of it, rather, it is self-understanding *Dasein* itself" (Heidegger 1996, 310). The being that we are is engaged with the project of its own meaning. To be a human is to be encumbered with framing, and to desire to frame, our own existence within the projects of meaning that we reveal to ourselves. To be is to self-understand and to move toward that which we are.

We have been noting, with Heidegger, how our structure as human being, our structure as *Dasein*, is that of a thrown project. We have also seen that, by means of a structural exploration of our guilt (or finitude) and conscience, we call ourselves back to being a whole within a situation in which we find ourselves. This being a whole is a global, active projection of care and resoluteness. It is the method by which, by way of our creativity, we poetically redeem or "release" the latent, implicit meaning in the situation in which we find ourselves by taking up ourselves as time, as the living through of the moments that we conjoin: "Coming back to itself, from the future, resoluteness brings itself to the situation by making it present. Having-been arises from the future in such a way that the future that has-been (or better, is in the process of having-been) *releases* the present from itself" (Heidegger 1996, 311).

It is on behalf of our future self, the one that we strive to be within this situation, that we make present the situation in its possibilities, in its referents, in its terms of endearment or resistance. We *"release"* the present from itself when we take the time to understand and to enact the meaning of our position within a particular situation. And this meaning is "released" when we enact time—when we conjoin the present, past, and future from within a structure of anticipation of what is to come by means of our involvement. A situation is not simply to be endured. It is to be described, to be discussed, to be created and directed from within the factical limitations that it sets before us.

In our stance of anticipation and resoluteness, we therefore *are* time. We are the unity of the moments of past, present, and future. And we are time not as an indifferent act of the flow of consciousness. Rather, we are time as the very project of meaningful attending. We are the release of the present into a dialogue of meaning that sweeps these moments along in a course that is multi-directional and multi-dimensional. We are the very unity of the experience of time by way of caring about the meaning of the situation in which we find ourselves and by way of projecting ourselves always in and toward actions that take up that situation.

We are time and we are action—and what more is our poetic expression than a weaving together of time and action—and those two are intimately linked so as to be the very possibility of being a whole person: "Only because *Dasein* is determined *as* temporality does it make possible for itself the authentic potentiality-of-being-a-whole of anticipatory resoluteness which we characterized. *Temporality reveals itself as the meaning of authentic care*" (Heidegger 1996, 311, my emphasis). We enact ourselves when we "take our time" and recognize the demands of the situation that we are set before and thrown within.

Heidegger thus pursues the meaning that we are by means of the time that we are. We "disclose," we "release" the situation into a narrative, into an enactment. We disclose and release ourselves, too, as returning to ourselves from a previous "entanglement" or "lostness" in an indifferent tradition of distraction. This is authentic care. It is a coming back toward oneself by taking one's time. Time is the meaning that one must become within the existence that one is.

But such a "disclosedness" is not a simple, mechanical process. It matters to us, this act of disclosure. And it matters, quite often, in such a way that it throws us into a mood, a mood of anxiety. Coming back to oneself as thrown into a situation, anticipating what is to come within a stance of resoluteness, is not very often joyful. Rather, this becoming a whole is most often felt within a mood of anxiety.

> Anxiety is anxious about naked *Dasein* thrown into uncanniness. It brings one
> back to the sheer That of one's ownmost, individuated thrownness . . . anxiety
> brings one back to thrownness as something to be possibly *repeated*. And thus
> it also reveals the possibility of an authentic potentiality-of-being that must, as
> something futural in repetition, *come back* to the thrown There (Heidegger
> 1996, 328, my emphasis).

Anxiety then is not something that necessarily dooms us. Anxiety supports us; anxiety offers us a coloring, a shading of our comportment to
ourselves. It is the very pressure of our whole as it offers the way forward.
Anxiety is the sign that we are authentic and in the process of care, in the
process of resolving with ourselves to become the whole that we are . . . not
yet.

Anxiety is not flight from the fact that we are thrown into the world
without a complete grasp of ourselves. Anxiety, rather, is the ability to *feel*
our wholeness in an intelligent yet not dominating manner. Anxiety *reveals*
that thrownness is something we can "possibly repeat." We can take our
thrownness and, as it were, throw ourselves into it. We can move toward that
which is most overwhelming about having to be finite, about having to die.
And if we become aware that it takes our decision to throw ourselves wholly
into a situation in order to navigate it, then we become able to "come back"
to our There, the There which we are as *Da-sein.*

All this means that anxiety presents very concretely to us the fact that the
situation is no longer solely or already interpreted for us by others. Rather,
anxiety is the "uncanniness" that we feel in recognizing that it is our task as
hermeneutical beings to "disclose" or to discern the meaning for ourselves.
Anxiety helps us maintain the resoluteness and the appreciation of our finitude in order to repeat for ourselves the situation in which we find ourselves,
to repeat our own understanding of the meaning of that situation, and to
reckon with it differently. We may be thrown into things, relationships, situations. But we can face them and begin to participate directly in throwing
ourselves.

Anxiety for Heidegger is thus not fear. It is the preparation for courage.
As such, anxiety as the recognition of our limit is not something to be
reduced through antidepressant medicines. It is not something that shuts us
down. It is rather a structure of self-awareness that we live, that we feel, and
that can therefore open us up. But anxiety is not our reason for being, and it
cannot, by itself, win the day, either:

> One who is resolute knows *no fear* but understands the possibility of anxiety
> as the mood that does not hinder and confuse him. Anxiety frees one from
> "nullifying" possibilities and lets one become free for *authentic* possibilities
> (Heidegger 1996, 328–329, my emphasis).

To be free for "authentic possibilities," especially of acting meaningfully within a situation, means to see anxiety as one's companion. It is not something that would "hinder and confuse" us. Rather, anxiety is the possibility of seeing time itself as entwined with the activity of making something.

Using the lens of our own finitude, which is given to us in the mood of anxiety, we see that time is the way we gather ourselves together, from the future, and move within this situation toward the meaning it will have, it will have had, once we have been "released" from it. And this means that anxiety reshapes our understanding of time as the very process of hermeneutics.

From within anxiety, from within a stance of anticipatory resoluteness, we see that time is our doing: "Temporality *temporalizes itself* as a future that *makes present*, in the process of having-been" (Heidegger 1996, 334). Again, time is not linear and is not a substance. Rather, time is something that *Dasein* enacts. Within our anxiety, our temporality can "temporalize itself," can generate the meaning of itself.

In acting resolutely within our anxiety, our being as time concretizes itself in such a way that we come *toward* time as the beings that unite past, present, and future toward the meaning that we strive to disclose. We do not flee time in our fantasies of eternity. Rather, we turn to time as the miraculous way we are engaged in the process of "making present" that which is meaningful.

If time were strictly linear, or if eternity were the lens through which to grasp time, then no meaning would be released within the present situation because we could not "see" according to past and future. We could not see that which might become. We would not feel the conscience that called both within ourselves and "from above" backwards and forwards from and to that which is now.

Having spoken about our thrownness, our being a whole, our anticipatory resoluteness, and our hermeneutic existence as temporality, Heidegger then points out a kind of concrete metaphor of stretching. It is important for this meditation on religious experience because it suggests a kind of bodily discipline. It may even suggest, for Christians, the crucifixion, the stretching of the divine who was human across dimensions of space and time in an offering of self toward the situations of danger and suffering.

As so determined, the phenomenon of stretching is a crucial way in which its ecstasies of time (past, present, and future) are our own enactment. That is, whether authentically or inauthentically, "in moving from day to day, [*Dasein*] *stretches itself along* temporally" (Heidegger 1996, 353, my emphasis). However, this insight about stretching, Heidegger claims, is not just about our movement "from day to day," but it also is about our lives as such, since, in addition, "*Dasein stretches along between* birth and death" (Heidegger 1996, 356, my emphasis).

The total situation of our life is to be thrown between an inaccessible beginning and an inaccessible ending. Our role as *Dasein* is thus to make sense of our limits and in so doing to create for ourselves our own time as this life: "*Dasein* does not first fill up an objectively present path or stretch 'of life' through phases of its momentary realities, but stretches *itself* along in such a way that its own being is constituted beforehand as this stretching along" (Heidegger 1996, 357). Much as a child stretches when she awakens from a deep sleep, *Dasein* is always stretching itself. It is always trying to unite itself to itself, to be toward its beginning and ending, to keep the relevance of its past within its orientation toward the future. And thus *Dasein* gives itself to itself as the very bodily enactment of a self in motion—in stretching as both preservation and evolution, i.e., as growth.

This being between birth and death, this being oriented toward the body as both origin and end of itself—this is what "care" is. It is because I am a bodily existence that cannot ever be fully clear to itself that I develop a life in which I can care for other things, other people, projects, etc.: "As care, *Dasein is* the 'between'" (Heidegger 1996, 357). The situation of a bodily life is to be between events that can only mean what they mean within the context of a life setting out to perform a hermeneutics on them.

It is something like finding out that "I was born for this." From out of the future, a possibility offers itself in which we take up the entire meaning of our lives and then perform a retroactive narrative. This hermeneutics is the way in which we really *are.* It is the event of our lives: "The specific movement of the *stretched out stretching itself along,* we call the *occurrence* of *Dasein.* . . . To expose the *structure of occurrence* and the existential and temporal conditions of its possibility means to gain an *ontological* understanding of *historicity*" (Heidegger 1996, 358).

With the phenomenon of stretching, then, we are not just temporality as a concept. We are "historicity," a life, a finitude that takes on a certain bodily character. Our structure as *Dasein* is visible not just in our consciousness but in our bodies as emblematic, as pertaining to, as existing our consciousness. Our job is to "expose" what it means to "occur," what it means to have *meaning* suddenly push up into the realms of existence and to take its rightful place as the motor of *being.*

I stretch myself out to myself and thereby create for myself the sense of my own finite, historical narrative. I make there be time—the time that I live through and toward. I make there be an experience of being involved in time because I am broken off from and reuniting with myself at each moment.

Time as something universal, time as that which we are all in together, is also an experience we have, but it is secondary. It is secondary because it is derived from the fact that each of us stretches ourselves along "somehow" in a life that is our own and yet not just our own. My life is my own and is also about the care I take about others' lives. My life intersects with theirs and is, as a hermeneutic project, about making sense of those relationships.

We therefore have time "in" us and have an experience of being "in" time—and we have these two experiences at the same time: "historicity and within-time-ness turn out to be equiprimordial" (Heidegger 1996, 360). It is this dual experience of time (time as our act of stretching, time as that in which we find ourselves) that makes our life "release" itself toward its future and interrogate—and remember—its past.

Resoluteness, the ability to act as a finite whole within a mood of anxiety, a mood which is essential to *Dasein* and not merely a temporary feeling to be avoided, is not a possibility arising solely within one's own will. Instead, resoluteness lies within oneself as something motivated by, and answering to *tradition*, to a community of others. It is the others with whom we live who motivate or challenge our resolve. It is the others we are with who reaffirm, by way of their already worked out understanding, that there is a way forward into the stretching out that one needs to do. Though *Dasein* is both thrown into a world and must die alone, though each must take its own death and birth as the hallmarks of a finite project—nevertheless that finitude gathers others within itself and toward itself. *Dasein* is always already a being-with and a being-toward other people.

And this openness to others from within our ontological structure means that the hermeneutics we place upon our own temporality, the narrative we tell about our own lives, is never static and never simply repeated. Rather, the fact that each *Dasein* is, together, the stuff of temporality guarantees the necessity of poetry in the description of our life as both together and as singular. Each of us looks, together and alone, toward the past from the future. Each of us guides our hermeneutical project into the release of the present by way of our received entanglements: "the resoluteness in which *Dasein* comes back to itself discloses the actual factical possibilities of authentic existing in terms of the *heritage* which that resoluteness takes over as thrown. Resolute coming back to thrownness involves *handing oneself over* to traditional possibilities, although not necessarily *as* traditional ones" (Heidegger 1996, 365).

Phenomenology, for Heidegger, is thus always already a hermeneutical project. It is a disclosure of meaning based on a "heritage" that relates us to our un-relatable birth. This "heritage" requires that we "hand ourselves over" to a past that is shared, to a "tradition" of meaningful enactments. But since *Dasein* is equally alone in its togetherness with others, the way that *Dasein* hands itself over is never simply to reaffirm a tradition that did not begin with us. Rather, it is to take up the tradition and make it new by virtue of the fact that we are new, that we are born into this tradition and that we are making a future for it by means of our "guilty" assertion of ourselves within it.

Whether or not Heidegger has talked about *Dasein* as intimately connected with religious experience throughout *Being and Time*, then, and I certainly would argue that he has, it certainly seems true that this connection is strongest toward the end of the book. For it is in the coming to terms with the stretching we do together, within a tradition that is never simply repeated, that we see that we are broken open to the meanings that are to come and that are both within and above us. *Dasein* is a kind of repeated binding oneself to a community. And, with anticipatory resoluteness, this binding is creative and receptive to a power that is shared among those with whom *Dasein* is striving toward.

In other words, *Dasein* is an ongoing act of choice. A choice to bind oneself to others in the shared repetition of that which is most necessarily to be repeated and yet which is most intimately creative and personal. Through its conscience, stretching, and anticipatory resoluteness, *Dasein* shows itself, in its community with others, to open onto the transcendent within the immanent: "in resoluteness the choice is first chosen that makes one free for the struggle over what is to follow and fidelity to what can be repeated . . . repetition neither abandons itself to the past, nor does it aim at progress" (Heidegger 1996, 367). *Dasein* is a kind of creed, handed down for generations—a belief that one's participation in the heritage or the tradition has some impact on the transcendent in its coming to appear. *Dasein* is the hope that that which cannot be named is nevertheless still possible in the shape of the to-come.

B. *Phenomenology of Religious Life—*
Situation, Enactment, Living Time

In the *Phenomenology of Religious Life*, which later was a lecture course Heidegger gave in 1920–1921, many of the themes he brought together in *Being and Time* can be found rather explicitly in the hermeneutical reading Heidegger gives on some of Paul's letters in the New Testament. In a way, then, this lecture course was a kind of applied phenomenology, using Paul as a particular instance, I believe, of authentic *Dasein*. In those letters, Paul stressed the call of conscience as necessitating anticipatory resoluteness and the act of stretching himself toward the others with whom he desired to share a religious existence.

Finding himself "thrown," quite literally, from his horse, Paul feels the urgency of attending to his situation both as a Jew and, through a turning around toward Christianity, as a believer in the Christ who will come again. This urgency, Heidgger claims, manifests itself in Paul's own writing in the Letter to Galatians as a struggle: "Paul must be seen in struggle with his religious passion in his existence as an apostle, the struggle between 'law' and 'faith'" (Heidegger 2010, 48).

The law is structure; law is having-been. Faith is openness to the future; faith demands that we use what is to-come retroactively, that we learn to see the to-come as already latent in the having-been, in the law. And thus, this struggle between law and faith is, for Paul, a hermeneutic struggle. How ought Paul, how ought his reader, make sense of his life as a whole, which is stretched between law and faith, between past and future? How ought one to read the present?

Heidegger further clarifies Paul's struggle as precisely a hermeneutic struggle of explication:

> Paul finds himself in a struggle. He is pressured to assert the Christian life experience against the surrounding world . . . it is an *original explication* from the sense of the *religious life* itself. It can be further formed out in the primary religious experience. At issue is a return to the original experience and an understanding of the *problem* of *religious explication* (Heidegger 2010, 50).

Paul therefore finds himself in the midst of the original question of religious experience: How is one to talk about it? And what is one to say?

Religious explication then is a "problem" that demands urgent reflection. Experience can throw one off, can come from the future with new, surprising demands. But this new experience is not simply singular, though it certainly is that too. The new experience, the religious experience, roots itself immediately in a "religious life" that embraces it. This life is "formed out" and rises to meet the experience. How then to talk about the life in relation to the particular experience? How does Paul name who he is in relation to his thrownness and, more particularly, to being thrown toward other people who desire for him to explicate himself in relation to the divine?

This struggle for explication of the religious life of Paul, who stands in for the others to whom this kind of religious life could produce similar religious experiences, is one of the explication of time. And, Heidegger says, Paul is a particularly poignant example of how religious life gathers time within itself, how religious life *lives* time: "Christian experience lives time itself" (Heidegger 2010, 57).

What does this mean, that Christian experience "lives time"? It means that the anticipation of the second coming of the Christ, which Paul asserts is the organizing principle of Christian religious life, must take on its own form. The anticipation of Christ is not a general structure of waiting or enduring. Rather, it is a new way of releasing the present, of releasing those who take it up within their present.

When Heidegger later discusses Paul's relation to the Parousia, or the experience of authentic Christians of the second coming of Jesus, he says something similar: "It is a time without its own order and demarcations. One cannot encounter this temporality in some sort of objective concept of time. The when is in no way objectively graspable" (Heidegger 2010, 73). The phenomenology of time, the experience of time, in light of the parousia is a new manner of lived time. Christian time is lived in a specific, committed, bodily way that allows the Christian religious life to transcend the notion of time as objective, to transcend the idea that time is a container in which the anticipation of the second coming requires the same kind of anticipation as the arrival of Santa Claus.

Time, then, for Paul, is related to action. If "Christian experience *lives* time itself," then that is because there is a different kind of enactment that this religious life requires. And this enactment, by which each Christian comports herself, is itself a hermeneutics. Each Christian's enactment is the disclosure of meaning of the phenomenon of the parousia, of Christ, and of religious community: "In the enactment and through the enactment, the phenomenon is explicated" (Heidegger 2010, 57).

But Christian temporal "explication" is not a given. It requires something. Indeed, what Paul's hearers or readers require (in order to "enact" their role as explicators within their experience of Christian time), according to Heidegger, is empathy.

Paul wrote within a certain historical situation. He experienced the parousia within a certain set of finite limitations. Our ability to take on Paul's life as relevant to our own, as making demands on our own enactment, if we take it up, requires that we are sensitive to the way that the having-been, the tradition, is precisely what the future calls to in the parousia.

Our empathy arises here and now, but through it we move back to Paul by means of orienting ourselves toward the same parousia: "Empathy arises in factical life experience, that is to say, it involves an original-historical phenomenon that cannot be resolved without the phenomenon of *tradition* in its original sense" (Heidegger 2010, 59).

Paul's religious life, his conversion experience, was never simply private. And it is less and less so as we read and reflect upon it. Religious experience founds tradition, and gathers up that time and propels us forward toward the to-come in ways that Paul could not fathom. Nor can we. And yet there we find ourselves—on the road to explication as Paul was to Damascus.

We find ourselves asking the same questions as Paul did: how do we talk about his letters, about his life, about our own, about this divine? What do we say?

But we are not left simply with Paul's words. Rather, Paul's words gather our own, gather our time into his: "Explication means: if it is explicated toward a particular direction of sense, the remaining directions of meaning are *co-projected* into it. In this it is important to determine the *How* of the *co-projection*" (Heidegger 2010, 62, my emphasis). We find the meaning of our time "co-projected" into Paul's, and Paul's into ours. We find the very ground shifting under our feet, in order to bring the way we live time closer to one another by having, again, to explicate the time of the second coming and the way it holds sway over the lives of believers.

Our ability to read and understand Paul's letter, our ability to empathize with the essence and the historical particularity of his situation, is not a simple matter. The co-projection is not simply that we abstract ourselves from our own particular lives and project ourselves as if we were Paul. Even with historical-critical or theological study, it is not simply the case that we co-project ourselves into the objective historical self-understanding or circumstances of Paul.

We do not try to live in 53 AD when we read his text. Rather, we project ourselves into his situation, which is of a piece with that history but allows us, as we target the whole, not to be caught reducing Paul to his circumstances.

Reading Paul's letter, the "remaining directions of meaning," the rest of the whole of his situation and of the references to the tradition and to the parousia that remain within it, announce themselves. It is the potentiality of being-a-whole that Paul's letters offer. But the whole has always meant not only the past and the present but also the anticipation and enactment of a certain, particular way of anticipating the coming of Christ. And that futural orientation, especially that, is part of the "remaining directions" and so the task of explication is hardly exhausted by learning what life was like for someone like Paul in 53 AD.

Paul's conversion experience was a turning around. One might say that Paul was turned from a simple identification with the past toward a future that is always to-come and so reads itself back into the past. This turning around, this conversion, is a re-reading of the situation into which one is thrown with greater facility, with a proper sense of anxiety or uncanniness, and with an orientation toward the others, past, present, and future, who also experience or could experience in his life the calling of that which is both within and above them: "The turning-around from the object-historical to the enactment-historical lies in factical life experience itself. It is a turning-around to the situation" (Heidegger 2010, 63).

Paul has something to say. He had a conversion experience. He had a situation in which he reflected and wrote. This "having" is the very possibility of his explication and ours: "Insofar as that which is 'like an I' *has* something, the departure for the situation can be taken from here. For what is *had* seems to give itself objectively. It offers a starting point for the carrying out of the explication" (Heidegger 2010, 64, my emphasis). We respond to Paul's "having," to his enactment, because his situation and his having of it calls to our own.

Paul's "having" of his experience, his enactment of it *within the writing of it*, is what can sustain a prolonged identification. His description of his experience calls to us structurally and personally. Structurally, his description enforces a kind of identification with the character of Paul, much as reading a novel enforces an identification with the narrator. Structurally, he brings to mind the fact that we as *Dasein* can be with others fundamentally.

Personally, Paul's highlighting the specific experience of Christian lived time as concrete and unique brings to mind the fact we can be *most* clearly with others only when we begin to move toward their perspective. We are not just a bare possibility of empathy. We are empathy insofar as we slide into the way they act and the way they take up or "have" a situation. We may not be able to take on every concrete facet of Paul's life in 53 AD; however, we can take on what is "had" by means of the specificity as such of the finite situation in which Paul finds himself. Even if it is difficult to know what it was like to live in 53 AD, we can pursue, by means of our desire to be with him, our own ability to take on the style of his "having." His words, and, more importantly, his projection toward the perspective of the Christ who is to-come, begin to work their way into our understanding. "Being thrown" from the horse means something. And we are off.

Most essentially, what we are identifying or empathizing with when we read Paul's letters is not even Paul or Paul's perspective, though that is a part of our experience. Most essentially, we are empathizing with the structure of Paul's conflict.

We are empathizing with the perspective of Christ who is to-come. We are living toward the perspective of the futural one in his coming toward us. We are learning to see ourselves as futural according to the future that is moving toward us.

In this way, we empathize with the anxiety of Paul, and thus, with the perspective of the one we will be within the to-come of the second coming. We are not simply in the past when we read Paul's letters but are thrown, by means of them, toward the future that will redirect it.

But why is it important for *Heidegger* to speak of Paul? Why point out the phenomenological structures of religious life from within the Pauline Christian situation? It seems that for Heidegger Paul offers the proper starting point. For Paul knows, in his conversion, that he has become attuned very directly both to the divine and to himself in his having been turned. For Heidegger, Paul is the instantiation of *Dasein* as conscience and as care—for it is as if from something within him and above him, as if by conscience, which is the knowledge of one's own enactment of time that Paul begins to reshape theology: "Knowledge of one's own having-become is the starting point and the origin of theology" (Heidegger 2010, 66).

Any religious life, then, must begin with the turning of *Dasein* toward the temporal enactment of life. Any religious experience that does *not* do so cannot proceed toward the transcendent. For it is in the clarification and renewal of the experience of temporality as the existence of *Dasein* that we find the motivation and support in our struggle for anticipatory resoluteness and stretching. To renew temporality (and to *disclose* it) is the very means by which others can discover their own lives as a co-projection into the life of the divine.

There is, however, another reason: Paul's account of his conversion also suggests another essential moment of temporality, of religious life, and of religious experience: anxiety or insecurity. To have a religious experience of conversion toward the to-come is not to be secure. It is to be thrown back onto one's own existence as one's own project within a call from the divine. Religious experience is not a dogma but a way of being, a way of living time in a certain kind of emotional specificity and thickness. Religious experience is a thrownness into the mood of anxiety: "There is no security for Christian life; the constant insecurity is also characteristic for what is fundamentally significant in factical life. The uncertainty is not coincidental; rather, it is necessary" (Heidegger 2010, 73). One's "factical life" derives its capacity to discern "what is fundamentally significant" only if one rests within a certain kind of insecurity. Only within a structure of waiting that is not simply passing time but rather living it.

If religious experience announces itself as uncertainty or anxiety, however, then that means that it must always and again be concerned with its explication, with its meaning. Hermeneutical circle that we are, we must, *especially within religious experience*, strive to critique both ourselves and the apparent divine that we encounter there. For we are finite. And thus to live as *Dasein*, even and especially in religious moments, is to always be vulnerable to falling, to projecting ourselves not toward the to-come but only toward the having-been.

Even in religious life, we can find ourselves not paying sufficient attention and thus always already moving toward the persecution of others and of ourselves within a fallenness or an ordinary language that sees nothing important or significant in the situation: "In order to escape the Antichrist as Antichrist, one must have first entered into the complex of enactment of the religious situation; for the Antichrist appears as God" (Heidegger 2010, 77–78). Religious life is a "complex of enactment." It is something which one "enters" and can remain within only with careful reflection and with discipline. And it is something that requires ongoing vigilance, for what "appears" demands that we test it with respect to the "whole" that is us and that is transcendent.

But even if religious experience is so dangerous, all hope is not lost. As always already having the possibility of authentic care, we can maintain our perceptual selves within our conversion. That is, we always already have within us the tools for right discernment. As *Dasein*, we always already are understanding, the understanding of time, of eternity, and of God. And these phenomena all appear only as meanings that we participate in, relate to, and enact: "The meaning of temporality *determines itself* out of the fundamental relationship to God—however, in such a way that only those who live temporally in the manner of enactment *understand* eternity. The sense of the Being of God can be determined first only out of these complexes of enactment" (Heidegger 2010, 83–84). Time, the new time of Paul's conversion, the time that is the seeing of the Parousia, is rooted in his "fundamental relationship," in his "enactment." And this relationship, this enactment, this "understanding"—these mutually implicated phenomena are open to us as well.

For Heidegger, then, Paul concretizes in a new kind of religious life, a new kind of experience and of a writing about that experience—in a new hermeneutics—an authentic approach to one's own existence as *Dasein*. Within the Christian religious life, God is both the author of "the meaning of temporality" and also the product of our enactment.

The "how" of the religious experience in Paul's Christian life is thus that of a "fundamental relationship" that is always already a mutuality. To live within it is to be thrown toward the possibility to "understand eternity" and "the Being of God." To understand as if a gift from the God with whom Paul is in relationship. But this understanding is equally our own doing, the product of our own enactment.

The meaning of Christian time "determines itself" out of the relationship. And the meaning of the to-come, of the parousia, is only something to be commented on within that act of life which stretches itself back toward Paul and forward, by means of a tradition that is not simply a dogma. To have a right to say something about Christian time is given not through official channels only but is given by means of those who take and read, those who orient themselves toward that which is to-come as revealing itself in surprising, organic ways within the Christian who has always already been active, even if she knows not yet how, in its determination.

By reading Paul's letters as involving situation, living time, and enactment, then, Heidegger has been able to show the hermeneutical position of *Dasein* as opening onto religious experience. It is not an experience of dogma, which "as detached content of doctrine . . . could never have been guiding for Christian religiosity" (Heidegger 2010, 79), but of anticipatory resoluteness toward the situation of enactment that Christianity requires. The focus of the Christian is toward the future coming again of Christ, which makes demands on Christians' lived experience. The parousia requires that one see Christ as "leaping ahead" in order that the Christian enactment have the strength for "the retrieval of the relational complexes" (Heidegger 2010, 87) between the divine and the human, and between each human and one another.

Paul's focus on the parousia is thus an important part of Heidegger's understanding as to how the structural analysis of *Dasein* can become concretized in the call of conscience, in anxiety, and in anticipatory resoluteness. One's own existence in Christian religious life, in light of the parousia, becomes an issue and one feels the deep "distress" of having to dwell completely within one's finitude, one's ecstatic character, without losing oneself in the world: "There remains only yet a little time, the Christian living incessantly in the only-yet, which intensifies his distress. The compressed temporality is constitutive for Christian religiosity; an 'only-yet,' there is no time for postponement" (Heidegger 2010, 85). This distress is a necessary mood, required by the experience of one's "compressed temporality." Such a compression is the experience of the future as putting us in direct contact with our past and our becoming—all at once.

This "compressed temporality," finally, is what Madeleine L'Engle might call a "wrinkle" in time. It is the way in which we begin to discover, like Meg Murry, that the requirement to save Charles Wallace on Camazotz is entering into an enactment that requires a kind of conversion, a becoming that depends on the divine as on an "above" of one's own conscience. Like Meg, the Christian understands that "entering into such complex of enactment is almost hopeless" and that "this facticity cannot be won out of [her] own strength but rather originates from God" (Heidegger 2010, 87). The future, conscience, the authentic resoluteness within the call—these provide the hermeneutics for *Dasein* as a being that seeks the meaning of Being and even Being itself within the context of a finite life within the world.

LITERARY PRACTICE: *A WRINKLE IN TIME* —
MOVING TOWARD ANGELS, MOVING AWAY FROM IT

A. Moving Toward Angels:
Mrs. Who, Mrs. Whatsit, and Mrs. Which

We learn late in *A Wrinkle in Time*, from the character of Calvin, that the three characters introduced to us in the first three chapters of L'Engle's novel are in fact "Angels! . . . Messengers of God!" (L'Engle 2007, 210).

This moment in which Calvin figures out how to translate who these three beings are to Aunt Beast and to the other beings on that strange planet of Ixchel is a particularly poignant one. Meg Murry, the central child in the story, is hurt, possibly dying, from close contact with a demonic sentience called the Black Thing. And their friends, Mrs. Who, Mrs. Whatsit, and Mrs. Which, who have proved powerful, are not there with them on this new planet. Communicating with a new group of beings about the power and the ontology of these three "women" forces Calvin to review the terms of his experience of them. When he finds the words it is because his "face [was] tense with concentration" (L'Engle 2007, 210) and because his review of his experience showed him something that was not there before. A relation to the divine. These three beings are themselves the relationship to the divine.

So powerful is this moment that, at first, it seems not to be powerful at all. Calvin's description, his explication of what has remained implicit in the appearances of the three characters, falls, as it were, on deaf ears. The beings of Ixchel are nonplussed: "How strange it is that they can't tell us what they themselves seem to know" (L'Engle 2007, 210). And yet Calvin's saying, the telling, the explication out loud for all to hear is in fact powerful and essential. Immediately afterwards, "a thundering voice reverberated throughout the great hall: 'WWEEE ARRE HHERRE!'" (L'Engle 2007, 210–211).

Calvin's bit of phenomenological description, "messengers of God," has allowed the response from those who are in direct relationship with the divine. His description has allowed them to appear. His description calls for a response. And his shouting, his concentration, calls for their "thundering voice."

It is true that the community the humans have discovered, the beings on Ixchel, do not yet understand. But they too are part of the appearance, part of the experience and intuition of Mrs. Who, Mrs. Whatsit, and Mrs. Which as angels. For it is as the interlocutors of Calvin, it is in their communal *striving to understand him,* that the angels appear to everyone. It is in the taking up of the text of their experience again that everyone, those of Earth and those of Ixchel, discover the latent religious meanings and symbolism that form that experience.

Let us now turn to these angels, who present themselves as women in the first three chapters, and see what L'Engle can prompt from us. What divine messages might we shout out when we turn again to see, again, what we have read?

Chapter 1 begins with a hurricane and with Meg being scared. Her first worry, it would seem, is that she feels compelled to "*show* everything" (L'Engle 2007, 9). Meg is thus in a relationship with her body that is not exactly seamless or happy. She is expressive and without control over that expression. She cannot hide what she knows or what she feels. As the novel progresses, we will see how the expressivity of her body is the very possibility of religious experience and of power.[1]

It is to this worried girl, who has lost her father, who wears what she is thinking and feeling on her face, and to Meg's little brother Charles, who reads Meg's face like a text,[2] that Mrs. Whatsit comes on this dark and stormy night. Dressed as if an old woman, this angel comes as a thief in the night, quite literally. She has stolen sheets off a line and is struggling to create the impression that she too is embodied, is expressive as a bodily being would be. Mrs. Whatsit is worried about "sprained dignity" (L'Engle 2007, 26) and about encouraging Meg and Charles to face the loss of their father head on.

Again, this angel blows in as a thief in the night. She is involved in some kind of theatrics, which present her as a cross between a bat and a witch, but she is there to encourage them all, even Mrs. Murry: "Speaking of ways, pet, there is such a thing as a tesseract" (L'Engle 2007, 27). This particular confirmation from Mrs. Whatsit provides hope, implicitly, for Mrs. Murry that her husband is all right or at least alive. And the angel's self-translation into a disoriented, disorienting older woman allows the family to interact with her, to begin the journey toward the divine and toward the reconciliation and re-membering of the father with the family.

Chapter 2 begins with the family trying to make sense of Mrs. Whatsit's visit. Mrs. Murry tells Meg, "You don't have to understand things for them to *be*" (L'Engle 2007, 29). This insight allows for the children to progress once again toward the angel of the night before. And it allows them to know that a pre-comprehension or a pre-maturity (as Merleau-Ponty emphasizes in "The Child's Relations With Others") inhabits their desire to know more. It is being that promotes understanding, and it is the irreducible, insurmountable otherness of our objects of experience, their ontological resistance to us, that propel us on the hermeneutic path of phenomenology.

The hermeneutics begin, in chapter 2, with absence. The father of the Murry children is missing. They feel him in their lacking of him. And Calvin's family is uncaring. He feels the lack of definition, and of love, in a similar way.

The hermeneutics, the intuitions by both Charles and Calvin, also begin with a sense of urgency. They begin with, as Calvin relates, "a feeling about things. You might call it a compulsion" (L'Engle 2007, 39). Something propels the children out of one realm of experience, that of their family relationships, toward another. It is this urgency about the absence of love that animates their movement, their being-toward as Heidegger would say. It is an urgent absence that compels us to have to pursue experience at the edges, at the periphery, that generates more meaning.

But this being-toward is something done together, as a group. It is not only Charles or Meg or Calvin alone that is compelled to witness the angels at the haunted house. It is all three of them together. As they enter the house, Meg is enfolded within a community of care: "Calvin put a strong hand to Meg's elbow, and Fort pressed against her leg. Happiness at their concern was so strong in her that her panic fled, and she followed Charles Wallace into the dark recesses of the house without fear" (L'Engle 2007, 41).

Many times in the book there is evidence of moving together, of supporting each other, of touch. In the shared touch, there is the ability to progress toward the source of meaning within the experience. And something about this shared project is also reminiscent of phenomenology. It can only be shared and be about sharing, about intercorporeality and intersubjectivity.

The meeting with Mrs. Who, the second of the two angels, then provides the opportunity for this second angel to exhort the children to come together, to eat, and to prepare. Their community must be reinforced if the revelation of meanings is to impact them, to have a home in their own experience.

And this "having a home" is precisely how Calvin takes the whole brief encounter: "I've never even seen your house, and I have the funniest feeling that for the first time in my life I'm going home!" (L'Engle 2007, 44). If hermeneutics and phenomenology are performed as a kind of communal project toward meaning, toward the genesis of meaning, and toward the fruition of experience, they would have exactly this structure. The insights of phenomenology, the insights as to what experience means, is in fact the recognition of truths as both new and old, as desired insofar as they are meant to be part of us.

As chapter 3's title indicates, the children next meet the third angel or messenger of God, Mrs. Which. But unlike their meetings with Mrs. Whatsit and Mrs. Who, this third meeting requires a good deal more preparation. This fact becomes understandable, for Mrs. Which is the most challenging and least corporeal of the angels.

The dinner that the children share is not the only preparation. There is also the sharing of oneself. Calvin talks about his life at home with Meg and concludes by saying, "You don't know how lucky you are to be loved" (L'Engle 2007, 47). This reckoning is immediately followed by Calvin being hopeful: "Things are going to happen, Meg! Good things! I can feel it!" (L'Engle 2007, 47). The content of the children's experience, their lives in their families, becomes the subject that they must articulate and judge. But in judging it, in acknowledging their own tendency to care and to be cared about, they also look forward. It is because they take the viewpoint on their own families and lives that they *can* look forward.

However, as we see in Calvin's remark about feeling good things coming, their preparation isn't just about *looking* into the future. The children primarily feel toward it. Throughout the novel, L'Engle makes it clear that emotions are themselves intelligent and create the possibility of meaning by being so. Calvin feels toward the future, and his sharing is a way that he feels toward the love that would create in him the power to experience more keenly: "I'm not alone anymore! Do you realize what this means to me?" (L'Engle 2007, 51–52).

In Calvin's epiphany, in his passage from confusion about "how did all this happen" to the enjoyment of the experience of being with others who accept him, lies the seeds of further thought. Meg and Mrs. Murry talk about the difference of Charles Wallace after dinner, and Mrs. Murry says it is "in essence" (L'Engle 2007, 54). Something about the way Charles Wallace is perceived immediately provides those who see him clearly, those who love him, with an intuition that confirms itself without its being understood. It is this reflection on how Charles Wallace appears to them that leads Meg and Mrs. Murry to talk about how they would "have to accept it without understanding it" (L'Engle 2007, 54).

This acceptance without understanding is not the end of the story, though. Neither Meg nor Mrs. Murry resigns herself to not knowing as to a disappointment. Rather, Mrs. Murry talks about "a willing suspension of disbelief" (L'Engle 2007, 55) in the reality of the angel Mrs. Whatsit because of the essence of Charles Wallace. It is his essence that turns her perception toward what is even stranger and allows her to suspend something in herself that would block that experience. So the acceptance of the essence of Charles Wallace is not a resignation of thought but the very possibility of reflection. It allows the experiences that relate directly to Charles Wallace (who already knows these three angels in some way of his own) to come to light.

This "willing suspension" might ordinarily be something we think of as the requirement to watching a movie or a play or reading a story, like one by Charles Dickens, in which coincidence drives the plot home. But that is not enough here. The suspension that Mrs. Murry is talking about is toward the revelation of experience on its own terms, allowing it to come to be as it wills within one's own consciousness. The suspension is for the sake of one's own participation in a story that has not yet been written but is written in the taking it in. The suspension, before judgment, is the beginning of phenomenology.

This suspension contrasts with the way people are often certain about what they are seeing by means of a limited, pre-established set of categories. When Mrs. Murry repeatedly writes to Mr. Murry, the postmistress makes snide comments. But that is because the postmistress does not enact the kind of suspension that is required: "They can't understand plain, ordinary love when they see it" (L'Engle 2007, 59).

Within a proper suspension, the understanding, then, ought to be rooted in the givens. And it cannot develop if the categories pre-exist the experience. Rather, understanding will always stray apart from experience if it does not let that experience dictate the terms of its explication.

The third angel cuts in with "a sharp, strange voice" (L'Engle 2007, 63) only after Calvin has attended to Meg's distress and seen the beauty in her eyes. Only then are the children prepared internally to perceive together, having left their previous concepts suspended. In Mrs. Which's voice, we discover that language can be used differently, since Mrs. Which speaks with doubled and tripled consonants. Something spoken differently, something appearing differently, not fully materialized—this is the path on which love leads them and which it will support them. Seeing together into the unknown, into the dark, requires a suspension. But it will require something much more—a sense of community and of purpose that transcends previous understanding and experience.

B. Moving Away from the Black Thing and IT

From chapter 4, entitled "The Black Thing," through chapter 9, entitled "IT," L'Engle's book weaves its way through the children's and the angels' encounters with darkness or evil. It is noteworthy, in a book that is most notably about love, that we as readers spend the majority of our time aware of how vulnerable and threatened the main characters are by evil.

This raises a fundamental question for the phenomenology of religious experience. Can a religious experience present itself without also presenting that which threatens or challenges the divine? Can a religious experience appear simply as a peaceful affirmation of the experiencer within the care of the divine?

The book does not answer this question directly. However, in chapter 6 we are presented with the experience of the Happy Medium. And it serves, at least for the children, as a brief respite before encountering, in the next chapter, the man with red eyes. If the book causes us to make a judgment, then, about religious experience, perhaps it is this: there are moments of peace and warmth along the journey of a religious encounter, but they are moments. The whole is an engagement with urgency and with ethics: there is always something to DO in religious experience other than contemplate and rest.

Let us look more closely at the way the children experience the Black Thing, the man with red eyes, and IT. In chapter 4, the beginning of the children's journey is announced with wind and confusion. Meg feels "completely alone," and her anxiety grows, in part, because "she had lost the protection of Calvin's hand" (L'Engle 2007, 64).

Not only losing her companions, Meg also loses the experience of her own body: "Where was her body? . . . The corporeal Meg simply was not" (L'Engle 2007, 65).

The travel that the angels initiated through the tesseract has been a suspension of the childrens' bodily experience. As the children feel toward their bodies on the other side, as it were, they come to see that they have traveled.

Mrs. Who tries to soften the experience of abrupt bodily changes by quoting from famous authors, as she has done in the book to this point. The first thing she quotes after the trip is, very fittingly, a line of Shakespeare's *Macbeth* in which one of the witches asks the others, "When shall we three meet again, in thunder, lightning, or in rain?" (L'Engle 2007, 68).

This line is full of foreshadowing, as the second witch in the play answers, "When the battle's done." Alas, Mrs. Who does not elaborate. She simply laughs with Mrs. Whatsit. No doubt the children have questions. But they do not ask the one question that they might ask: why are the angels named FOR questions?

The reader must keep up with Mrs. Who's quotes, some of which are not attributed, and keep asking herself who this quote is from and what significance it has. And in Mrs. Who's habit of quoting there is something irritating and revealing. For Charles Wallace, who is worried about Meg's late arrival through the tesseract, Mrs. Who's quoting is not helpful: "Mrs. Who, I wish you'd stop quoting!" (L'Engle 2007, 69). But there is something important in the practice of Mrs. Who, as Mrs. Whatsit sees: "But she finds it so difficult to verbalize, Charles dear. It helps her if she can quote instead of working out words of her own" (L'Engle 2007, 69).

Perhaps as readers we ought to pause and consider the practice of quoting more urgently. Why would L'Engle create a main character who quotes instead of "working out words of her own" throughout the book? It may be that there is much at stake in Mrs. Who's practice.

If religious experience is not just about oneself or about one's own family, then perhaps we need to ask how much a religious experience embraces. Does each religious experience embrace all of one's knowledge, all of one's culture? Does the divine want to save all the inspired works from ancient times (Mrs. Who quotes Horace and Euripides as well as Shakespeare) up to the present? If so, the journey of the children seems to be about all of their civilization, all of their history, as well as all of their future. The divine then would not just transcend history but work in it to gather it all together and make explicit what rides through it.

Another question arises: what do texts have to do with religious experience? It would seem that describing religious experience, describing temporality, describing the limits of bodily experience and the possibility of transcending them in, say, resurrection, needs some help. It would seem that religious experience can be not only direct but also indirect—and sacred texts may help to engage the sacred within an ordinary life and its quest to bring the good to fruition.

If I trust in a text, say the Gospel of Luke, to say something important about faith and about the way God cares about me, and if I have a religious experience in which something like the divine opens itself up to me, then perhaps I am encouraged to think about it *more* if I have a text that provides a foundation or a backdrop. Perhaps, too, that same text might be itself opened up for a new interpretation by means of that experience.

Mrs. Who, for example, uses Shakespeare and the discussion of the three witches as a touchstone. But in doing so, she shifts the very ground of the text away from a literal repetition and toward the coming plot of this, new, book. It is not so much that she is faithful to Shakespeare as it is that she is faithful to the unfolding experience and to the children whose eyes and ears are not yet trained to understand what they nevertheless have a pre-comprehension of.

As Mrs. Who continues, it seems that Meg learns what she needs to learn: "if you want to help your father then you must learn patience" (L'Engle 2007, 71). The patience that Meg needs is the patience to be open to the experience without having it thoroughly explained by others. It is the patience to go back to the references Mrs. Who offers and to think them through in their intersection with the experience that is unfolding now. It is to consider how time and this experience are engaged together.

When Mrs. Which tells the other two angels to show their true form, the experience of their beauty is rather overwhelming. But this beauty, as the beauty of the whole of the planet Uriel, is for something else. The beauty is for the sake of the children's further encounter, an encounter with the Black Thing. And it is for the sake of this further encounter that Mrs. Whatsit takes the children on her back and works to translate the song of the creatures on Uriel, which loosely translated was a reading from the prophet Isaiah.

The translation, the explication, is something that Mrs. Whatsit does for the children to understand. And in the making explicit, the joy that the children experience is shared and magnified: "Calvin's hand reached out; he did not clasp her hand in his; he moved his fingers so that they were barely touching hers, but joy flowed through them, back and forth between them, around them and about them and inside them" (L'Engle 2007, 77).

Something about a religious experience, which Mrs. Whatsit marks out in her translation, then, is magnified when shared. Something about a religious experience can be beautiful, can be restful. It can be joyful. A religious experience can be marked out and understood by means of the emotions that it brings forth.

Again, however, the experience of beauty and the communal religious experience seems to be for something beyond contemplation in this book. It is for strengthening the children to look at "the dark shadow" (L'Engle 2007, 81) and to feel their own vulnerability to it and the urgency that beauty calls them toward—toward the battle with it as bearers of the beauty of the divine.

In light of the experience of the dark shadow, and the way it wends itself into the children's consciousness by hurting them and causing them to fear, the angels who named themselves as questions (or nominatives formed of questions) now try to tell the children how they will travel closer to the dark shadow—by means of the tesseract.

It is at this point, close to the midway of the book, that Mrs. Who tries to help the children understand what they do not yet understand (time-space travel) by means of their experience. She quotes Cervantes who says "experience is the mother of knowledge" (L'Engle 2007, 85). This quote forms the very heart of the book and relates directly to the title, as the ability to "wrinkle" in time is explained by means of folding a skirt so that the distance between two points shrinks. It is by means of their already developed spatial experience that something beyond their experience can come to be intuited directly as the kind of thing that it is—namely, a different way of participating or moving in time and space.

The explanation, the use of the skirt, the discussion of dimensions, helps. It prepares for the intuition that builds on the previous intuitions: "'I see!' she cried. 'I got it! For just a moment I got it! I can't possibly explain it now, but there for a second I saw it!'" (L'Engle 2007, 88–89). What this kind of physics requires, then, is not only explanation but "getting it" or intuiting its meaning in a form that is perceptible or quasi-perceptible. Experience then really does come before knowledge. Or rather, experience gives birth to knowledge, which flows out of it and reorders the experience that it has emerged from.

In traveling with the angels, the children have been given a method to their experience. With the three angels, their experience has proceeded in steps, gently. There has had to be an introduction to beauty first and then to the Black Thing and then to tessering. Science is helpful but only in context, rooted to its for-what. And if the children were going to be able to continue drawing knowledge from experience and not instead to feel despair and be unable to continue, they needed this method of preparation and its rootedness in an emotion of joy: "That's another reason we wanted to prepare you on Uriel. We thought it would be too frightening for you to see it first of all about your own beloved world" (L'Engle 2007, 99).

The method of introduction, then, is gradual. And it involves interrogating experience for its structures and its limits in order to move to those very limits themselves and to see the experience from another viewpoint. The method of this religious experience is to pause for beauty in between the battle against the dark shadow. It is to reckon with emotions, since they are part of the strength of the children, since emotions too are part of the experience.

In chapter 6, the children stop to visit the Happy Medium with the three angels. The medium has the power to enable the children to see their mothers, which for Calvin is a scene of disappointment and for Meg and Charles Wallace a scene of sadness. But in the discussion of these visions, the children understand there is much more at stake than their families.

In seeing her mother long for her father, Meg feels anger. This anger, it would seem, is very important for what is to come for the children: "You will need all your anger now" (L'Engle 2007, 110).

Then the angels take the children to Camazotz, passing through the Black Thing. It is here that Meg, Charles Wallace, and Calvin will have to try to rescue Mr. Murry. It is interesting that Calvin is set upon this mission with the other two, since he is not from their family and has not even met Mr. Murry. But Calvin in some sense is stronger, physically and emotionally, than the other two. And he loves them and is genuinely moved by Meg.

Mrs. Whatsit gives them parting gifts—a strengthening of Calvin's "ability to communicate" and a quote from Shakespeare's *The Tempest*, the recognition and affirmation of Meg's faults, and a reminder for Charles Wallace that he does not know everything.

This gifting of the children's own finitude and limits puzzles them, but also reminds them, like the affirmation of Meg's anger, that to be human (and not to will domination or power over others) is itself a gift. Correct self-description and honest wrestling with the meaning of one's limits—these apparently are part of the religious.

Charles Wallace, the youngest, is most prone to ignore his limitations. And so Mrs. Whatsit is explicit with him: "Beware of pride and arrogance, Charles, for they may betray you" (L'Engle 2007, 114).

Through these middle chapters, we see that the children's religious journey requires honest self-appraisal, an exhortation to virtue, and the recognition of community. They are bound together by sad pictures of their mothers and a quest to rescue the Murrys' father from his own mistake, from his own vulnerability. But they enjoy being together because their community, their friendship, is supported by their relationships with the messengers of God.

As a final affirmation of her support for Meg, Mrs. Who gives Meg her glasses. Something about insight is happening in this gift. Something about seeing as God does or as the messengers of God see. It is not enough for any of the children to simply be on the journey. There are requirements, too. Each one must use her or his own powers of perception to see things for what they are, for what they give themselves to be, in order to become closer to the divine.

The first experience of Camazotz is the rhythm of the people in the houses and the children at play outside of them. Meg, Calvin, and Charles Wallace try to make sense of the "perfection" and maddening sameness of the people and their interactions. They seem to have no script, no schema, on which to place this. And the fear of the people whom they encounter directly, that they will be punished for deviance, does not yet make sense for them.

When they enter CENTRAL Central Intelligence, the children remind each other that they need to pay attention to their experience. Meg reminds Charles Wallace that he will know their father when he sees him, and Calvin reminds both of the Murry children that his initial intuition that he should come to the haunted house is repeating itself in a way—he is now certain of a kind of forboding concerning their entry into CENTRAL.

In chapter 7, the children enter into CENTRAL holding hands. They find inside a central processing unit of the entire city. And their differences, their irregularity, provokes a man to report them. There is talk of reprocessing and of IT.

Everywhere around them there is a lack of freedom, a subjugation of self, and an acceptance of a foreign governance. Everywhere there is scientific accuracy and no creativity. There is no beauty grounding the legitimacy of science on Camazotz. The children feel the cold walls and see the sameness of the people and begin to realize that there is something of pain and punishment in all this order.

Meeting the man with red eyes is a first lesson in how the citizens have decentered or lost themselves and reformed themselves around a tyrannical authority. The red-eyed man tries to enter Charles Wallace's thoughts and to force the children to recite the multiplication tables. In so doing, he claims he merely wants to take on "all the burdens of thought and decision" (L'Engle 2007, 135). It is the lure of the demonic, which pretends to be divine.

The children resist his control by quoting nursery rhymes or Lincoln's Gettysburg Address or simply, in Meg's case, calling out for her father. In these acts of resistance, the children show that they are in some ways aware that the taking over of their experience, the mechanization of their consciousness, would do away with the very heart of their identity.

There is a strong sense in which the Black Thing or IT wants to argue its way into a position of standing for or imitating God. The God of the monk or the nun who rewards contemplation, who forms the telos for the rule of the order—this God sounds an awful lot like IT's self-description: "To come in to me is the last difficult decision you need ever make" (L'Engle 2007, 144).

But the difference—the fact that divine peace, the peace that passes all understanding, *rests* on taking responsibility and on self-creativity—is an important difference. Rest is the reward for taking responsibility for each moment—whether in Judaism, Islam, or Christianity. IT requires self-annihilation, requires slavery, not service. And this would be a rest that does not facilitate self-awareness.

In chapter 8, the children are taken by the enslaved Charles Wallace to see Mr. Murry. The evil of IT is discovered: IT puts to death any person who is ill or is disabled or different. Meg and Calvin declare that they are different from others and that that is important to them (L'Engle 2007, 155).

This emphasis on difference provides an experiential touchstone that allows the children to access the experience of the divine. The divine would not require them to manifest sameness. The divine lives in difference, desires difference, and celebrates it.

The chapter ends with Charles Wallace disapproving of Meg's and Calvin's resistance to IT and to the punishment or training of difference into sameness, as witnessed by the boy who is shocked each time he fails to bounce the ball appropriately. And then they see Mr. Murry imprisoned in the transparent column.

In chapter 9, Calvin and Meg discover that Mr. Murry has had the possibility of mutual recognition taken away from him: "We can see him, but he can't see us" (L'Engle 2007, 161). This freezes Mr. Murry in a kind of paralysis.

Calvin focuses on Charles Wallace and repeats the words of *The Tempest* that Mrs. Who had given to him. It is not just Mr. Murry who is in a "cloven pine," but also Charles. It is Charles who is locked in by a witch, not Meg or Calvin. Calvin, whose name is remarkably close to Caliban, tries to call Charles back. He fails because IT intervenes with violence against Charles (L'Engle 2007, 163).

The only way forward comes not in attacking Charles Wallace directly or in appealing to his former humanity as if it were simply hidden. The way forward comes when Meg puts on Mrs. Who's spectacles. Then she can move into the transparent column and help her father to take her back out. But Charles Wallace seems completely taken over by IT, and her father does not know exactly what to do.

It is this recognition that the family ties cannot save them, that evil is greater than the parent's power, that provokes the crisis of the book—the leaving behind of Charles Wallace on Camazotz. Meg is in despair at the loss of her brother, who is leading the four of them to IT: "Do something, Meg implored her father silently" (L'Engle 2007, 173).

But Mr. Murry can do nothing to help Charles, it seems. And so Meg, Calvin, and Mr. Murry are led by Charles to see IT, which is "a disembodied brain" (L'Engle 2007, 174) and "the most repellent thing" (L'Engle 2007, 175). It is the thing that is *only* a thing, that is not opening onto meaning in a generative, creative way. IT is a thing locked in itself. A thing in itself.

Against the rhythm of IT, Meg now recites the Declaration of Independence. Like Calvin had done with the Gettysburg Address facing the man with the red eyes. Channeling the behavior of Mrs. Who, quoting what is most important to them, that which thematizes individuality and freedom, they make some progress away from the pulsing, evil rhythm that would take over their very hearts with its own beating.

But in that momentary escape from IT, in her figuring out that like and equal were not the same at all, the question comes to Meg. She cannot or might not be able to destroy this disembodied brain that somehow lives. For if she could, would not everything connected to it die also?

In this scene, as in all of these middle chapters, the children's religious experience then addresses the limits of human finitude. They are presented with the dangers of becoming lost in the rhythms of objectification. But in so doing, these chapters also involve the presentation of a kind of validation that is called salvation, or, at the very least, of a desire for being saved, for being at home and safe.

In the end of chapter 9, Mr. Murry then does what he can do—he tessers after Calvin reminds him to do it. He tessers but without Charles Wallace. And it is this finite act that will force Meg to a resolution.

C: Enacting the Proper Response: Resolution

Chapters 10–12 are ones of suffering, healing, and determination. They are the moving on from a direct encounter with evil toward a more humble acknowledgment that fighting evil directly on its terms is not the way toward the divine. Instead, the novel appears to claim, the method of religious experience is not conflict, not strength and violence, but love.

In chapter 10, entitled "Absolute Zero," Mr. Murry, Calvin, and Meg are on a new planet, Ixchel, where Meg is slow to recover. Tessering away from the planet has caused them to pass through the Black Thing or Dark Shadow and she has been severely injured as a result. Mr. Murry was almost at the point of collapse into resignation—re-signing himself to IT—but the children's appearance allowed him to regain some strength. As he tells Calvin on their escape to Ixchel, "I had almost come to the conclusion that I was wrong to fight, that IT was right after all" (L'Engle 2007, 181).

Mr. Murry, it seems, found his way to Camazotz and to IT by accident. His refusal of IT's dominance, then, allowed him to survive the contact. But Charles Wallace, whom the three left behind with the man with red eyes—Charles "thought he could deliberately go into IT and return. He trusted too much to his own strength" (L'Engle 2007, 182).

Resistance and direct aggression against IT have their limitations. Staking out one's experience as a negation of IT will not work. The resistance of the star that the three children saw with the Happy Medium may be praiseworthy, but it is not ultimately what will allow religious experience to continue. What is needed is not direct conflict but something else.

As Meg regains her ability to experience, after listening to Calvin and her father speak, she realizes that she is ice cold, injured, and bereft of a fundamental hope: "Her father had not saved her" (L'Engle 2007, 187).

This sense of being bereft of one's moorings, of one's loved ones, seems to be particularly problematic for Meg. What is unspoken by Meg is that her father had in fact tried to save her. He had tried to return her gift, but she rebuked him. Her definition of being "saved" is what is most problematic. She cannot believe that there are limits to what her father or she can do. She is disappointed in her own vulnerability and in her own finitude. She has misunderstood what it means to be a parent or a human being: "All her faults were uppermost in her now, and they were no longer helping her. . . . Disappointment was as dark and corrosive in her as the Black Thing" (L'Engle 2007, 189).

This sense of abandonment and failure pulls not only Meg but also Calvin and Mr. Murry in its wake. They are paralyzed and cannot figure out what to do. In addition they have no sense of self-righteous anger, since their own health is a witness against them in favor of Meg's very real, very dangerous condition: "She did not realize that she was as much in the power of the Black Thing" (L'Engle 2007, 190).

In their paralysis, however, Calvin and Mr. Murry seem to still have hope. And they hope within their limitations for a transcendent God that will work with them: "all things work together for good . . . to them who are called according to his purpose" (L'Engle 2007, 190).

The comparison of IT and God hinges on the difference, as Meg said when confronting IT, between like and equal, between slavery and freedom, between erasing finitude and celebrating it. The question that the three are left with on Ixchel is how to determine the method of goodness, or love, or the divine such that it can open their experience toward what it is that they should do.

They already know that experience cannot simply be the passive resignation toward another's will. It has to be, instead, an active taking up of something that lies implicit in the being called, being sent. There is something given that can shine forth like a star if the person attending is in the proper attitude. But they cannot go any further without others, without a tradition and a community to support them.

At the end of chapter 10, the three "Things" approach Mr. Murry and the children, and they bring healing and understanding. It is in their touch, which is more powerful than the touch or the voice of her father and Calvin, that Meg first experiences healing and hope: "a reassuring sense of safety flowed through her . . . as the beast touched her" (L'Engle 2007, 193).

As chapters 11 and 12 unfold, we see that these Beasts, who are without eyes and therefore are literally unseeing, help to re-educate Meg toward returning to the proper attitude. They help her again, as if for the first time, to immerse herself in the enactment of religious experience. Relationally and emotionally oriented, these beings offer her their care, their touch, their food. And it is through them that Meg heals. It is with them that she comes to see that religious experience is not only an emotion of anger or a political argument—not fighting or resistance—but rather a love that stakes its claim as a response to the other. It is hospitality that is the code of religious experience, as well as its method and its attitude.

In chapter 11, indeed even in its title, we see that Meg is able to enlarge the notion of family toward an inter-species concept of care. The Thing, the Beast, that cares for her is something she begins to call "Aunt." And it is the Aunt that helps to assuage the disappointment at the father or the mother (as for Calvin). It is the extension of love away from a centrifugal, private realm toward a more global reach that allows religious experience to unfold in times of great challenge and difficulty.

It is as strangers that Calvin and Mr. Murry speak to the inhabitants of Ixchel. And it is as offering hospitality that the creatures of Ixchel respond to them, even though they are unhappy that the Murrys and Calvin have come from Camazotz.

The creatures are less moved by Mr. Murry's story than by Meg's injuries. They see that she was injured by the Black Thing and that she is in danger. It is toward her that they move to save her from the icy coldness of IT's lingering effect upon her. Despite Meg being a different species, despite the danger to their own society that Meg might represent, the creatures help her. They provide care and comfort, which for Meg, makes a very clear distinction between IT and goodness: "IT could only give pain, never relieve it" (L'Engle 2007, 197–198).

This care and hospitality that the creatures, the beasts, offer—this goodness or healing or beauty—is the opportunity to further mutual recognition. No longer trapped in a "cloven pine," the humans do not need to see the other person's face to experience togetherness. But this recognition comes slowly and by means of great challenge. For the humans, Meg, cannot understand how touch, feeling, could be the primary sense that a body could have. And the beasts, in their turn, cannot understand how touch could be submerged in a human in favor of the foregrounding of sight as the most discriminating sense: "We do not understand what this means, to *see*" (L'Engle 2007, 199).

The diversity in body, then, is not insurmountable. In fact, it appears again as necessary. For in the reckoning with difference, all of them come to see more clearly the common capacity to seek the good, to welcome and attend to one another, to understand. And it is this unity by means of difference that marks out the shared journey of religious experience.

Difference is what provides the intuition of a shared method—a method rooted in bodily affirmation, in bodily attentiveness to particularities. It is not by causing bodies to be undone or mechanized, ignored or surpassed, that religious experience comes. Rather, religious experience is possible only by causing bodies to be respected, cared for, and centered around a mutual understanding. Religious experience is therefore an affirmation of finite bodily life and about seeking the meaning of bodily togetherness, in its multiplicity and overlap, but most especially in its diversity. We are many bodies and our togetherness is predicated on and arises out of our fundamental differences and possibilities of insight.

This hopefulness, however, is hard won. What is hardest for Meg is that the hospitality is itself limited. Hospitality does not on its own determine what should be done. Out of hospitality comes rather the urgency of determining what to do and the resolution to do what is appropriate, with full knowledge of the risks. Because the host and the guest are intimately linked, they need to talk together about what is to be done. Each bears responsibility to the other. In a shared decision, each must be involved. And thus, Aunt Beast says, it is not appropriate "to go rushing back to Camazotz," as Meg has suggested, but instead Meg "must wait until [she is] more calm" (L'Engle 2007, 202).

To be a guest is to share responsibility for one's body. And so Meg begins to learn that waiting seems to be as important as Aunt Beast's caring for Meg's wounded body. It is in the waiting that the proper action will show itself. Hospitality requires time to reckon with each other and, through that reckoning, to approach the divine, who is always implicated in hospitality, in the right way. It takes time to rescue each other such that the shared journey toward the divine, toward the goodness that stands in for the divine, can proceed.

When Meg awakens from a deep sleep brought on by the singing of Aunt Beast, she learns something important. To Meg, Aunt Beast attests that the beings on Ixchel are in fact "fighting the Black Thing" and that "Good helps us, the stars help us, perhaps what you call *light* helps us, love helps us" (L'Engle 2007, 205). This is the first inkling to Meg that love, not fighting, is the method by which religious experience unfolds. That religious experience unfolds not solely in setting oneself *against* the Black Thing but in setting oneself *with* those who are also allied with love.

In chapter 12, Meg is caught in the quandary that defines the book. The angels are finally there on Ixchel with them, but the angels cannot help. Rushing in to save Charles Wallace "is not our way," Mrs. Whatsit says (L'Engle 2007, 213). And this means that Meg has to look more carefully at herself, at her rages and unhappiness, and at her relationship with Charles Wallace. Meg discovers that it is she who must go back to Camazotz. However, she must go in the right way, or she will not save him. As Mrs. Whatsit reminds Meg, "We want nothing from you that you do without grace . . . or . . . without understanding" (L'Engle 2007, 215).

Meg must proceed on the drive to save Charles Wallace, on the active and teleological facet of religious experience, by "grace" and "understanding." She must understand that the task is given to her as hers from elsewhere. She must understand that the givenness of the task is also the preparation and the support that she has received throughout her journey. The hospitality and friendship and love *gives* the task, enacts it as one's own. Finally, she must see that very understanding as itself grace, as itself the proof of itself. It is not only grace and understanding that work in tandem; rather, they are the same thing or close to the same thing and mutually refer to one another.

When Meg sees this, when she sees it must be and thus that it can be she who saves Charles Wallace—when Meg sees that it is her whole relationship with her brother that enables her to reach him, then all the effects from the Black Thing drop away. It is her commitment to him that provides her with the understanding. It is her recovery of their relationship, of her having been given him by grace, that enables her to go to him.

Helping her father and Calvin to understand this, however, proves diffi-cult. It is not by chance then that Mrs. Whatsit teaches them about sonnets. Only by remarking on the vicissitudes of form in a poem can they understand that religious experience makes its demands by way of simultaneously af-firming their freedom: "You're given the form, but you have to write the sonnet yourself" (L'Engle 2007, 219). The form is given. The sonnet is tradition. But within that tradition, the expression is what one finds when one bears the form into the time of one's own lived experience.

When Mrs. Which then takes Meg to Camazotz, she leaves Meg with another gift: "Yyou hhave ssomethinngg that ITT hhass nnott. Thiss ssome-thinngg iss yyourr only wweapponn" (L'Engle 2007, 223). Alone, Meg must find her way and find her way to use this "wweapponn." As she walks toward IT and Charles Wallace, Meg reckons with the moments of religious experi-ence that are personal and isolated, even if the whole is not, even if the whole opens out onto the community. And this reckoning is necessary for her. For there IS something personal about this whole journey: "I have to resist IT by myself" (L'Engle 2007, 225). For each person, for Meg, religious experience is "mine."

When Meg reaches CENTRAL, she remembers that she is loved: "Mrs. Whatsit loves me" (L'Engle 2007, 226). This memory of love, perhaps the memory of Calvin's kiss and her father's concern and hug and terms of endearment—these memories stand her well.

For it is love that is a weapon by not being one. Not a weapon of domina-tion or power or violence. Love instead is what attests to and affirms and recovers relationships. Love is the method, even better than a weapon, that overcomes the challenges of religious experience as it connects people to-gether: "Love. That was what she had that IT did not have" (L'Engle 2007, 228).

By loving Charles Wallace, who appeared before her with IT, she was able to separate him from IT's dominance. For there is nothing that love cannot conquer, Meg is sure of that. And while she cannot love IT, she can love her brother. And suddenly he, Charles Wallace, is freed and there with her. And just as suddenly they are tessered back to earth, having dealt a huge blow to IT (L'Engle 2007, 230).

The ending of the novel is the accomplishment of two rescues, Mr. Murry and Charles Wallace. But it is also the possibility of joy and love, which all those around her feel in light of being tessered back to earth. It is a joy and love that goes even further than the restitution of the family: "Meg . . . felt a flooding of joy and love that was even greater and deeper than the joy and love which were already there" (L'Engle 2007, 232).

Religious experience is ultimately, for L'Engle's novel anyway, about love and, through love, joy. It is ecstatic reconnection with friends and fami-ly, with other strangers. It is the opening outward toward the divine that rushes in to affirm and grow that experience toward the infinite possibility of these emotions.

CONNECTING HEIDEGGER AND L'ENGLE

Having explored Heidegger's works and L'Engle's novel, I would now like briefly to connect the two in ways that have been implicit throughout the previous sections. In doing so, I hope to open the reader onto further research possibilities within the phenomenology of religious experience.

First, however, I would like to take up a review of scholarship on the novel. Unfortunately, while there has been some critical reception of L'Engle's work and of *A Wrinkle in Time* in particular, there has not been much. What has been written is mostly polemical, with one side faulting L'Engle for missing the boat with respect to contemporary feminism or for ineffective plot resolution or for being either too religious or not religious enough, and the other side defending her from these claims. I will share some examples.

First, the detractors. Katherine Schneebaum in "Finding a Happy Medium: The Design for Womanhood in *A Wrinkle in Time*" argues that Meg is a central character who simply repeats an injunction for women to be traditional models of femininity. Thus, Schneebaum faults L'Engle for not writing a more explicitly feminist narrative: "Meg is portrayed as in her element, her 'happiest medium' as it were, when she is operating in the traditionally feminine sphere of maternal love as redeeming force. The final message is that a girl becomes a woman only when she voluntarily takes on the role of moral leader and keeper of love, subordinating her other interests and capabilities to this one" (Schneebaum 1990, 36). This characterization of Schneebaum's, I think, misses the entire possibility of Meg as bending her own gender, of the multiply-gendered power of the three angels, and the androgyny of Aunt Beast. The "howl" of IT as Meg vanquishes it suggests that Meg has not "subordinated" other interests to love but rather refused to subordinate herself and instead empowered herself by means of love for all other good things. Hospitality is not gendered feminine. It is, as xenia demonstrates in ancient Greek texts, a move toward the divine. (And Anne-Frederique Mochel-Caballero in a more recent article, agrees.)

From a different standpoint, William Blackburn hounds L'Engle for her mischaracterization of evil, her dogmatism with respect to her inclusion of Christian elements in the text, and her ultimate failure to help real children develop their real identities in a literary way. His backhanded compliments to L'Engle aside, Blackburn's piece is close to a full-tilt opposition to the novel. And thus his appraisal is interesting.

When Blackburn suggests that L'Engle's characterization of evil is too simplistic, he argues that IT is a code for any "signatory to the Warsaw Pact" (Blackburn 1985, 129). But this is a throwaway criticism. It just sets up Blackburn to address what he thinks is a knockout blow at the novel: "Evil is always presented as foreign to [Meg's] nature and to that of her brother" (Blackburn 1985, 131). This, it seems, is the way that L'Engle fails to do as good a job as C. S. Lewis or Hawthorne or any of Blackburn's favorite books for children.

Blackburn of course is rather silent on the way that evil is within Meg after she passes through its shadow. And of course it is true that Charles Wallace has in fact chosen evil by thinking himself superior to it and entering it. But Blackburn is out to put the novel in its place. And thus his reading of *A Wrinkle in Time* is more political than phenomenological.

In contrast to Schneebaum and Blackburn, Karen Schiller and Susannah Sheffer see a value to Meg, especially in her pedagogical possibilities. In "Inviting Children to Imagine Peace," Schiller argues that Meg's love is an important lesson to other children about politics: "Without our love and this attendant grace, we tend to fall prey to authoritarian thinking, to conformity, and to inaction and despair. The love for ideas and values, for the wonder of nature and science, and a grace-filled love for others are what enable Meg to ultimately take down IT and save her family" (Schiller 2019, 68). This I believe is an important point, as the novel does make political arguments relevant to children who believe that religious experience, for example, should be taken into their everyday relations with others. But Schiller does not push the implications very far.

Sheffer in "Breaking the Rules: A Defense of *A Wrinkle in Time*" writes against those who would ban *A Wrinkle in Time* by emphasizing the pedagogical possibilities for the young readers who are most likely to take it up. Sheffer claims that L'Engle's novel shows children "it is not only superheroes who triumph. It is regular children, regular people . . . who gather the courage to act, who don't necessarily end up more beautiful than when they began, but who do nonetheless end the book with someone's hand in theirs because it is possible to be loved anyway" (Sheffer 2002, 456–457).

Having looked briefly at some of the critical work on L'Engle's novel, I hope it will become clearer how a phenomenological reading can obviate polemics in favor of seeking out what is given in the novel in the manner in which it is given. This story can in fact be seen as offering something far more significant than a story to our judgment. Rather, it can be viewed, in connection with Heidegger's work, as making possible a concrete meditation on the meaning of a religious project and of a finite, human existence. Having already suggested this fact above, I will now briefly call the reader's attention to a few salient points about resolve, stretching, and enactment.

Finally freed of her deep disappointment at the end of the novel, Meg's willingness to go rescue her brother is the product of anticipatory resoluteness being demonstrated by all those gathered on Ixchel. Meg's decision, in light of their support and in light of the tradition of Christian readings of the human history of great texts, is a total commitment to what the situation may entail. Her calm approach, her gathering herself back in, means that she is capable of understanding, of disclosing, to herself first and to the others gathered there, the possibility of her being a whole. This wholeness gives a determinate place to all her faults, and allows her to leap ahead of the others to engage in an authentic, resolute process of proceeding toward her brother.

However, this resolve is not possible without a sense of her heritage, without taking up a stand on the tradition of religious experience that has come before. Now I would argue that the tradition in the novel is most clearly represented by Mrs. Who and her quotations. These quotations, and the works from which they come, stand in stark contrast to the novelty of the physics experiments that Mr. and Mrs. Murry have enacted.

It is by means of the works of these past authors, and most particularly those of literature, that Mrs. Who serves and supports the children by connecting their future, which she has some knowledge of, to their having-been. She connects the children to a time they did not know—but which has helped to create them—by making it part of the reflection on what and how they have learned within their experience of school.

To be human beings is to be exposed, through a process of education, to a heritage into which they are thrown. Furthermore, this human heritage, Mrs. Who implies, makes possible not just an act of mutual understanding but a journeying toward the horizon of religious experience. This human heritage prepares them for the call of conscience.

Provided that they take up this heritage and interpret it, providing they become hermeneuticists, the children can find their own ability to encounter angels, to seek goodness, and to suspend evil. Provided they dwell with this heritage, the children can move resolutely into a creative leaping ahead such that others follow.

A most salient moment of taking up the tradition comes in Meg's echo of Mrs. Whatsit's confession of love. She is quoting Mrs. Whatsit to herself, in the face of IT. But in hearing those words to her in a new context, Meg starts to become aware that she can really love, that she is made, even in anxiety, to direct herself toward a community in which each *Dasein* is herself or himself an ownmost potentiality for being a whole. And in this love she moves out of herself in a very genuine, very resolute way.

In front of IT, in front of the direct challenge to both her future and her having-been, she knew it was dangerous to stand there and to love. But it was in the danger, in her inescapable, authentic being aware of death and of herself that allowed her to be for Charles Wallace. It was in being free for death that she could be free to become what she was not yet. Only as seeing, with Mrs. Who, the whole of the tradition of those "stars" which illuminate their lives can Meg see her act as "a possibility that [she] inherited and yet has chosen" (Heidegger 1996, 366).

This choice of Meg's, to go where her situation and her past have cast her, is to stand within the parousia of Paul. It is to enact a rather hopeless looking stance of weakness in order to make the comportment of one's life ready for the interruption of the divine. In this moment in which she chooses to go back to Camazotz, Meg becomes for the first time a particular, historical actress that, as soon as she enacts the choice, resonates retroactively through her life: "the resoluteness of the self against the inconstancy of dispersion is in itself a steadiness that has been stretched along . . . in such a way that in such constancy it is in the Moment for what is world-historical in the actual situation" (Heidegger 1996, 371). Her resolution, in other words, has been prepared or "stretched along" from the first moment of her longing for her father. Far from being subject to her emotions as to alien things, Meg shows that what truly defines her is the "constancy" of being loved and of loving such that in this "Moment" she approaches a historical choice for the situation.

In going back for Charles Wallace, Meg makes authentic history—the ability of love to take on a specific form and style, a specific way of defeating that which would defile love—and in doing so goes beyond the quotations of Mrs. Who and the long-standing powers of the stars who became angels. Meg is not billions of years old. She is 13. And in being 13, Meg does something momentous. In the words of Heidegger, Meg "*undoes* the character of making-present of the today and weans one off of the conventions of the they" (Heidegger 1996, 372).

The ones on Camazotz, with their submission, are the they. They follow IT. But Meg "undoes" IT and makes possible the retrieval of creative, future-oriented enactment not just for her but for others as well. It is Meg whose efforts cause IT to "howl." And in IT's weakness, the Angels can come in and take Meg and Charles Wallace home.

No longer is Meg "caught up unexpectedly in shadows" (Heidegger 1996, 372) but instead she engages in what Heidegger might call "a historical destruction" (Heidegger 1996, 372)—or what Derrida might call a deconstruction—whereby what we thought we knew about God or about love or about little girls, doctrinally and dogmatically, must be repeated and undone by way of Meg's enactment of her own, quite powerful existence.

NOTES

1. Phenomenologically, we might enlist Meg as we follow Derrida in *Structure and Genesis* who says that, even for Husserl, intentionality is not just theoretical but also existential. Meg

lives her understanding in her body. Her experiences of objects and others are lived. They are not just thoughts.

2. Charles has a reputation for being able to read other people's minds. But what he himself says is that he is capable of paying attention quite closely (L'Engle 2007, 36). Charles sees relationships. And his power of explication is the complement to Meg's power of intuition and expression. Charles sets in motion. Meg follows through.

Chapter Five

Toward a Phenomenology of Education in *Merci Suárez Changes Gears*

INTRODUCTION

In previous chapters, we have seen how a phenomenology of temporality or of emotion or of religious experience or of gender and child development can help to appreciate the complexity of children's literature. In each case, phenomenology as a method of reading allows for those who would teach these books to or share them with children to investigate, together with those children, what meaningful tensions or contradictions emerge.

In this final chapter, I would like to turn our attention to something that has been implicit in all of the novels we have examined so far—namely, a philosophy of education. Novels for children or about children almost always describe a situation of learning, usually though not always within a school, in which the child finds herself or himself thrown. Indeed, in our own discussions here, whether it was about the mouse child, who forms a school, or about Wilbur the pig who learns to read and write by means of Charlotte the spider's life-saving sacrifice, or about Scout's reckoning with her school pageant—we have already been enmeshed in stories of education.

The way we will approach a philosophy of education in this chapter is, consistent with the other chapters, by means of phenomenology. Our literary focus will be on the recent Newbery Medal–winning book, *Merci Suárez Changes Gears*, by Meg Medina. It is the story of a sixth-grader, Merci Suárez. The focus of the story is the back-and-forth motion she performs between the independent school she attends, Seaward Pines, and the intergenerational, Cuban immigrant family she lives with at home. Our phenomenological focus will once again begin with Husserl and Merleau-Ponty. But it will shift quickly into two figures who have taken up phenomenological themes in education, John Dewey and Paolo Freire.

What we will see by examining Dewey's *Democracy and Education* and Freire's *Pedagogy of the Oppressed* is that education must take its method to arise from and remain rooted in the lived experience of the students. And this means that education must be committed to helping students to reflect on their situation, to identify its tensions, and to affirm and empower their resolution of those tensions by means of a program of deep reflection. These insights coming out of Dewey and Freire will be ones that I hope to show as a necessary conclusion for any rich phenomenological description.

My reason for that conclusion is that I see the logic of phenomenology as inherently democratic, as involving a shared task whose method is mutual recognition. Phenomenology has disproven a mind-body dualism and, using its richer descriptions of embodied consciousness, has gone on to demonstrate quite clearly that we are these embodiments within an ongoing situation of intersubjectivity and intercorporeality. These demonstrations thus support the idea that phenomenology's trajectory, its telos, is the enactment or the ongoing development of our possibility for a shared democratic life.

The chapter first returns to a discussion of the phenomenology of Husserl and of Merleau-Ponty. It will do so in order to move toward later figures who write explicitly about education. In doing so, this chapter will bring phenomenology back to its roots and open it onto its future in order to argue that the vision Meg Medina gives of education in Merci's life is a phenomenological one. And it is one that any of us (who are concerned to mirror or to model our communal life on our experiential structures) should try to bring about.

Medina's description of Merci's family and of Seaward Pines coming together is a plea for a vision of education that centers itself around the attempt to reduce oppression and to empower reflection by means of using Merci's lived experience and her relations with other people (her teachers, her fellow students, and her family members) to build her up and to resolve what appear to be the contradictions of her life. Merci moves, as any phenomenologist and any committed person should, toward the democratic values of mutual recognition and shared governance. And she does so by taking her concepts and categories, her acts of understanding, from within the structure and events of her lived experience.

PHENOMENOLOGICAL THEORY:
HUSSERL, MERLEAU-PONTY, DEWEY, AND FREIRE ON
THE PHENOMENOLOGY OF CHILDHOOD AND EDUCATION

A. Husserl and Merleau-Ponty on the Method of Thinking

In "Human Sciences and Phenomenology," Merleau-Ponty describes the essential project of Husserl's phenomenology as the following: "the essence of his project is the assertion of a rationality which is tied directly to experience, and the investigation of a method that empowers thinking *simultaneously* about interiority and exteriority" (Merleau-Ponty 2010, 320, my emphasis). This "empowered" thought that brings together a thought about what is immanent to me (my experience) and what is transcendent to me (what my experience is *of*) is once again an assertion about the centrality of intentionality. Our reason is "tied directly to experience," and our ability to use concepts and develop categorial distinctions emerge from that experience and not from somewhere else. What is "exterior" to me is always tied to the noetic acts by which I make sense of it. And my acts are always making use of the previous givenness of the noema whose appearance I focus upon.

What is new here, perhaps, is that my thinking as a phenomenologist is for Merleau-Ponty to be "simultaneously" about inside and outside. If for Husserl we phenomenologists use a zigzag approach to description—first the noematic layer and then the noetic or vice versa—for Merleau-Ponty we need to begin to think in terms of "both/and." As intentionalities, we are required to empower ourselves to move not only back and forth but further outward and onward, toward the origin and toward further insight that take both the object and the subject up together, as does the situation itself.

Part of what empowers the possibility of this simultaneity was already visible in Husserl's early work. As Husserl says in *Ideas*, "everything is *connected* by eidetic relations, thus especially noesis and noema" (Husserl 1983, 227, my emphasis). Because the object and the subject, because the noematic appearance and the noetic act, are given together as participating in the larger interaction, because noesis and noema are taken up together within the higher essence of lived experience as such—therefore the perceiver can come to see any essence of a concrete lived experience as rooted in her or his own capacity. I see this *as* what it shows itself to be because I am ready for it. Because, as Husserl claims, the noema or object of intuition is "an index, pointing to a noetic intentionality that pertains to it" (Husserl 1960, 45–46). The object and I are simultaneous because it presents itself to me as the route toward my not-yet, toward the person I will become in getting to know it better.

In light of Husserl's characterizing the object as an index for my acts of recognizing its meaning, Merleau-Ponty describes the process of seeing and hearing a concert. This concert, perhaps of Mozart, is presented in a flow, right now, in which myself, the rest of the audience, the musicians and the music are given together, simultaneously.

However, my grasp of the *meaning of the simultaneity* is not. Rather, the concert "is not understood in an instant, for it appears in the executions of the artists" (Merleau-Ponty 2010, 327). When I do hear the concert as a good "execution" of a number of pieces by Mozart, for example, that is because I "thematize" the work and, in so doing, allow the concert itself, and the movements of the artists, to bring to the fore of my consciousness an educative reflection on what the concert is to be heard *as* being: "through concrete experience, I grasp an intellectual structure *which imposes itself* on my ego. It *exceeds* my singularity and the contingency of the everyday by *conferring a sense* on the series of events, although this sense is not immediately given" (Merleau-Ponty 2010, 327).

The simultaneity of the givenness of musicians, audience, and music that my thinking appropriates by reflecting on the flowing situation of the concert, then, is a period of education. I "grasp" meaning "through" experience. And this education, this grasping, occurs because experience takes time to unfold and because experience makes demands on me to see and hear it (and my union with it) more than as what it initially appears to be.

The fact that I am always late in my arrival to the significance of the concert, as it were, and that I have already been hearing it as what I finally grasp it to be—these are facts that are tensions propelling the motion of my education along. As Merleau-Ponty notes, the thing, the concert, "imposes itself" on me such that, in "exceeding" my grasp of it, it nevertheless *gives* me something. It "confers a sense" that exceeds the manner in which the concert was initially given in my experience while also *always already having been that*. It reaches into my past acts of listening, into my current understanding of music, into the possibility of my being both a perceiving and a reflecting person at the same time, and presents itself to me *as* having the essential structure of a concert presenting the works of Mozart, a classical music concert, and a very good execution, etc.

I do not necessarily stop listening to the music when I "get" its significance. My reflection occurs "through" my hearing and develops it. The simultaneity of the situation's components (musicians, music, audience) give me to myself in a simultaneity that is also a back-and-forth between perception and reflection. Any grasping of the significance, even after the concert is ended, projects itself within the flow of the perception. I hear or perceive toward concepts within experience.

On the way toward my simultaneously grasping the concert and myself as a concert-goer and a subject who is learning about music, there is newness—I have learned or brought home to myself what it is—and there is continuity—it has already engaged me as what it is in coming to see it as such:

"thought envelops the object, but *at the same time* concrete perception is guided by the essence as something that it presupposes" (Merleau-Ponty 2010, 327). My empowered thinking, then, comes to see how the essence of the concert that I have established has also been the concert's own gift to me. I have "enveloped" the concert in my thought "at the same time" that I have been "guided" by that concert itself. In my education I have never left behind perception for reflection. Rather, the situation has helped them work together.

Learning, then, involves being led by experience to find its essential structures. Learning involves a transcendence of the limits of this or that particular experience toward an essence that remains rooted in the particular, immanent givens of each situation. Learning is coming home to simultaneity as the situation of intentionality, as the co-development of perception and reflection *with* and *in* the world, the situation, the relationships with others.

Pedagogy, meanwhile, for phenomenology, at least as Merleau-Ponty's argument would go, would therefore be the process of empowerment. It would involve helping oneself and others attend to the way in which experience transcends itself by imposing itself, the way in which I transcend myself and become capable of a "both/and" grasp of not only the concert but my act of perceiving it. Pedagogy would be holding together two things that *seem* to be distinct so as to allow them to show me their origin and goal together in the event of meaning.

In this way, empowerment just is the simultaneous understanding of interior and exterior, preparation and fulfillment, passivity and agency. Pedagogy just is the ability to use experience as the motor of my education and of my becoming more and more capable of perceiving complex meanings: "in reality what Husserl sought . . . was . . . a notion of spontaneous organization which transcends the activity-passivity distinction of which the visible configuration of experience is emblematic" (Merleau-Ponty 2010, 330). Teaching, learning—if it is to be phenomenological—can be neither simply active nor passive. It must, instead, be "spontaneous" and "transcend" that "distinction" and pursue a greater resolution, a way back into the experience itself that takes account of my—our—perspective and life.

B. John Dewey's *Democracy and Education*

Like Edmund Husserl, Dewey bemoans the continued adherence to the conviction that the mind is separate from the body. Such a dualism does not get experience correctly and, sadly, is still the dominant assumption in the methods and practice of education. Dewey's major work *Democracy and Education* is therefore an attempt to rid education of this dualistic prejudice.

Dewey spends a great deal of time trying to describe and define what experience is as such. First and foremost, experience for Dewey is "not primarily cognitive" (Dewey 1916, 164). This is because what happens in experience is an interaction between us and things, between us and each other, which is bodily and emotive. When we divorce the body from the school experience we commit both teachers and students to "strain" and friction:

> the nervous *strain and fatigue* which result with both teacher and pupil are a necessary consequence of the abnormality of the situation in which bodily activity is *divorced* from the perception of meaning. . . . The neglected body having no organized fruitful channels of activity breaks forth, without knowing why or how, into meaningless boisterousness (Dewey 1916, 165).

For Dewey, then, although he does not speak in terms of intentionality or of embodiment as do Husserl and Merleau-Ponty, it is clear that "bodily activity" is itself the "perception of meaning." And thus what both teacher and student must do is to realign their perceptions, together, toward the simultaneity of action and meaning, interior and exterior. The danger of not doing so, then, is not just "strain and fatigue" but a wholesale rejection of the very process of education which at worst is violent outburst and at best "meaningless boisterousness."

The way to achieve the simultaneity of body and meaning for Dewey is to require any pedagogical theory to show its pedigree. It must come out of experience, since it is in experience that theory can be creative and fruitful: "an ounce of experience is better than a ton of theory simply because it is only in experience that any theory has vital and verifiable significance" (Dewey 1916, 169). We cannot make a child, or anyone, think a certain way if her or his experience provides a compelling alternative.

We are not in control, ever, of how another person thinks. At best, for Dewey, we can persuade others by means of rooting our theory in their experience: "Thinking is thus equivalent to an explicit rendering of the intelligent element in our experience" (Dewey 1916, 171). In other words, phenomenologically, our pedagogy must make explicit what is already implicit.

What Dewey sees as the edge of pedagogy, a pedagogy that in 1916 was already fractured and fragmented, is the deadening of human beings. As Charles Dickens showed in *Hard Times* with the Gradgrind approach, we need to concern ourselves with what goes on in school as it connects with what goes on outside of school:

> No one has ever explained why children are so full of questions outside of the school . . . and the conspicuous absence of the display of curiosity about the subject matter of school lessons. Reflection on this striking contrast will throw light upon the question of how far customary school conditions supply *a context of experience* in which *problems naturally suggest themselves* (Dewey 1916, 183, my emphasis).

Human beings rely on experience for a "context" for their concepts. Experience is not the vague sketch of truer, eternal ideas. Rather, experience is the petri dish of ideas. The "problems" that education runs on, its motor, "suggest themselves" within experience and concepts arise out of the resolution of those problems.

If, as Dewey believes, "all thinking is original" (Dewey 1916, 187), then it seems that what teachers ought to do is to think like and with their students. If they pose problems within the student's grasp of the world and of other people, the student will come to the ideas as her or his own "original" creation. And thus learning in each case will be the student's very own. This process for Dewey relies heavily on a rather phenomenological notion of "situation."

First and foremost for Dewey a child who is authentically to learn needs a "genuine situation" that sustains her or his interest "for its own sake" (Dewey 1916, 192). Constructing this "situation," the teacher then removes herself or himself from the role of authority as much as possible so that a "genuine problem" can develop in this situation that stimulates the child's thought and responsibility for further investigation and solutions (Dewey 1916, 192). There is, then, even at the level of pedagogy, a commitment to democratic structures and the disappearance of central authority.

This commitment to democracy is so far-ranging, however, because it is not simply a political conviction. Rather, democracy is in the nature of the simultaneity of things and meaning, of embodiment and meaning, of experience as such: "It is the nature of an experience to have implications *which go far beyond* what is at first consciously noted in it. Bringing these connections or implications to consciousness *enhances the meaning* of the experience" (Dewey 1916, 255, my emphasis). What is implicit takes us to a new "far beyond" place, which is unstructured politically or personally. Learning is a commitment to transcendence.

Dewey turns to the practical carrying out of an educative program when he brings together an integrated curriculum and an integrated society:

> the tendency to assign separate values to each study and to regard the curriculum in its entirety as a kind of composite made by the aggregation of segregated values is a result of the *isolation* of social groups and classes. Hence it is the business of education in a democratic social group to struggle against this *isolation* in order that the various interests may *reinforce and play* into one another (Dewey 1916, 292, my emphasis).

If math or science is to matter to human beings, these subjects must not be "aggregated" but rather reflect a whole curriculum that appeals to whole persons. "Struggle" against "isolation" and thus against the tendency to create separate "groups and classes" is thus a problem both for pedagogy and for government. And for the same reasons. One cannot be fully human if one is not able to "reinforce" one's concepts by being free to "play" with others. One cannot understand math without music and literature.

Such a vision of education, though, runs up against the tendency of schools, even now, to view the classroom as a model factory job. The students are at work. Their play is often an enactment of *Lord of the Flies* on an unsupervised aggregate of swing sets and dangerous ground. Rather than seeing education to be enforced work, Dewey instead declares that "the problem of education in a democratic society is . . . to construct a course of studies which makes thought a guide of free practice for all and which makes leisure a reward of accepting *responsibility for service*, rather than a state of exemption from it" (Dewey 1916, 305, my emphasis).

Study and play, school and home, are not opposites. Rather, there is a continuity of "service" and "responsibility" that allows education properly, i.e., democratically, conceived to reward "free practice" with increased agency. Play then would be another name for student-directed activities, which would be of a piece with teacher-led activities.

This vision of study as play, of responsibility as rewarded, entails the superseding of custom by creativity. For Dewey, this means that the classroom, like the democratic society in which it occurs, must value diversity of persons:

> A society based on custom will utilize individual variations only up to a limit of conformity with usage; uniformity is the chief ideal within each class. A progressive society counts individual variations as precious since it finds in them the means of its own growth. Hence a democratic society must in consistency with its ideal allow for intellectual freedom and the play of diverse gifts and interests in its educational measures (Dewey 1916, 357).

There can be no dichotomy between school and society. If the society is based on mutual recognition and participation, then the school must exemplify that. Each person as an "individual variation" must be valued for their "diverse gifts and interests." The child, the student is not meant to answer to a dictatorial authority. Rather she or he is meant to bring a self to bear on the process that has the potential to shift that process as "individual variations" press forward together toward "growth" of the group and of the practice of education itself.

There is no place in a curriculum, Dewey implies, for borders to be artificially imposed. If the students are to be able to experience learning as a desire in itself, as a responsibility they freely and willingly take on, then what occurs in school must be able to be applied, exemplified, modified, and extended by what occurs outside of school: "The learning in school should be continuous with that out of school. There should be a free interplay between the two. This is possible only when there are numerous points of contact between the social interests of the one and the other" (Dewey 1916, 416).

Education, then, is "numerous points of contact." It is the "interplay" between family, school, and society. Education is the development of citizens who are not compartmentalized but are, rather, empowered.

This democratic vision that Dewey codified in 1916, with the publication of *Democracy and Education*, is something he remained deeply committed to throughout his career. As late as 1938, in response to the growth of fascism worldwide, Dewey continued to develop and refine his earlier insights. These insights are collected in a series of lectures from the 1930s entitled *Experience and Education.*

Continuing with his earlier phenomenology of experience, Dewey later spoke even more directly of the need to derive education's force from the lived experience of the students. The role of the educator, however, becomes more and more important insofar as it is a student's experience that generates the possibility to pose and solve meaningful problems.

In order to be effective at freeing students to be democratic, the educator must be able to see further and see according to what is latent or implicit in each experience she sets up for her students: "it is the business of the educator to see in what direction an experience is heading" (Dewey 1938, 32). This long or future-oriented view of the teacher, what one might call with Husserl a horizontal view, must also, however, be accompanied by a view of the conditions or contexts that the present experience carries with it.

By paying attention to the way in which the context of each experience arose, by paying attention to the situation in which the students live, the educator would also become better able "to utilize surroundings physical and social that exist so as to extract from them all that they have to contribute to building up experiences that are worth while" (Dewey 1938, 35). It is only in seeing his students as complex human beings, with a past and a culture and a tradition that do not disappear once they enter the building, that the futural orientation can be possible. It is as situated within a lingering past, as embedded members of families and social groups, that students move toward the future.

This simultaneous vision of the teacher—toward both the future and the past—means that her art is an attempting to introduce students to the apprenticeship of democratic freedom. By means of seeing their futures and their pasts within the present, the teacher understands that "experience is truly experience only when objective conditions are subordinated to what goes on within individuals having the experience" (Dewey 1938, 37). In other words, with each activity, with each lesson, *she* must reach *them*.

In this way, teaching is the art of negotiating with students' lived experiences of complex, always already given situations: "we always live at the time we live and not at some other time, and only by extracting at each present time the full meaning of each present experience are we prepared for doing the same thing in the future" (Dewey 1938, 51). The teacher must be alive to social groups within her classroom, to students' tendencies to revert to less than democratic family prohibitions and permissions, to the allure of subservience in the face of difficulty.

Taking on the situation of the students, the teacher would demonstrate that the power of education lies in its multiplication: "the primary source of social control resides in the very nature of the work done as a social enterprise in which all individuals have an opportunity to contribute and to which all feel a responsibility" (Dewey 1938, 61). Students are controlled best by working together on projects in which they take an active, responsible role. They are controlled best when they control themselves at the behest of the interesting problems that they themselves desire to solve.

Such a vision of education is an admission of how difficult democracy is to achieve. An appeal to the students' lived experience can end, as many democracies can do, in disaster. For what seems easy to say, that we should all govern ourselves by means of a common project, does not arise without a great deal of work and commitment. And this is the basic insight of Dewey as he continued to advocate for democratic pedagogy. The teacher's work of power-sharing and problem-posing is not easy and is not easily taken up by the students: "community life does not organize itself in an enduring way purely spontaneously" (Dewey 1938, 61).

A classroom community, like a national one, needs constant attention and constant, and universal, buy-in. Revisions to pedagogy are as frequent as the shift of situational contexts. For the goal is not rote memorization but engaged desire. And this means that the classroom must be continuously self-modulating so that education remains "conducive to community activity and to organization which exercises control over individual impulses by the mere fact that all are engaged in communal projects" (Dewey 1938, 64).

To educate in a democratic society, then, Dewey says, is to have to plan all the time and yet never to plan too much. It is to plan for the obsolescence of teacher and of subject matter insofar as "planning must be flexible enough to permit free play for individuality of experience and yet firm enough to give direction toward continuous development of power" (Dewey 1938, 65). The student, Dewey asserts over and over, is developing her "power." And if that is true then she too must be involved in the governance of her situation within education.

C. Freire's *Pedagogy of the Oppressed*

Dewey's focus on developing power and shared governance, on diversity and connectedness, is shared by Paolo Freire in his revolutionary *Pedagogy of the Oppressed*. Resting much more explicitly on Husserlian and Sartrean phenomenology, Freire's work from beginning to end notes the liberatory potential of an education that involves the students in their own learning.

The reason that I move from Dewey to Freire here is to show how one might make an explicit argument about how to educate children toward their own free self-actualization. The thoughts in Dewey about the isomorphism between pedagogy and democratic politics only obliquely, and occasionally, imply liberation as the goal of education. By contrast, Freire renders a version of Dewey's focus on democracy more explicitly as turned toward the eradication of social classes and of the corresponding oppression that drives their continued existence. In what follows, I will demonstrate Freire's employment of phenomenological concepts and descriptions. And then I will move on to show how liberation is a possibility for a pedagogy that is the shared responsibility of teachers and students.

Before I begin, however, it is important to remember that Freire is writing about an even more polarized society than our own. He is writing about Brazil in the mid-twentieth century, in which class distinctions are so rigid and codified that there is almost no hope of upward mobility. He is also writing from within an experience of the lower classes' utter poverty and subservience.

This might suggest that his insights have limited application to our own. However, I believe that "oppression" is not limited to countries in which the degree of poverty is significantly higher overall than in our own. Rather, oppression can be seen even in wealthy societies, particularly in the way we treat and educate children. Though it may sound strident, naming the experience of forced servitude in the schools as "oppressive" seems both to do justice to students' lived experience and to structure a way forward.

Freire's vision of a liberating pedagogy comes from his identification of the current state of schooling as a process of rote memorization and of the preservation of the status quo, i.e., oppression of the lower classes by means of the higher. This means that schooling is the perpetuation of a narrative of student inferiority and that it involves a method that Freire calls the *banking model* of education: "the 'banking' concept of education [is that] in which the scope of action allowed to the students extends only as far as receiving, filing, and storing the deposits" (Freire 1968, 72).

If students are viewed as empty vessels into which the teacher deposits concepts and skills, then these same students are not seen as co-participants in learning. They are nothing but apprentices, and poor ones at that, within a structure of indentured servitude. The teacher simply "banks" on them following directions and throws a variety of punitive fits when they do not.

For Freire, if left to its own banking model, this traditional education will continue to decline as a result of its "narration sickness" (Freire 1968, 71). Seeing the students as inferior and as tasked with uninteresting, disconnected learning will only exacerbate the tensions and contradictions that are lived in the class struggle of the lower classes against the punitive measures of the upper class.

Instead of perpetuating a hostile, oppressive system, Freire exhorts teachers to leave behind the banking model for a problem-posing model:

> Those truly committed to liberation must reject the banking concept in its entirety, adopting instead a conception of men and women as conscious beings, and consciousness as consciousness intent upon the world. . . . "Problemposing" education, responding to the essence of consciousness—*intentionality*—. . . epitomizes the special characteristic of consciousness: being *conscious of* not only as intent on objects but as turned in upon itself . . . consciousness as consciousness *of* consciousness (Freire 1968, 79).

This problem-posing education then takes the root of phenomenology—intentionality—seriously. To be intentional, to be united with things and with other persons and with oneself (as self-conscious) means something specific with respect to education. It means that education itself must reflect, in its logic, the logic of consciousness. Education must respond "to the essence of consciousness." And its response must be such that the child or the student *sees herself* within the act of learning.

This idea, that the pedagogy and the course of study reflect the essence or the logic of consciousness as such, does not mean simply that the subjects taught promote self-awareness. Rather, Freire means that the lived experience, the situation, of students must be the very *content* of the coursework:

> no pedagogy which is truly liberating can remain distant from the oppressed by treating them as unfortunates and by presenting for their emulation models from among the oppressors. The oppressed *must be their own example* in the struggle for their redemption (Freire 1968, 54, my emphasis).

Math, science, music, literature—the student must be able to see herself within them, as relevant to them. This is because there is no other way to make them relevant to her. She must become able to use "her own example" and thus to make herself visible as implicated in what she studies. Only so can the pedagogy truly be intentional—i.e., only thus could education show the student the entangled togetherness of herself with the objects of her study.

The way in which problem-posing education can become a reality, Freire argues, is through the dismantling of the power dynamics that haunt many, if not all, teacher-student relationships. Only by educating the students to a new sense of their responsibility can the teacher promote a life of the mind that is at one and the same time a life of the community which can be democratic and answering to a plurality of views.

This is a major role reversal for the teacher: "Education must begin with the solution of the teacher-student contradiction by reconciling the poles of the contradiction so that both are simultaneously teachers *and* students"

(Freire 1968, 72). For this new vision of education requires that the teacher give up her seat at the table or—perhaps more clearly—get a bigger table.

The action of education is no longer to be a one-way deposit without a corresponding withdrawal of funds. Rather, it is to be a multiply determined, interconnected focus on a reality that transcends everyone and that transcends all existing concepts:

> Her [the teacher's] efforts must coincide with those of the students to engage in critical thinking and the quest for mutual humanization. His efforts must be imbued with a profound trust in people and their creative power. To achieve this, they must be partners of the students in their relations with them (Freire 1968, 75).

To form partnerships with the students, however, is to have to share the activity and the situation. It is to "trust" the "creative power" of the students in order to uncover possibilities of learning that have not yet surfaced.

A teacher's job, then, becomes infinitely richer in its potential. And it becomes more difficult but also more rewarding. For at stake in this liberating education is the development of the phenomenological insight of intentionality toward the recognition that the world people share is always a world of "process" and of "transformation":

> In problem-posing education people develop their power to perceive critically *the way they exist* in the world *with which* and *in which* they find themselves; they come to see the world not as a static reality, but as a reality in process, in transformation (Freire 1968, 83).

By posing problems that already have their root in the students' lived situations, the teacher calls each student to be conscious of their own acts of perceiving and of the ways that the objects and structures of those perceptions are indices for future action. Posing problems that arise out of experience, in other words, teaches the noetic-noematic correlation of Husserl without having to read *Ideas.* Rather, it is to live out the insight of the life-world from within it.

By means of forming, critiquing, and sharing problems, then, the teacher and the students both gain power and effectiveness. They both move toward one another and the world. And it is in movement, as we saw in *To Kill a Mockingbird*, that a person and a community can thrive:

> [problem-posing education] affirms women and men as beings who transcend themselves, who look forward and look ahead, for whom *immobility represents a fatal threat*, for whom looking at the past must only be a means of understanding more clearly what and who they are so that they can more wisely build the future (Freire 1968, 84).

As we now transition into a discussion of the novel *Merci Suárez Changes Gears,* perhaps we could reflect on the way in which this Brazilian, Latinx author predelineates for us a possible way of seeing the necessity of movement, of change, and of transformation of a Latinx immigrant family, who look to education to support their own process of becoming acclimated to a new land. For it is by affirming herself and her family as self-transcending, as not simply caught by their past, that Merci will be able to "build the future."

LITERARY PRACTICE: A PHENOMENOLOGICAL READING OF *MERCI SUÁREZ CHANGES GEARS*

Meg Medina's *Merci Suárez Changes Gears* is a novel for children about a variety of interconnected learning experiences in the life of its main protagonist and narrator, Merci Suárez. A grandchild of Cuban immigrants, Merci finds herself thrown between two worlds—that of an upper-class independent school, Seaward Pines, and that of her lower middle-class family home. As the novel progresses, Merci, finding no mercy at her school, and finding it difficult to reconcile changes in her grandfather and her family, feels increasing pressure to "change gears" in order to unite the fields of her experience and to continue to strive as a whole person on unfamiliar terrain.

Merci's brother, Roli, is a high school student at Seaward. Interested in all things scientific and medical, he is constantly studying biology or chemistry or physics and is, even at home, engaged in watching medical documentaries or talking with the adults about scientific findings. Roli seems to be able to navigate the social class distinctions, the discipline, and the academic challenges of Seaward very easily.

Merci is a sixth grader. She feels thrown into the school by her mother and by her family's desire to be upwardly mobile within a relatively well-off surrounding area in Florida. As thrown by her family into her school situation, Merci feels that her status as a scholarship (or need-based financial aid) student haunts her much more than it seems to haunt Roli. As a case in point, Merci does not feel the equal of a student named Edna, who appears as Merci's main nemesis, so to speak, in the novel and who, unlike Merci, seems effortlessly to organize their peers inside and outside of the school.

One of the foundational relationships for Merci is the one she has with her grandfather, Lolo. Lolo calls her his "preciosa," spends a great deal of time with Merci, and gives her things that become important to her sense of self and to the way she tries to integrate seemingly contradictory facets of her world and of herself into a whole:

> Thank goodness Lolo gave me an azabache to protect me. Mami says mal de ojo is nonsense, that no one can hurt people with just an evil eye. But I believe.

The world isn't all logic the way she and Roli think. It's got mystery the way Lolo says. So I wear my protection on a chain next to the gold cross I got for Holy Communion (Medina 2019, 36).

Thanks in part to Lolo, Merci is a synthesizer. She unites and feels loyalty to everyone and everything. She feels proud of Roli and interested in the subjects at her school while also feeling grounded in her family's rather long (and, to Merci, mysterious) history in Cuba and the Philippines. She unites logic and mystery, science and the humanities, immediate and extended family, old world and new world. She wears *everything* on two chains around her neck.

Merci is uncomfortable being asked to do community service as a Sunshine Buddy, a formal greeter and friend for new students: "I've already decided that I'm going to ask Miss McDaniels to switch me to some other community service. I'm barely comfortable at this school myself. How can I help anybody else?" (Medina 2019, 39). But her discomfort, although possibly signaling a moment of rebellion, is quickly passed over or ignored. For her family (and their pride and their poverty) requires her to accede to the demands of the school in the person of Ms. McDaniels.

Facing her forced community service, Merci then comes to see school as another place, another opportunity, to work at her own notion of synthesis. And there are moments of agency for her. Facing Edna and other girls who are forced to work together in class to complete a map, Merci has an idea. At first, the other girls scoff at her, especially Edna, the daughter of a wealthy podiatrist, who has assumed an air of popular authority. But Merci does not give up, and she tries to bring her family, her father and abuela, in to help her navigate the school terrain: "For a second I think of backing down. . . . But then I think of Papi. . . . So I use a sales skill that Abuela has perfected. . . . Give your idea calmly, she says, and find somebody else to say it's brilliant" (Medina 2019, 66).

Not everything fits into Merci's synthetic acts, though. One such thing that does not fit is racism, which receives mostly oblique treatment in the novel. However, when Roli is tasked with taking Merci downtown to meet her classmates at the movies on a weekend night, the family briefly describes the possible racism and abuse of Hispanic young people by the police. Specifically, their parents mention "what to do if he's stopped by police, where not to be, how your hands never go into your pockets" (Medina 2019, 107). This is one of the first indications that we get as readers that Merci's agency will have real limits on her own.

After the movie night in town, after Edna's dad picks her up and leaves, Merci notices that it is not just she who experiences Edna as the sole focus of their group: "We look at one another, and suddenly our mouths feel sticky from sugar and empty" (Medina 2019, 116). The group does not know how to come together without a central authority. What else is there to the group but the seemingly obvious pull of wealth and popularity that Edna embodies?

Merci's father is not a wealthy podiatrist like Edna's father. Rather, Merci's Papi owns his own house painting company. Merci's mother is a physical therapist. They work very hard and do not have very much. Merci recognizes the inherent class consciousness and racism that dominate the Florida landscape. Once when she is helping her Papi and Lolo paint a municipal bathroom near the beach, a woman "with a brass name tag" accosts her and wants to know her business: "Some customers watch us, as if we might take things when they're not looking" (Medina 2019, 143–144).

In truth, ever taken with synthesis, Merci has herself taken something. But nothing that should concern others: "I fish in my pocket for my phone and snap a picture of the ocean. Sometimes I take pictures of ordinary things" (Medina 2019, 143). This attention to "ordinary things" proves to be one of Merci's dominant strengths. For it is because of all these pictures that she takes that she is able to synthesize or make a Christmas gift of an album of family memories for her Lolo, who is in the onset of Alzheimer's.

The pressure of Lolo's increasing symptoms of Alzheimer's means that Merci's mom will not allow her to try out for the soccer team at school, soccer being the sport that Merci is very good at and might allow her to gain some social capital. This prohibition, combined with the family's attempt to keep Lolo's condition a secret from Merci, means that her education, her agency falls short, and she spirals into a kind of resentment and depression: "*Everything. I hate everything,* I think as I run inside the girls' bathroom to hide" (Medina 2019, 157).

This depressed and disenfranchised Merci then begins to participate in what Dewey might call "meaningless boisterousness." When Michael, Merci's white, male Sunshine Buddy and the one she is supposed to "serve," teases Merci that she could not hit a baseball that he pitches to her, she makes a bet with him and then drives the ball into his face. This is one of the first times that we as readers are made aware that the teachers at Seaward are inconsistent with their supervision of the children at the school (the baseball equipment is not to be touched until the teacher is there). And it is one of the first times that Merci's behavior leads to the pain of another student.

Because she got into trouble for using the sports equipment without supervision and for hurting Michael, even if accidentally, Merci's parents get involved in her situation. Papi explains to Merci about her responsibility to Michael (and writing the apology letter the school requires) and to the Sunshine Buddy program: "we don't pay for tuition like most of the other families. So the value you add to the school has to come from *you* because it's not coming from our wallets" (Medina 2019, 174–175). This "added value" however is forced upon her like a banking concept. It has no real hold on her without a mutual responsibility within her family and within the school environment to shared suffering, namely that of Lolo and of Merci.

The way forward toward the resolution of Merci's suffering comes from a teacher encouraging the students to take responsibility for their own learning. The sixth grade class, under the leadership of the social studies teacher, Ms. Tannenbaum, is doing a series of assignments on ancient Egypt. When Merci is allowed to have a say in what the class is doing, she becomes more able to return to her strength of synthesis and to explicating her situation and her life for its creative potential.

Ironically, once Merci learns of Lolo's illness and the family includes her within the discussion, Merci begins to bring her school and her home worlds together. Inviting Michael over so that her Abuela can make their costumes for class celebration of the Egypt unit, inviting Hannah and Lena to come over and work on the sarcophagus and then having them stay for dinner—the home becomes not just a refuge from school but an extension of it. Michael tries empanadas, Hannah and Lena interact with Merci's twin cousins and share in Merci's emotional anxiety about her grandfather's Alzheimer's. This is what helps Merci begin to achieve an emotional and personal balance again, somewhat like removing the training wheels and learning to ride.

The revelation of Lolo's Alzheimer's to Merci also allows other family members to come to her aid. Roli, for example, takes his scientific knowledge and teaches it to Merci in an attempt to help her see the situation more clearly. As he unravels what he understands to be the symptoms of Alzheimer's, however, Roli does something even more important. He lets Merci be angry at him, at all of the family, for not disclosing the disease Lolo has. And when Merci then begins to take the model of the brain into her own hands and learn the parts, she has questions. And Roli waits and takes her seriously: "And when I finally start to ask all the questions I can think of, Roli answers every single one" (Medina 2019, 268).

This emphasis on a synthetic understanding of the body and the brain, of school and home, is something that Merci needs in order to make sense of more than Lolo's disease. Her synthesis is important as she comes to terms with her own life, with her own body and consciousness. Her own left eye wanders, and she often cannot control it. Her hair curls more than she likes in the rain or the wind. She has a crush on a Latinx movie star and not on Michael, the white boy in her class.

Merci's body, in its relation to the bodies of others, is something that Merci strives to understand. She is trying to take account of herself in different situations and to synthesize her own process together into a life. At stake, then, in her working through her family and school worlds is her capacity to be a confident young woman and a person who understands and is responsive to the bodily needs of others—such as those of Edna whose eyebrows she inadvertently glues to the inside of the sarcophagus and then advertently cuts off to get Edna out.

As she progresses through the novel, which really only defines a timeline of several weeks, Merci clearly grows, and grows more attentive by asking important questions. When Lolo tells her what is happening to him, from his own point of view, Merci is stressed, angry, and hurt. But she thinks in the midst of, and from within the energy of, these emotions: "Lolo is right here, talking to me, the same as always, but he's disappearing a little bit at a time. How can a grown-up forget how to walk across the street and come to explain himself the next day?" (Medina 2019, 273). These questions about memory and forgetting are part of her life. They are implicated within the very logic of remembering in any normal person. But when faced with the degree of forgetting in Lolo's life, Merci has no choice but to become explicitly self-referential. What is life if it forces us to forget?

In what is surely the most moving moment of the book, Merci knocks over the game of dominoes Lolo has brought in to play with her, his *preciosa*. Lolo understands that Merci is frightened, that she is, even according to her, trying to express the logic of her own thinking: "This is what it's like when someone changes and scares you. How do *you* like it?" (Medina 2019, 274). In this moment, Merci uses herself as an example. In the face of the family who has decided, finally, to involve her in their understanding, Merci demonstrates quite clearly the way in which this understanding comes to be part of her. It is the destruction of a childhood space of play, the destruction of an experience of joy as embodied by the game of dominoes. Lolo's destruction and forgetting are paired with her own, since she fears that that part of her which is Lolo will also die or fade away.

The emotion is educative, the destruction exemplary, and Lolo knows it: "I am frightened too," he says. "We all are. But we are the Suárez family, Merci. We are strong enough to face this together" (Medina 2019, 275). And so the example is a return to the power of synthesis. Make sense of this with me, he seems to say, for I cannot do it without you.

Merci's new emotional terrain, which occurs because of her new understanding of Lolo, becomes dangerous out of school. But it is also dangerous in school. The unit on ancient Egypt is of a piece with Lolo's illness: "No matter what, all of it comes back to death, which comes back to Lolo being sick, and *that* makes me so sad that all I want to do is stare out the window" (Medina 2019, 279).

When she has to go to see the principal, Dr. Newman, she dreads being confronted about her choice to cut Edna out of the sarcophagus. Certainly, as privileged people in the community, Edna's parents are furious, as is Edna, for her missing or distorted eyebrows. And Merci receives the lion's share of the blame because she is the one who volunteered to rescue Edna from the sarcophagus that Lena, Hannah, and Merci built around her body. But Merci, again, is also the victim of inconsistent oversight. As Ms. Tannenbaum attests, "It's my fault they were unsupervised" (Medina 2019, 317).

Merci it would seem is at the mercy of adults who are inconsistent and are not fully self-aware of their role in building and affirming the power of their students. However, Ms. Tannenbaum does defend Merci, and Ms. McDaniels does as well. It is because of this support that Merci makes her way back toward Edna by means of an apology and a gift (an eyebrow pencil). She buys the gift with money she had been saving for a bike. She buys the gift at the expense of her own movement, which seems to identify her with Edna, who was immobile in the sarcophagus the girls built around her.

Toward the end of the novel, after the class's presentation of the Egypt unit and the sarcophagus, Ms. Tannenbaum has clearly recovered her capacity to unite and affirm the budding power of these Egyptologists. She tells the students she is very happy with them and their ability to work within a problem-posing system of education: "You have a lot to be proud of, third hour. I want you to know that a project like this takes a lot of planning, research, teamwork, and problem-solving. Not everything went smoothly, but you didn't let that stop you" (Medina 2019, 338).

If Merci's strength throughout most of the novel is her power of synthesis, of joining things together, what shows at the end of the novel is that she has moved on to a new power, one of creativity. No longer a "banker" in the Sunshine Buddy program, Merci now sees that what was first an enforcement of her status as a scholarship student has now become an opportunity to extend and develop the value of community service. Now, she and Hannah and Lena are planning "the new volunteer club we want to start. . . . I thought students could visit the Lourdes Killington Residence for seniors who don't see their families enough" (Medina 2019, 342). She is still bringing her concerns, her family life, into her life as a student. But she is doing it with others, and she is creating the possibility for extending their family and school lives into the larger community.

In parts equally synthetic and creative, Merci's final gift for her family, the scrapbook for Lolo with all the photos she has taken on her phone as well as some from back in Cuba when Lolo was much younger, is a huge success. It unites the past and the present and anticipates the future. She has "left lots of pages blank in the back" (Medina 2019, 353) and she ties her act of giving it to him to the memorable Nochebuena festivities, which means that the photo album will become something of a tradition that enables memory to function even when it becomes difficult for Lolo.

These initiatives from Merci—that of the volunteer club, that of the scrapbook, even that of hitting the baseball from Michael or cutting out Edna from the sarcophagus—mean that she has learned the role of finitude and of change: "Staying the same could be just as sad as Lolo changing. . . . I can handle it, I decide. It's just a harder gear, and I am ready. All I have to do is take a deep breath and ride" (Medina 2019, 355). She is moving, and as moving, is self-transcending.

CONCLUSION

In this chapter, as in each of the chapters that came before, what I have tried to show is that phenomenology is so effective as a method of description because it takes its methodology from the way experience actually unfolds. In each case of reading a novel phenomenologically, it is less a matter of reading something *into* the story than it is of showing how the story *already* portrays a phenomenological logic.

This is true, perhaps especially, of this last novel. Merci realizes on her own terms that her yearning to be free from the contradictions of class and race are impossible without being shared. As Freire has argued, a student can only be free if "when they discover within themselves the yearning to be free, they perceive that this yearning can be transformed into reality only when the same yearning is aroused in their comrades" (Freire 1968, 47).

Binding herself together with Lena and Hannah, and allowing them to have an equal say in the construction of the class project, allows for the other two girls to affirm Merci and Lolo. It allows them to share meals and time together.

Her trajectory, which began to look like depression and withdrawal, changes because all three are liberated from the lure of popularity and wealth. And they are given rather to new forms of community. Had Ms. Tannenbaum and Ms. McDaniels, had Papi and Mami and Roli and Lolo, not affirmed Merci's potential to develop herself, she would have never been able to take responsibility authentically, to move from synthesis to creativity. For, again with Freire, the lack of engagement with students enriches nothing and extends suffering: "When their efforts to act responsibly are frustrated, when they find themselves unable to use their faculties, people suffer" (Freire 1968, 78).

As phenomenological readers, it is our responsibility to be alert to suffering, to be alert to others. Moreover, it is our job to see children as philosophical creatures, beings for whom Alzheimer's, finitude, death, and loss are already latent realities that make sense to them. Children are nothing if not prescient, and a pedagogy that takes them seriously, whether in an independent or a parochial or a public school, needs to take that prescience and allow children to become better able to reflect on and to impact their own lived situations.

There are a number of other scholars in phenomenology who have worked on Dewey and Freire and who have made it possible to develop a philosophy of education that roots itself in the lived experience of children or students. It is important, I think, to explore and acknowledge their work here.

Laura McMahon and Gregory Trotter offer recent articles in which the insights of Dewey generally in terms of what it means to be an experiencing self are compatible with Merleau-Ponty and Husserl, respectively. McMahon claims that Dewey's *Democracy and Education* allows us to see that "we can derive from the human capacity for *growth* a normative criterion for conceiving of the health of both individuals and the environments that support or hinder their natural tendencies" (McMahon 2018, 609). This "normative criterion," McMahon continues, helps to bring out the meaningfulness of Merleau-Ponty's *Phenomenology of Perception*, particularly with respect to the narratives of health and illness that are within that work.

Trotter maintains that Dewey in fact expresses the same insight into intentionality that Husserl does, and that this fact enables both philosophers to recover a sense of what nature and the world offer (against rationalism) to experience as such: "Husserl and Dewey both recognize the importance of the experiencing subject in the process of knowledge, and both recognize that attempts to isolate subjectivity from its position within experience are misguided" (Trotter 2016, 33).

Turning more explicitly to Dewey's vision of pedagogy, we see Andres Muro working to bring together Husserl, Dewey, and Freire around the issue of creating the experience of education as one of liberation. Working with the El Paso Community College to create an education program for GED students that allows them to reflect critically on their consumption of images and speech about immigrants and Mexicans, Muro blends a concern with the articulation of the structures of consciousness with the liberation of self-awareness in a historically challenging situation. As Muro says, Dewey and Freire seem designed to work together: "Dewey develops a pedagogy that appears less political than Freire's and does not use the phenomenological language of intentionality. Yet, Dewey's pedagogy clearly frees the intentionality of the students to explore their own context and history" (Muro 2017, 42).

Finally, I would be remiss not to mention the work of David Kennedy on Dewey and education, especially insofar as Kennedy tries to comment on how education ought to be more responsive to the anarchic, to the needs of all students, and to children most importantly. In particular, I think it is crucial to read Kennedy's recent (2017) piece about developing a dialogical practice of schooling that does not answer to received norms but is rather open-ended. There Kennedy works to

> identify an archetype of "school" understood as a specific type of intentional community—an experimental, neotenic zone in which participants are allowed and encouraged, through explicitly dialogical practice, to develop the personal

and relational habits that make authentic democracy possible—a communal form that gives practical meaning to Dewey's oft-cited notion of school as "embryonic society" (Kennedy 2017, 553).

Kennedy's long familiarity with phenomenology and with Dewey is noteworthy throughout his work. And this article in particular brings the notion of the uncovering of experience as intentional into conversation with the open-ended character of democratic politics.

This brief review of some of the recent literature on phenomenology, Dewey, and Freire should help the reader find more to explore. Certainly Medina's novel about a relatively wealthy, independent school displays that certain Deweyan insights and certain liberatory potential remains in education now. But these insights require ongoing vigilance to avoid the kind of dispersion into acts of punishment and suffering that the novel relates.

Conclusion

Embracing Failure and Leaping Ahead

Years ago, Georges Poulet wrote an important piece entitled the "Phenomenology of Reading," which makes the case that the act of reading involves each of us, as readers, in a kind of otherness. I become another person when I fill in for the narrator, whether first, second, or third person. Reading is thus a passive activity that inducts rather than educates. [1]

What Poulet does not discuss fully enough is the fact that many of us fail to read adequately and fully. In fact the hermeneutic circle is possible only *because we fail*, because the whole that we have just read still transcends our grasp.

Before leaving the reader with a program for further study, what I would like to do here is to use Husserl's descriptions of intentionality, pairing, and of essential intuition to show how Poulet's discussion can be brought to a more phenomenological conclusion. I will pair Husserl here with Virginia Woolf's *The Waves*, a novel whose structure evinces many of the same points as Poulet's article but whose conclusion is that authentic reading *embraces reading problems* or *failures* and yields an apprehension of intersubjectivity between the children who are its main characters.

Woolf's phenomenological novel, then, is not a piece of children's literature. Yet it is, as so many nineteenth- and early twentieth-century adult novels are, about children and education. And so this current book, as it turns toward the possibility of educators and parents and scholars to make a phenomenology of education more concrete and present in the world, does well to open onto the world of adult fiction. It is my belief that the terms, arguments, and readings of the previous chapters propel the reader forward into her own relationships with texts in a phenomenological way. And I hope that

this last analysis of Woolf's novel can motivate the reader to turn her attention toward any piece of literature with an eye to the liberating possibilities it
offers—all by way of intentionality, intercorporeality, existence, and phenomenological description more generally.

POULET'S ARGUMENT

In "Phenomenology of Reading," Georges Poulet marvels that, in reading,
our consciousness "behaves as though it were the consciousness of another"
(Poulet 1969, 56). When I read, I experience an alien subject in me and thus
"I am *on loan* to another, and this other thinks, feels, suffers, and acts within
me" (Poulet 1969, 57). This other who demands my transfer to her or to him,
the other to whom I "loan" myself—this other, however, is still not a tyrant,
for the other depends on my offering of myself, of my time. The text, the
author, the narrator, the characters—these wait for me to endow it as a living
thing to whom I subordinate my sense of myself.

For Poulet, then, insofar as I am "as though" another, my reading is not a
pure activity of my own. Nor is it a pure activity of the text itself. Rather, in
the reading act there is a passive, reciprocal pairing and a mutual transfer of
sense. There is mutuality insofar as I return its "consciousness of another,"
insofar as I return the one who I become, to its own self-consciousness: "I
give it not only existence but awareness of existence" (Poulet 1969, 59).
There is mutuality insofar as the work allows me to fade away from my own
view in favor of the work's own life as an alien consciousness. The enjoyment or immersion that I experience is the emotional clue to the reciprocity.

Poulet's description of reading, then, involves a kind of active and passive synthesis of subjects, a kind of intersubjectivity, a sharing of consciousness: "we start having a common consciousness" (Poulet 1969, 59). However, this intersubjectivity is not a simple or complete identification. There is
still "a lag [that] takes place, a sort of schizoid distinction between what I feel
and what the other feels" (Poulet 1969, 59). My unity with the work, in other
words, is as much about the gaps in the pairing as the pairing itself: I am
"aware of a certain gap, disclosing a feeling of identity, but identity within
difference" (Poulet 1969, 60).

Thus far, Poulet seems to have followed Husserl's description of pairing
with the other person quite closely. His extension of the other to the text itself
is quite noteworthy, and presages all kinds of deconstructive work that would
follow in the work of Derrida and others.

Having discussed the experience of identifying with and being "on loan"
to the text, Poulet then speaks of six critics, each marking out a different kind
of reading. Each of the six takes a different stance on the identification of
reader and narrative subject.[2] I will now explain each of the six readers

Poulet presents, and I will, later, map each of these onto the characters in Woolf's novel *The Waves*.

The first critic or reader Poulet examines is Jacques Riviere. Riviere emphasizes the senses and tries to see what the author saw. However, Riviere understands that he cannot live through the author's eyes, since all that is given is the text. So, Riviere reads the text in order to perform "the tactile exploration of surfaces, through a groping exploration of the material world, which separates the critical mind from its objects" (Poulet 1969, 60). The text is thus an index of object experiences that calls out to be enacted by the reader. They are stones or breadcrumbs left in the forest, all of which lead "home" to the textual subject. For Poulet, Riviere fails to account for how reconnecting a series of object experiences could lead to the intimate relationship of the reader with said subject.

The second reader or critic, Jean-Pierre Richard, is a bit more successful in Poulet's view. Richard begins with the assumption that it is possible to "undergo the same experiences," in order to imitate and apprehend not the person but the *style* of the author (Poulet 1969, 61). Richard goes beyond breadcrumbs and stones. We do not piece together the world of the author and thus build up the author's whole subjectivity out of parts. Richard instead insists we can get directly to the whole of the authorial body through the reading of the author's world-experience as a whole. We can get to that, Richard argues, through a kind of imaginative mimicry, with "mimicking physically the apperceptual world of the author" (Poulet 1969, 61).

The failure of Richard's view comes from its position. Richard as reader remains *outside* the world of the author and thus at best mimics only a surface whole. The world of the author is not empathized or lived from within.

Richard's description is tantamount to someone trying to play football like Pele simply by watching Pele play several times on television. It is this kind of imitation of a bodily whole or style, without careful attention to the detail of the specific bodily motions and practices that make up that style—it is this naivete that prevents Richard from being able to identify how the subject of the text and the reader enter into union. If all we do is watch Pele play, we would never play like him. If all we do is see the world of the author or textual subject, we would never identify with her from the inside, as it were.

The third reader that Poulet treats is Maurice Blanchot. Blanchot opposes both Riviere and Richard since Blanchot "would abolish the object and extract from the texts their most subjective elements" (Poulet 1969, 61). Blanchot is someone Poulet finds more amenable to his own phenomenology. For Blanchot, the point is not to identify completely with the author but to make the work as strange as possible, in order that the reader's identification can appear as full of gaps, as an identification that does not stop being a kind of naked opposition of stranger to stranger. It is Blanchot's task to reduce the author to something so naked, so *other*, that the author is no longer bodily. For Blanchot the reading act is thus an ongoing act of identification that is never fully at home with itself, since my bodily whole and the author's subjectivity never fully pair, never clearly see within and through each other.

But Blanchot, like Riviere and Richard, also lacks something important. Poulet compares the three together and argues that each of them, in their own way, simply promotes one side of an oscillation "between two possibilities: a union without comprehension, and a comprehension without union" (Poulet 1969, 63). Neither a close identification nor an overemphasis of the author's or text's alien character can be a proper description of the act of reading for Poulet. Instead, for Poulet only if the description of the act of reading accounts for its dual character—making possible both immediate and mediated identification, both intercorporeality and intersubjectivity—can it be sufficient to describe what we always already do.

And so Poulet moves on to a fourth reader, Starobinski, who seems to unite the senses and reflection in a "kind of reciprocation and alternation," or "a reading of bodies which is likened to the reading of minds" (Poulet 1969, 63). However, Poulet claims, Starobinski abandons the integrity of the text and instead moves "imperceptibly toward a dominating position" (Poulet 1969, 65). For Poulet, a phenomenology must always account for the element of desire, of mutuality, of love. One reads because one loves the relationship that is the act of reading. Moving toward "domination" of the text by oneself, or vice versa, is to abandon reading for violence.

After Starobinski, Poulet evaluates the descriptions of Raymond and Rousset. However, these readers also neither accurately nor fully unravel "the interrelationship between subject and object, which is the principle of all creative work and the understanding of it" (Poulet 1969, 67). Like all the accounts before theirs, Raymond's and Rousset's descriptions seem to presume a false dichotomy or limited choice. Either the reader starts with the objects described in the work and moves toward the author or the subject. Or the reader starts with the global style or body or "life" of the subject and moves toward the objects as that subject experiences them. In neither case can a phenomenologist account for the immediate, total, and intimate identification of the reader with both the subject and the world of that subject— an intimacy which reading already offers us when we are engaged in it.

Unfortunately for us, Poulet sees the failure of these six readers as requiring him to move beyond Husserl's descriptions of intentionality and of pairing. For Poulet simply says that reading is understood as an experience when we see that "the subject present in the work disengages itself from all that surrounds it and stands alone" (Poulet 1969, 68). We read successfully, Poulet says, when we no longer see the particular objects of the work, no longer see the particular experiences of the author or narrator, no longer move in a zigzag fashion from the object to the subject. Rather, for Poulet reading involves a kind of disappropriation of the text's subject from her world, considering the subject itself in its purity, such that we have an intuition of

> an *essence* that I was not able to perceive, except by *emptying* my mind of all the particular images created by the artist. I [then could become] aware of a subjective power at work in all those pictures, and yet never so clearly understood by my mind as when I had *forgotten* all their particular figurations (Poulet 1969, 68, my emphasis).

Reading then involves a kind of intuition of an "essence." But this intuition, contra Husserl, is not a fullness, which appears by means of a kind of overlaying of particulars, but rather, for Poulet, a process of "emptying" one's experiences and "forgetting" the particulars of the text and of the textual subject's relation to objects. Doing that will allow the reader to understand the lure of the text's subject, the real or true presentation of her "subjective power."

This is clearly a violation of the principle of all principles, for Husserl, and also of the insight into intentionality. For Poulet, reading is the passive experience that *cannot be described phenomenologically* because the phenomenological tools we have conceal the real truth, namely, that we have fallen in love with a subject whom we cannot see and whom the text itself cannot reveal *except by a kind of radical disappropriation that we bring to it.*

Reading the subjectivity of the text means grasping simply one subject with another, one mind with another, and thus grasping the Other without a world to mediate her:

> It seems then that criticism, in order to accompany the mind in this effort of detachment from itself, needs to annihilate or at least momentarily to forget the objective elements in the work and to elevate itself to the apprehension of *a subjectivity without objectivity* (Poulet 1969, 68, my emphasis).

Not by paying careful attention to our experience, then, but only by ignoring it can we reach what for Poulet seems to be the pure Being or radical transcendence of a text that has captured and subordinated us to its mystery.

But if the textual subject is what I pair with as "a subjectivity without objectivity," then it is unclear to me how Poulet accounts for its power. It is precisely because the other has a view on the world and on our shared things and experiences within it that she shows her power. It is in her challenge to my world that we have a shared world at all. There is no way that a disembodied subject of a text can offer any resistance, opacity, or "gap." Poulet's author is simply either fantasy or divinity, but in either case cannot be directly experienced as the subject of a text, which is always a text of a world and of objects.

No, Poulet's description is inadequate. Children, most of all children, do not read texts in such a way as to leave behind the world and the objects and experiences presented there for some disembodied, divine lover. Children, who are, as we have seen throughout this book, reflective and intelligent, pair because they *like the person they identify with.* And they identify with the one who shows herself *in* the text.

HUSSERL RETURNS TO POULET

What then are we to do with this presentation of the phenomenology of reading by Poulet? Is there more to do than to reject it? I would answer, yes. Poulet reminds us of the necessity to remain with phenomenology in order not to impose metaphysical nonsense on the education of children. And he offers us an occasion to think through the way in which we actually experience not only pairing and intentionality but, in addition, the intuition or perception of essences.

In *Phenomenological Psychology, Experience and Judgment,* and *Analyses Concerning Passive and Active Synthesis,* Husserl describes essential intuition in the same terms as he describes the pairing with an alien other person. What we find in both descriptions are the same crucial terms, *awakening* and *overlaying* [*wecken, decken*]. We are awakened to each other in pairing. We are awakened to the essence in essential intuition. We overlay each other in pairing. The different experiences of related particulars overlay one another and support our awakening to the essence as a separate, higher-order experience.

Because we pair with other persons, because we are always already over-reaching, awakening and overlaying ourselves with all other subjects we encounter, we can perform the activities whereby our particular experiences of things can yield to us their essences, essences that make the explication of those very experiences possible and rich.

We perceive essences, therefore, on behalf of our community with others and not through a process of "emptying" or "forgetting." We perceive essences because we perform a "transition" between particulars and hold onto them while leaping ahead toward the essence that gathers them into itself:

> In this *transition* from image to image . . . all the arbitrary particulars attain overlapping coincidence [*Deckung*] in the order of their appearance and enter, in a purely passive way, into a synthetic unity in which they all appear as *modifications of one another* and then as arbitrary sequences of particulars in which the same universal is isolated as an *eidos.* Only in this continuous coincidence [*Deckung*] does something which is the same come to congruence, something which henceforth can be seen purely *for itself* (Husserl 1973, 343, my emphasis).

Seeing an essence then, like reading, takes time. It requires us to move, like Scout in *To Kill a Mockingbird*. And it requires us to see that which appears as arising "for itself."

The identification we perform with other persons, the "overlapping coincidence" that awakens us to a shared world, is the essential act of reading. The pairing of our perspectives, which occurs not despite but *by means of our bodies,* allows us to see our own world and our perspective on it as part of a system of perception, which Husserl calls a *functional community*: my body and the other's body, my perceptual system and hers "are so fused that they stand within the *functional community of one perception*" (Husserl 1960, 122)

In seeing essences, then, whether of things or of a text, we are enacting others' lived perspectives and taking them on "as if" in a shared way, "as if we were there." We grasp the essence, the universal, only because we grasp that our entire consciousness is already pulled into a universal, bodily pairing, into actual and ongoing encounters with others. Reading then is possible not because we can empty ourselves and forget the other's world. Reading is possible because the world of the other has already done its work in us. And we approach the textual subject as something visceral, which demands that we turn to how the trace of the textual subject is already within the way we experience the world.

When Poulet says that he needs to "empty" his mind, to "forget" the particularity of the textual subject's variation from his own, this is not phenomenological. An essence shows itself *through* the particulars as they become arbitrary (but not meaningless). It is across and through the gaps between these particulars that the eidos shines through. It is in the *way* that Van Gogh painted a table, a bed, a vase of flowers—more, it is in the way that that style is *inseparable* from the apparition of these (and not other) furniture and flowers, that the essence of Van Gogh shines through. It is as much looking into these objects as past them that gives the subject, Van Gogh. Similarly, the act of reading—it is as much reading into and with the characters as it is reading "beyond" them that gives us clarity as to the experience of the textual subject, who is more concrete the more we see how she sees.

Husserl continues his description of essential intuition, and the inseparability of the particular variants that make it possible, in the *Analyses Concerning Passive and Active Synthesis*:

> [the universal] can only first be ready for possible thematic grasping, by carrying out the activity of grasping uniform objects separately in the synthetic *transition* from the one to the next. . . . The direction of interest toward the universal, toward the unity as opposed to the manifold, is not that of determining the one uniform object in relation to the other being uniform to it; rather what *awakens* interest is the One being actively constituted *in* the coinciding [*Deckung*] of *individually grasped* uniform objects; the One is the same, and is

the same over and over, no matter what direction we may pursue in passing *from one to the next* (Husserl 2001, 349–350, my emphasis).

An essence is thus recognized as a light shining up through multiple overlaid transparencies on an overhead projector, a light which preserves something of the transparencies' coloration and density. The One is recognized, the essence is recognized, the subject of the text is recognized, by children as by critics, in making real, concrete steps from one perspective, one object, one character to another. The ultimate or sufficient reading, then, would not detach the textual subject from the objects that *give it* to the reader. Rather, the ultimate act of reading is performed only when one describes the intentionality of that textual subject through its own evidence, its own transcendence in immanence.

Reading, in short, is intentional. Poulet misses this. And yet he can still offer us something important. Each of the six critics Poulet faults could be read as six "variants" on reading that, together, might give us insight into the full essence of an act we have always already begun, an essence we have already encountered and begun, hermeneutically, to pursue. Their failures, as the failure of Poulet, can be helpful to us who would move forward toward a better method of education as rooted in lived experience.

As we turn now to Virginia Woolf's *The Waves,* I will now leave behind Poulet's six readers for Woolf's children. I believe that Woolf's children will show us that the ultimate textual subject is given to us as the *relationships* that are carved out between the text and the reader. It is because reading that text is always already an encounter with a group of enworlded, embodied subjects, subjects we call characters, that that overarching subject (the author, the narrator, etc.) can become separated for the critic.

A PHENOMENOLOGICAL READING OF WOOLF'S *THE WAVES*

It is in Virginia Woolf's novel *The Waves* that we get the ultimate reading that Poulet has suggested but failed to give. Like Poulet, Woolf writes about reading. The novel is in fact a story of six friends and their individual experiences of reading blackboards, books, dinner parties, and each other. Like Poulet's six critics, each character embodies a different method of reading, and each one's reading is insufficient. Unlike Poulet, however, Woolf does not leave behind the six for an essence that is other to them. Rather, for Woolf, the community of these six readers forms the only "essential intuition" that can be given of reading as such. For her, the lived experience of reading is always partial, related to bodies and to objects, and can only start within the community, within the interrelationship of these limited, plural, fragile readers to one another.

In the beginning of the novel, while they are doing their Latin exercises, we as readers are introduced to the characters as children. Woolf gives us to see how each child sees the words on the blackboard differently. Susan sees them as "white words . . . like stones one picks up by the seashore" (Woolf 1959, 20). For Bernard, these words are animals who "wag their tails . . . they move through the air in flocks" (Woolf 1959, 20). Jinny sees the same words as "yellow" and "fiery": "they make her think of a dress for the evening" (Woolf 1959, 20–21). Neville focuses not on the words at all but on time, on the tenses that the words have; the tenses show him that "there are differences in this world, upon whose verge I step" (Woolf 1959, 21). In this small passage, one can see very different experiences of reading, different critical approaches.

For Susan, words are mostly disconnected; yet a single project can illuminate them. Picking up stones at a seashore gathers all the white stones together; fulminating before a book and a blackboard, the white words (from the chalk) are to be gathered slowly into a story, into her project of treasure-seeking.

For Bernard, words are already reverberating within some higher project of their own, alive, entrancing him. Jinny's experience of reading throws her back on herself, on her body, on the dress she would like; Jinny sees herself becoming the yellow, fiery words. Neville's experience of reading is one of opening a world, of time beginning and "differences" emerging. Reading is "only a beginning" (Woolf 1959, 21).

All of these successes in characterizing the act of reading—words as stones, fire, a flock of birds, the origin of time-consciousness—pale, however, in the face of the magnificent failure that is Rhoda's experience of reading. And it is with Rhoda's experience to the circle of friends that we clearly see Woolf's phenomenological superiority to Poulet. For Rhoda, reading and writing are "terror" (Woolf 1959, 21). Within the classroom, before the blackboard, Rhoda can neither read nor write. She sees "only figures" on the board. When the others go out to recess, Rhoda is left alone with the board and the figures: "the figures mean nothing now. Meaning is gone. The clock ticks" (Woolf 1959, 21). Reading was oppressive, was terrifying, even with people there in the room with her. But there is nothing left without the others. Reading is not an experience that is even possible without the other friends, at least for Rhoda.

Rhoda's character is important to a phenomenology of reading or of education because it suggests that problems with reading, problematic readers, insufficiencies, gaps—all these are not just the responsibility of the individual but of the community. An accurate phenomenology of reading would have to show, as Paolo Freire and John Dewey and Merleau-Ponty begin to do, how problems or failures in reading or in education generally encourage the building up of communities and institutions. Failure does not indicate reasons for dismissal.

In the novel, the others do not stop being friends with Rhoda because she cannot read. Rather, to show how their union takes their pairing seriously, how reading can in fact build itself up out of its failures, Woolf goes on to show the power of Louis's empathy, of his reflection, of his reading *of* reading.

For even more remarkable than Rhoda's problems with reading is the fact that Rhoda's difficulties in reading are visible to Louis. He sees that "as she stares at the chalk figures, her mind lodges in those white circles; it steps through those white loops into emptiness, alone. They have no meaning for her. She has no answer for them. She has no body as the others have" (Woolf 1959, 22). Louis sees her reading, experiences her body in its dumb, mute frustration. Reading is not just a mental act; it is the activity of having a body and therefore a power of resistance. Reading is not just essential to understanding the board. It must be done to answer the problems. It demands that it be taken up and answered, bodily. Reading requires response. And, if Rhoda is unable to respond, if she is unable to grasp meaning, then she is not in the world, she has no body, and she is, quite simply, oppressed.

Louis, however, has a body with which he can bridge the gap. He can help her to arrest the feeling of oppression, of being an outcast. Like Paolo Freire's or Dewey's educator, Louis carries his empathy forward into Rhoda's distance. He uses the world, interposes it once again between Rhoda and her experience. He gives her back her body by way of facilitating the redirection of the blackboard into a shared problem that makes sense of her situation and affirms it while leaping ahead toward its transcendence.

In this simple opening, with these six children, Woolf inaugurates a phenomenology of reading. She accounts not only for the differences we each have in the way we make our paths into texts, language, or situations. But she also accounts for the way that the act of reading is visible as such, with all its stylistic variations and failures. It is not that Louis is better than Rhoda; rather, it is that he adds to her, can help her, forms an essence *with* her by means of reading her act of reading. The failure that Rhoda enacts is part of the essence of what it means to read or to learn and is not simply to be forgotten or emptied or transcended. Any transcendence that is possible must root itself in the givenness of how education *always fails someone.*

What we learn from Woolf here in this initial scene is that reading is an act that each one does with her whole person, whole body, with emotions and projects. Reading musters our entire narrative, our entire identity. Only if it were so could we experience each other's investment or lack thereof, each other's ease or difficulty in reading or learning.

An educator who pays attention then to the givenness of reading as a commitment of each student's whole being-in-the-world can become, like

Louis, a facilitator of transcendence. Only by reckoning, with Woolf as with Heidegger, with the existential analysis of the human being as essentially hermeneutic can we see that to read is to form a community, to be paired. It is to commit oneself to the call of conscience insofar as even in reading we are implicit in one another's lives and perspectives.

Later in the novel, when the children are young adults, they come together for a dinner, ostensibly given to see Percival, their seventh friend, before he leaves for India. Bernard looks at the dinner and notices communion: "we are drawn into this communion by some deep, some common emotion" (Woolf 1959, 126). In articulating this communion, Bernard focuses on the perspectives, on the eyes of those gathered:

> We have come together . . . to make one thing, not enduring—for what en-
> dures?—but seen by many eyes simultaneously. There is a red carnation in that
> vase . . . a whole flower to which every eye brings its contribution (Woolf
> 1959, 127).

This synthesis of perspectives, of eyes around the one table, around the one noematic carnation—this synthesis of "making" but not "enduring," of transitioning toward an essence—this is what drives the multiplicity of interpretations of the dinner toward comprehensibility. It is because all are gathered that reading begins and begins to be complicated. It is in the gathering that oneness and multiplicity are constituted *at the same time*.

Is the dinner for Percival? Yes, but not only for him. The coming together is to focus as much on an arbitrary flower as on Percival. It is on the blossom of their togetherness itself, with all the objects that that togetherness discloses. If we are to be educators of children, we would do well to remember this point. It is the class itself that can be the subject of its own learning, just as for Freire it can be the peasants themselves. The classroom is the text, and reading it is something the children have always already begun to do *since the gathering of them together is the genesis of the project of meaning*.

Louis further develops Bernard's description by opposing it: "We differ, it may be too profoundly, for explanation. But let us attempt it" (Woolf 1959, 127). Reading, like intimacy, like phenomenology, like education, is an attempt. It is not always already given as an explicit, transparent accomplishment. Reading is a kind of pairing that must be synthesis with gaps, because of gaps. How could Bernard's discovery of difference occur without its being situated around the core of a presentation of community, of togetherness? And yet both the togetherness and the difference are already present together. To be together is to be apart, and hence the striving for solidarity by way of inclusion.

Reading carries loss, distance, and sorrow at its heart. We cannot meet Woolf in her novel, even when we do. And while we meet her, we anticipate the end of the act of reading and the shattering of the intimacy. The end does come, and sooner all the time. But reading is also a return to the intimacy that gets shattered. Reading is necessary, as Kierkegaard says, because "life fractures what is united in the pious simplicity of the child" (Kierkegaard 1983, 9).

By means of Louis's identification of their profound differences, Bernard returns to his red carnation in order to see unity in multiplicity, to see the essence of their togetherness as a prism that reflects light in so many different ways: "the flower, the red carnation that stood in the vase on the table of the restaurant when we dined together with Percival is become a six-sided flower; made of six lives" (Woolf 1959, 229). Reading is a living act, done with those who live together. One student who does well does so because of the contributions of those who raised their hands before him. One who fails does so on behalf of the teacher and the other students. Their failure is a stepping stone just as the other's success. In reading, in community, there are no grades.

Reading is a living act, done with those who live together. It is an act that is changed by the death of Percival. But the dead, the ones who have written and are now gone, cannot answer for the interpretation of their texts. Reading sediments and discovers loss. And as it moves along, there is something of a forgetting—a forgetting of loss. But it is a forgetting that one remembers and remembers by way of the necessary forgetting.

The seven petals become six. The ones who read are the ones who can speak. Percival, like Woolf, is gone. What remains is only the flower insofar as it is seen by the six. As Heidegger shows us, we too, we sevenths, are already being-toward-death. We already know the fallenness of our forgetting of loss and the flight from conscience that occurs when we cannot read our finitude. And yet we hear, as does Augustine, that we should take and read.

With Woolf, in the very image of the carnation, repeatedly engaged as the icon of the text, we are given over to our lives as hermeneutic. We are given over to our role as educators. We are given to the act of re-reading for the sake of ourselves and of those who, like Rhoda, are paralyzed by failure.

What we are given is a world, objects, and intentionality. We are given a phenomenological set of principles and concepts that can build a shared, communal structure that allows education to happen as much at a dinner party as in a classroom. For reading, perception, is always moving us toward the educative.

The subjectivity of the text is the subjectivity of a circle of friends. It is, following Husserl and Merleau-Ponty, an intercorporeality and an intersubjectivity that responds to and enacts its own style, its own life as shared, interlocking perspectives on a shared world. The life of the text, whether in one's own act of reading or in the classroom, is bound to the lives of those who form and inform it.

Woolf's textual subject does not confront the reader as a disembodied alien, contrary to Poulet. The other of that text, the haunting spectre of the novel, beyond Percival, is haunting because of its intimacy. It does not stand there and utter inscrutable admonitions within an armor of invisibility, as in *Hamlet*. Rather, her text invites the reader into itself, in order to enable the reader to be one of the circle of friends, which includes narrator, character, author, and any other textual subject who might appear.

The essence of the text is thus one that requires participation and liberation. We must be free to learn to read the text on its own terms. We must strive to liberate our perspective from its moorings in ideology. Particularly with Woolf's novel, we can struggle with our failure to proceed according to the stream of consciousness. We can feel that our immersion and identification are serially interrupted. We can feel condemned, over and over, to return to the text we might try to love by means of perspectives that we have not yet adopted or adapted to.

But that difficulty that the text presents is just the means whereby it offers us more of itself. In returning, we can come to see more because, in returning to it, we can see that we have become more. Like Heidegger's characterization of Paul, we too can realize that we have become caught between law and faith, between freedom and finitude. And we can thus refashion the practice of our reading by co-projecting ourselves more effectively, by way of the characters and objects it presents, into the text and into its subjectivity.

As phenomenologists, we cannot do otherwise. And thus a phenomenological education becomes a kind of religious experience. It becomes a means of grasping the transcendent by way of being a process of liberation.

That is, by the very practice of encouraging the students, the children, to attend to the text, by opening ourselves to their readings, we release them. We give up our demand that they master a set of information for the demands of the situation in the text in which we, in which they, find themselves. Like Charlotte the spider, a phenomenological education begins to weave the words we read into the fabric of our lives together, into our community as a whole class, so that we lift each other up.

NOTES

1. An earlier version of this conclusion appeared as the article, "Toward a Phenomenology of Reading: Poulet, Husserl and Woolf," in *Phenomenological Inquiry* 30 (2006): 36–48. I am grateful to Jeffrey Hurlburt for permission to use parts of that original article in this concluding section.

2. Wolfgang Iser in "The Reading Process: A Phenomenological Approach" offers the notion of the literary work as a third thing that is "not to be identified either with the reality of

the text or with the individual disposition of the reader" (279). The literary work is what is *created* in the intersubjectivity of text and reader. I find this a helpful addition to Poulet.

Further Reading

Interested readers who want further introduction to phenomenology would do well to read any of the recent books by John Russon. His *Human Experience, Bearing Witness to Epiphany*, and *Sites of Exposure* are a very helpful trilogy which employs the works of Husserl, Heidegger, and Merleau-Ponty within a very readable progression of chapters. Without engaging the jargon of the phenomenologists as directly, Russon makes the case for my reading of the themes of time, alterity, and education.

Most notably, Russon talks about the way that things are the bearers of our memories and of our meanings in *Human Experience*, the way that learning or education happens as a rhythmic, bodily appropriation of responsibility in *Bearing Witness*, and the way that religious structures open us onto the shared responsibilities of democratic life in *Sites of Exposure*. This current book obviously owes a lot to Russon's insights.

For each of the main figures I talk about here (Husserl, Heidegger, and Merleau-Ponty), there are a number of scholars whose books are essential for a developing understanding. For study of Husserl's works, I suggest the work of Robert Sokolowski, particularly his *Introduction to Phenomenology*. Dan Zahavi's *Husserl's Phenomenology* is also very helpful, as is Dermot Moran's *Introduction to Phenomenology*.

For further reading of Heidegger's texts, I view *How to Read Heidegger* by Mark Wrathall and Simon Critchley as helpful. I also suggest work by Matthias Fritsch, Charles Scott, John Sallis, and William Richardson, all of whom have contributed a great deal to my understanding of Heidegger.

For further reading in Merleau-Ponty, Susan Bredlau's *The Other in Perception*, David Morris's *The Sense of Space*, and Scott Maratto's *The Intercorporeal Self* are quite helpful. In addition, articles by Kym Maclaren, Kirsten Jacobson, and Jessica Wiskus have proven to be invaluable to my own understanding, and they each write with a view to the reader who is beginning the journey of close textual work.

There is a tradition of phenomenological literary criticism. *The Phenomenology of Henry James* by Paul Armstrong is one of the notable foundations of this tradition. The work of Hugh Silverman is also very helpful.

There is also a growing tradition of the phenomenology of religion or of religious experience. See work edited by Olga Louchakova-Schwartz and the Society for the Phenomenology of Religious Experience (SOPHERE). See also the work of Emmanuel Levinas and Jacques Derrida, each of whom maintains a close proximity to phenomenology in their discussions of the Torah, the Gospels, and the Koran.

Works Cited

Allison, Alida, ed. *Russell Hoban/Forty Years: Essays on His Writings For Children*. New York: Garland, 2000.

Blackburn, William. "Madeleine L'Engle's *A Wrinkle in Time*: Seeking the Original Face." In *Touchstones: Reflections on the Best in Children's Literature*, Perry Nodelman, ed. West Lafayette: Children's Literature Association, 1985.

Costello, Peter R. "From Confusion to Love: Russell Hoban's *The Mouse and His Child* as Phenomenological Novel." *Childhood and Philosophy* 11, no. 21 (2015): 93–103.

———. "Gift-Giving, Waiting, and Walking: The (Non-)reciprocal, (Im-)possible Apprenticeship of Frog and Toad." In *Philosophy in Children's Literature*, Peter R. Costello, ed. Lanham: Lexington Books, 2011.

———. *Layers in Husserl's Phenomenology: On Meaning and Intersubjectivity*. Toronto: University of Toronto Press, 2012.

———, ed. *Philosophy in Children's Literature*. Lanham: Lexington Books, 2011.

———. "Toward a Phenomenology of Reading: Poulet, Husserl and Woolf." *Phenomenological Inquiry* 30 (2006): 36–48.

———. "Toward a Phenomenology of Transition: E. B. White's *Charlotte's Web* and a Child's Process of Reading Herself Into the Novel." *Libri et Liberi* 5, no. 1 (2016): 13–36.

Derrida, Jacques. *The Animal I Therefore Am*. New York: Fordham University Press, 2009.

———. *The Problem of Genesis in Husserl's Philosophy*. Chicago: University of Chicago Press, 2003.

Dewey, John. *Democracy and Education*. New York: Macmillan, 1916.

———. *Experience and Education*. New York: Macmillan, 1938.

Freire, Paolo. *Pedagogy of the Oppressed*. Trans. Myra Bergman Ramos. New York: Herder and Herder, 1968.

Hakala, Laura. *Scouting for a Tomboy: Gender-Bending Behaviors in Harper Lee's* To Kill a Mockingbird. Georgia: Georgia Southern, 2010.

Heidegger, Martin. *Being and Time*. Trans. Joan Stambaugh. Albany: SUNY Press, 2010.

———. *Phenomenology of Religious Life*. Trans. Matthias Fritsch. Bloomington: Indiana University Press, 2010.

Heims, Neil. "'Were You Ever a Turtle?': *To Kill a Mockingbird*—Casting the Self as Other." In *Critical Insights:* To Kill a Mockingbird, Don Noble, ed. Pasadena: Salem Press, 2010.

Hoban, Russell. *The Mouse and His Child*. New York: Harper and Row, 1967.

Husserl, Edmund. *Analyses Concerning Active and Passive Synthesis*. Trans. Anthony J. Steinbock. Dordrecht: Kluwer Academic Publishers, 2001.

———. *Cartesian Meditations: An Introduction to Phenomenology*. Trans. Dorion Cairns. The Hague: Martinus Nijhoff Publishers, 1960.

———. *Crisis of the European Sciences.* Trans. David Carr. Evanston: Northwestern University Press, 1968.

———. *Experience and Judgment: Investigations in a Genealogy of Logic.* Translated by James S. Churchill and Karl Ameriks. Evanston: Northwestern University Press, 1973.

———. *Formal and Transcendental Logic.* Trans. Dorion Cairns. The Hague: Martinus Nijhoff Publishers, 1978.

———. *Ideas Pertaining to a Pure Phenomenology and to a Phenomenological Philosophy. First Book. General Introduction to a Pure Phenomenology.* Trans. Fred Kersten. The Hague: Martinus Nijhoff Publishers, 1983.

———. *On the Phenomenology of the Consciousness of Internal Time (1893–1917).* Trans. John Barnett Brough. Dordrecht: Kluwer Academic Publishers, 1991.

———. *Zur Phanomenologie Der Intersubjektivitat. Texte aus dem Nachlass. Erster Teil.* Ed. Iso Kern. *Husserliana Band XIII.* The Hague: Martinus Nijhoff, 1973.

Iser, Wolfgang. "Phenomenology of Reading." *New Literary History* 3, no. 2 (1972): 279–299.

Jacobson, Kirsten. "Heidegger, Winnicott, and the *Velveteen Rabbit*: Anxiety, Toys, and the Drama of Metaphysics." In *Philosophy in Children's Literature*, Peter R. Costello, ed. Lanham: Rowman & Littlefield, 2012.

Kennedy, David. "Anarchism, Schooling, and Democratic Sensibility." *Studies in Philosophy and Education* 36, no. 5 (2017): 551–568.

———. "John Dewey on Children, Childhood and Education." *Childhood and Philosophy* 2, no. 4 (2006): 211–229.

———. "The Child and Postmodern Subjectivity." *Educational Theory* 52, no. 2 (2002): 155–167.

Kiefer, Barbara. *Charlotte Huck's Children's Literature.* New York: McGraw-Hill, 2009.

Lang, Richard. "The Dwelling Door: Toward a Phenomenology of Transition." In *Dwelling, Place, and Environment: Towards a Phenomenology of Person and World*, David Seamon and Robert Mugerauer, eds. The Hague: Martinus Nijhoff, 1985.

Lee, Harper. *To Kill a Mockingbird: The 40th Anniversary Edition.* New York: Harper Collins, 1999.

L'Engle, Madeleine. *A Wrinkle in Time.* New York: Square Fish, 2007.

Lipman, Matthew, Ann Margaret Sharp, and Frederick S. Oscanyon. *Philosophy in the Classroom.* Philadelphia: Temple University Press, 2010.

Matthews, Gareth. *The Philosophy of Childhood.* Cambridge: Harvard University Press, 1994.

McMahon, Laura. "(Un)Healthy Systems: Merleau-Ponty, Dewey, and the Dynamic Equilibrium Between Self and Environment." *Speculative Philosophy* 32, no. 4 (2018): 607–627.

Medina, Meg. *Merci Suárez Changes Gears.* Crawfordsville: Candlewick Press, 2019.

Merleau-Ponty, Maurice. *Child Psychology and Pedagogy: The Sorbonne Lectures 1949–1952.* Trans. Talia Welsh. Evanston: Northwestern University Press, 2010.

———. *Phenomenology of Perception.* Trans. Donald A. Landes. New York: Routledge, 2012.

———. *The Primacy of Perception and Other Essays on Phenomenological Psychology, the Philosophy of Art, History and Politics.* Ed. James M. Edie. Evanston: Northwestern University Press, 1964.

Mochel-Caballero, Anne-Frederique. "Protagonists of *A Wrinkle in Time*." In *Dimensions of Madeleine L'Engle: New Critical Approaches*, Suzanne Bray, ed. Jefferson, NC: McFarland, 2016.

Morris, David. "Hegel on the Life of the Understanding." *International Philosophical Quarterly* 46, no. 4 (2006): 403–419.

Muro, Andres. "Toward a Liberatory Pedagogy Grounded in a Husserlian Phenomenology." *InterAmerican Journal of Philosophy* 8, no. 1 (2017): 35–49.

Murris, Karin. "Reading Philosophically in a Community of Enquiry: Challenging Developmentality with Oram and Kitamura's *Angry Arthur*." *Children's Literature in Education* 45 (2014): 145–165.

Nikolajeva, Maria. "Toward Linearity: A Narrative Reading of *A Mouse and His Child*." In *Russell Hoban/Forty Years*, Alida Allison, ed. New York: Garland, 2000.

Pantaleo, Sylvia. *Exploring Student Response through Picturebooks.* Toronto: Univeristy of Toronto Press, 2008.

Perry, Imani. "If That Mockingbird Don't Sing: Scaffolding, Signifying, and Queering a Classic." In *Reimagining To Kill a Mockingbird: Family, Community, and the Possibility of Equal Justice Under the Law*, Austin Sarat and Martha Merrill Umphrey, eds. Boston: University of Massachusetts Press, 2013.

Poulet, Georges. "Phenomenology of Reading." *New Literary History* 1 (1969): 53–68.

Pryal, Katie Rose Guest. "'Walking in Another's Skin': Failure of Empathy in *To Kill a Mockingbird*." In *Harper Lee's* To Kill a Mockingbird*: New Essays*, Michael J. Meyer, ed. Lanham: Scarecrow Press, 2010.

Schiller, Karen. "Inviting Children to Imagine Peace." *CEA Critic* 81, no. 1 (2019): 64–69. Johns Hopkins University Press.

Schneebaum, Katherine. "Finding a Happy Medium: The Design for Womanhood in *A Wrinkle in Time*." *The Lion and the Unicorn* 14, no. 2 (1990): 30–36. Johns Hopkins University Press.

Sheets-Johnstone, Maxine. *The Primacy of Movement*. Second Edition. Amsterdam: John Benjamins, 2011.

———. *The Roots of Thinking*. Philadelphia: Temple University Press, 2010.

Sheffer, Susannah. "Breaking the Rules: A Defense of *A Wrinkle in Time*." In *Censored Books II: Critical Viewpoints 1985–2000*, Nicholas J. Karolides, ed. Lanham: Scarecrow Press, 2002.

Stephens, John. "Questions of 'What' and 'Where,' and Contexts of 'Meaning' for *The Mouse and His Child* in the Late Twentieth Century." In *Russell Hoban/Forty Years*, Alida Allison, ed. New York: Garland, 2000.

Toolan, Michael J. *Narrative: A Critical Linguistic Introduction*. London: Routledge, 1988.

Trotter, Gregory. "Toward a Non-Reductive Naturalism: Combining the Insights of Husserl and Dewey." *William James Studies* 12, no. 1 (2016): 19–35.

Ware, Michele. "Gender and Power in Harper Lee's *To Kill a Mockingbird*." In *Women in Literature: Reading through the Lens of Gender*, Jerilyn Fisher and Ellen S. Sibler, eds. Westport: Greenwood Press, 2003.

Wartenberg, Thomas. *Big Ideas for Little Kids: Teaching Philosophy Through Children's Literature*. Lanham: Rowman & Littlefield, 2009.

White, E. B. *Charlotte's Web*. New York: Harper Collins, 2001.

Wilkie, Christine. *Through the Narrow Gate: The Mythological Consciousness of Russell Hoban*. Rutherford: Fairleigh Dickinson University Press, 1989.

Winnicott, D. W. *Playing and Reality*. London: Routledge, 2005.

Woolf, Virginia. *The Waves*. New York: Harcourt, 1959.

Young, Iris Marion. "Thinking Like a Girl: A Phenomenology of Feminine Body Comportment Motility and Spatiality." *Human Studies* 3, no. 1 (1980): 137–156.

Index

About the Author

Peter R. Costello is professor of Philosophy and of Public and Community Service at Providence College. He is the author of *Layers in Husserl's Phenomenology: On Meaning and Intersubjectivity* with the University of Toronto Press. He is also the editor of *Philosophy in Children's Literature and* the co-editor (with Licia Carlson) of *Phenomenology and the Arts*, both published with Lexington Books. Peter is on the board of directors of the Society for the Phenomenology of Religious Experience, the editorial board of *Sofia Journal of Philosophy,* and a co-editor with Barbara Weber of the Philosophy of Childhood series with Lexington Books. Peter has published numerous articles on phenomenology and is currently working on two manuscripts—one on Husserl's account of spatio-temporal experience and one on a phenomenological reading of the Gospel of Luke.

CPSIA information can be obtained
at www.ICGtesting.com
Printed in the USA
LVHW040430290822
726885LV00004B/148